Alcoholism
ITS FACETS AND PHASES

Alcoholism

ITS FACETS AND PHASES

MARVIN A. BLOCK, M.D.

THE JOHN DAY COMPANY
New York

© COPYRIGHT 1962, 1965 BY MARVIN A. BLOCK

All rights reserved. This book, or parts thereof, must not be reproduced in any form without permission. Published by The John Day Company, Inc., 62 West 45th Street, New York, N.Y. 10036, and on the same day in Canada by Longmans Canada Limited, Toronto

Library of Congress Catalogue
Card Number: 65-13751

MANUFACTURED IN THE UNITED STATES OF AMERICA

TO LILLIAN

Acknowledgments

ALCOHOLISM is a vast subject. In order to understand its facets and phases, one relies not only on one's own experience in the field but gleans from others their opinions and reactions. In writing this book, I am indebted to many for their stimulating and enthusiastic encouragement.

I am especially indebted to Dr. Milton G. Potter, who first awakened me to the necessity for dynamic action by the medical profession in the field of alcoholism. It was he who suggested that one should make a specialty of the prevention, diagnosis and treatment of this illness.

The late Dr. E. M. Jellinek was always an inspiration. Each hour of discussion I spent with him, both here and abroad, increased my respect for his enormous knowledge, and provided incentive for me to continue with my work.

To the leaders of the National Council on Alcoholism go my special thanks—Mrs. Marty Mann, Mr. R. Brinkley Smithers, Col. Harold Riegelman, the Reverend Yvelin Gardner, Dr. Harold Lovell and Dr. Ruth Fox—always enthusiastic co-workers.

In the American Medical Association, all of the Councils and Committees were extremely helpful in fostering interest in the subject. Much encouragement in the work was given me by its executives, Dr. F. J. L. Blasingame and Dr. Ernest B. Howard. The Council on Mental Health of the American Medical Association deserves special mention. Under its first Chairman, Dr. Leo Bartemeier, it enthusiastically espoused the program of its Committee on Alcoholism. Succeeding Council Chairmen Dr. Lauren Smith and Dr. Hamilton Ford continued to endorse the same principles. The members of my Committee on Alcoholism were exceptionally helpful. Mention must also be made of Dr. W. W. Bauer and Dr. Fred Hein, of the A.M.A.'s Department of Education, who were always ready to cooperate in our Committee's work.

Among the government departments to which I am indebted for cooperation is the National Institute of Mental Health, of which Dr. Paul Stevenson, formerly, and his successor, Dr. Carl Anderson, were particularly helpful. At state levels, the Advisory Council of New York State, the Alcoholism Divisions of Colorado and Utah, and the Division of Behavioral Problems of Pennsylvania were all helpful in furthering the work.

Others throughout the country whose work must be recognized are the members of the North American Association of Alcoholism Programs, and the various schools of alcohol studies. Leaders in these fields who were of great aid were: Clyde Gooderham of the University of Utah School of Alcohol Studies; Mrs. Frona McCambridge and Dr. Edward Delahanty of Colorado; Mrs. Vashti Cain of Mississippi; and Mr. Mark Keller of the Rutgers School of Alcohol Studies, and Editor of its Quarterly Journal.

Acknowledgment must also be made to those in other parts of the world who provided interesting and provocative discussions on alcoholism: Dr. Carl Biccard Jeppe, Dr. George Du Plessis, and William Osmund, of the Union of South Africa; Dr. John Hurt, Dr. John Moon, and the Health Minister of Australia, the Hon. W. F. Sheahan, Q.C., M.L.A.; Prof. J. E. Caughey and Dr. Lindsay McDougall of New

ACKNOWLEDGMENTS

Zealand; Dr. Hans Hoff of Austria; Dr. Leonard Goldberg of Sweden; Dr. Pullar-Strecker and Dr. D. L. Davies of England; Dr. Erik Jacobsen and Dr. O. Martensen-Larsen of Denmark; and Dr. Archer Tongue of Switzerland.

I am indebted to Dr. Arthur H. Cain, who wrote the challenging book, *The Cured Alcoholic: New Concepts in Alcoholism Treatment and Research.* Although we have not always agreed, our discussions were always stimulating.

Bill W., the surviving co-founder of Alcoholics Anonymous, helped me to understand the spiritual approach to the problem of excessive drinking, as did the non-alcoholic board members of that fellowship, Dr. John Norris and Dr. Harrison Trice.

Mrs. Marjorie Cronwell, my secretary, deserves special mention for her hours of hard work in preparing the manuscript for publication.

Last, but not least, are my patients—all of them—from whom I learned so much. There are numerous types of alcoholism and innumerable kinds of alcoholics, and there is something to be learned from each patient. After forty years of practice, I have found that alcoholic patients are in no way different from others. They are sick, unhappy, unhealthy, and in need of help. When this help is given to them in the proper way, they accept it and recover. They need the same encouragement that all patients need, and the same attitude on the part of the physician that he has toward any other type of patient. Over the years, I must say that in the field of alcoholism, as in the teaching profession, while treating these patients the teacher often learns more than the student. I can pay them no greater tribute.

—M.A.B.

Contents

	Acknowledgments	7
	Introduction	13
1	The Illness Called Alcoholism	19
2	Why People Drink	31
3	The Problem as a Public Health Matter	43
4	How Alcohol Affects Humans	50
5	Alcoholism and the Law	60
6	Understanding the Alcoholic	74
7	Treating the Alcoholic	82
8	Medical Treatment of Alcoholism	87
9	Effect of Alcohol on the Body	116
10	Treating the Abstaining Alcoholic	121
11	Skid Row: A Socio-Economic and Public Health Problem	133
12	Alcoholics Anonymous	145

CONTENTS

13	Women Alcoholics	157
14	The Government and Alcoholism	168
15	The Medical Profession and Alcoholism	182
16	Alcoholism and Industry	196
17	The Teacher and Alcoholism	211
18	The Hospital and Alcoholism	229
19	Necessary Components for an Effective Program on Alcoholism	238
20	The Nurse	246
21	The Clergy	254
22	Young People and Drinking	258
23	The Spouse of the Alcoholic	270
24	Mass Media and Communications	279
25	Lawyers and Alcoholism	283
26	The Social Worker and Alcoholism	287
27	Alcoholism in Other Countries	290
	Glossary	307
	Index	313

Introduction

THIS BOOK is intended as a source of information for those who seek a ready reference on the subject of alcoholism. It is written in simple, non-technical language that can be understood by anyone concerned with the care and treatment of the alcoholic.

The purpose herein is to fill a lack of information on alcoholism among the general public. Many persons misunderstand the illness of alcoholism and where it fits into our lives and our culture. Even supposedly enlightened people—persons of education and intellectual background—seem not to understand the character of this illness. Although many authors have attempted to supply this information, most have written of the disease only in its late and advanced stages. Certainly the emphasis has been on treatment and care once the disease has reached the advanced stage. Very little has been written of the incipient stages and the prevention of alcoholism, except in terms of prohibition of alcohol itself; and comparatively little has been written about the very early symptoms of the disease and the measures necessary at that stage to prevent its progress.

Persons suffering from alcoholism often have been subjected to criticism, even condemnation, by those, more fortunate, who can drink normally without ill effect. This attitude prevails in numerous professions and, even more important, has permeated our culture to the extent that the victims avoid help because of the shame they feel. Suffering the disease would seem to be preferable to being labeled an alcoholic, since so many victims of it refuse to seek help.

In the past, the behavior of mental patients was often so bizarre and frightening that the public, and members of the medical profession, punished rather than treated them. Most people tend to fear the unknown, and until mental illness was better understood it was often frightening to those who came in contact with its victims, including the physician. The mentally ill were for a long time thought to be possessed of the devil, or controlled by evil spirits. Treatment was administered in the form of punishment in an effort to drive out these evil influences.

An increase of knowledge in the mental health field has resulted in tremendous strides in understanding the disturbed. With it came consideration, compassion, and proper treatment. Even today, insufficient attention is paid to these illnesses and their victims, for society as a whole still ostracizes them although they may have recovered. They are feared even after they have been re-integrated into society and have assumed the responsibility of normal individuals. The medical profession has accepted the mentally ill as patients, but even so, many physicians continue to fear them and will refer them to a psychiatrist. The same is true of the patient suffering from alcoholism.

In the acute stage, the alcoholic patient often is guilty of antisocial behavior. It is true that he may act differently from the non-alcoholic, but the alcoholic and non-alcoholic, when drunk, are difficult to differentiate. Yet the individual who is not an alcoholic but who sometimes drinks excessively often cannot accept the uncontrolled drinker. Society as a whole frowns upon these sick individuals and refuses to believe that they cannot control their drinking, for it seems obvious to those who can that it is merely a matter of willpower and moral responsibility. The alcoholic, in this respect, represents an immoral weak person, one to be shunned.

Unfortunately, this same attitude was for a long time prevalent in the medical profession, the legal profession, and among the clergy. In recent years a number of members of these professions have recognized alcoholism as a disease. The recovery of many alcoholics has made it obvious that the condition is treatable, but there are still many in the learned professions who are prejudiced. It is with that in mind that this volume is being written. Perhaps when it is commonly understood how ill the alcoholic patient is, how much he requires and deserves help, and what a great degree of recovery he can achieve with the proper treatment, more of these people will be helped before the illness progresses too far.

The same lack of understanding is also often present among sociologists, social workers, teachers, and others who, because of unfamiliarity with the etiology and course of the disease, and because of the untoward reactions of the individuals involved, have avoided alcoholics rather than sought to help them. For this reason this book is divided into chapters especially applicable to particular fields. Those devoted to the professions are intended to give general information for specific treatment of alcoholic patients in a brief but practical manner. For the more complicated cases, further information from specialists may be needed. It is hoped, however, that this book will contribute to a greater understanding of alcoholism and the individuals suffering from it.

—MARVIN A. BLOCK, M.D.

Alcoholism
ITS FACETS AND PHASES

What are you like
under the influence —
What do you do?
— Personal House clay

CHAPTER 1

The Illness Called Alcoholism

CHRONIC excessive drinking, or addiction to alcohol, with its compulsive character and devastating effect, has become one of the great public health problems of the world. In the United States it ranks among the top four and is exceeded only by the mental illness and cardiovascular (heart and artery) diseases. Considered as an aspect of mental health, it is numerically the largest part of that particular problem.

There are many definitions of alcoholism. Every individual seems to have his own idea of what constitutes this illness. Definitions range from casual observations of laymen to the results of considered deliberation by scientists. All agree upon one point, however, and that is that alcoholism is characterized by excessive ingestion of alcoholic beverages. Therefore, wherever excessive ingestion of such a beverage occurs, the likelihood of alcoholism exists. Whether it remains a likelihood or becomes a fact depends upon a number of factors. Whether one or more of these factors is determinant depends upon a further study of the condition involved. Since, however, every illness has a beginning, any excessive ingestion of alcohol should be considered an early sign of alcoholism until proved otherwise. How can one prove it? By control.

If control of drinking is present, it is not alcoholism, but if this same control is absent, then the excessive drinking is characteristic of the disease.

The term *excessive ingestion* requires definition, since the meaning of the word *excessive* may vary considerably in the minds of individual observers. Excess in anything, even the good things in life, can produce untoward effects. It would be reasonable to assume, therefore, that an excess exists when the use of anything otherwise considered good begins to have undesirable results. For those in whom a minute amount of any agent would produce untoward results under any circumstances, even that minute amount is excessive. The fact that this very small amount might have no effect whatever on others in no way modifies the excessiveness for the individual who is susceptible to it.

Some of the definitions that have been used in describing alcoholism represent the considered opinions of many authorities in this field. "Alcoholism is a progressive disease characterized by uncontrollable drinking." This definition by the late E. M. Jellinek, Sc.D., former consultant on alcoholism to the World Health Organization, is brief and succinct, but depends to a great extent upon the definition of the various terms used, such as "progressive" and "uncontrollable." [1]

Howard J. Clinebell, Jr. prefers the definition, "An alcoholic is anyone whose drinking interferes frequently or continuously with any other important life adjustments or interpersonal relationships." [2] Though this definition is broader than the previous one, in my opinion it is not broad enough and can be applied only to what is alcoholism in a somewhat advanced stage.

Such definitions as "Alcoholism is a physical allergy

[1] *Disease Concept of Alcoholism*, E. M. Jellinek, Hillhouse Press, New Haven, Conn., 1960.
[2] *Understanding and Counseling the Alcoholic*, Howard J. Clinebell, Jr. Abington Press, Nashville, Tenn., 1956.

The Illness Called Alcoholism

coupled with a psychological compulsion," often used by lay people, or "Alcoholism is an allergy of the body and an obsession of the mind," often used by recovered alcoholics, are of little value, since they are confusing to anyone who understands any of the terms used. In no way does excessive drinking of alcohol resemble an allergy as it is known to the medical profession, nor does it produce the allergic signs and symptoms commonly observed with allergies. Further, there is no evidence that the individual who is allergic to any substance ever craves more and more of the same substance once the allergy has begun. That drinking is compulsive with many alcoholics is beyond doubt, but there is little in the way of allergic manifestation to characterize it as an allergy. Dr. Harold W. Lovell, former President of the National Council on Alcoholism, used the definition, "Alcoholism, then, is a condition characterized by uncontrolled compulsive drinking." [3] The key to this definition is the word "compulsive." An alcoholic is impelled to drink against his will or judgment, even if will and judgment are functioning. Furthermore, the will is powerless to stop the drinking. So far as alcoholism is concerned, the victim is completely without willpower, not weak-willed or wrong-willed.

The Executive Director of the National Council on Alcoholism, Mrs. Marty Mann, who is also its founder, describes alcoholism as a disease "which manifests itself chiefly by the uncontrollable drinking of the victim who is known as an alcoholic." [4] While these statements are true, and excellent descriptions of the disease, they are but descriptions of the manifestations of the illness and not definitions of the disease itself. The "official" definition of alcoholism, as reported by the World Health Organization's Expert Committee is a technical one and reads, "Any form of drinking which in its

[3] *Hope and Help for the Alcoholic,* Harold W. Lovell, M.D. Doubleday & Co. Garden City, N.Y., 1951.
[4] *Marty Mann's New Primer on Alcoholism.* Rinehart & Co., Inc., New York & Toronto, 1958.

extent goes beyond the traditional and customary 'dietary' use or the ordinary compliance with the social drinking customs of the whole community concerned, irrespective of the etiological factors leading to such behavior, and irrespective also of the extent to which such etiological factors are dependent upon heredity, constitution, or acquired physiopathological and metabolic influences." [5] A close study of this technical definition will reveal many factors not included in the other definitions. The definition is also broad, and covers all aspects of the disease without regard for the various etiological factors that might be involved.

While such definitions are of great value in trying to understand alcoholism, I feel that we must go back a great deal further. Every illness has a beginning. Any disease process is at its very inception difficult to differentiate from what is considered normal health. The early stage of an illness must represent but a slight variation from what was up to then considered the normal healthy state. Often the variation from so-called normal health is a generalized transition with no definite indication as to which course the disease may take. Not until definite pathways of symptomatology develop can a direction be recognized. Not until there is a focusing of the signs and symptoms can a diagnosis be made.[6]

The professional medical mind is continually alert to many kinds of symptoms and deviations from normal. The behavioral sciences, a comparatively new area associated with public health, have in addition to recognizing and labeling a disease process, focused much attention on a number of chronic diseases that are profoundly influenced by social phenomena hitherto considered nonmedical. Such phenomena as social pressures, patterns of group behavior, occupation, education, and recreation influence to a great extent the

---

[5] *Alcoholism as a Medical Problem*, H. D. Kruse, M.D., Editor. Hoeber-Harper, Paul B. Hoeber, Inc., New York City, 1956.

[6] "Approaching the Problem of Alcoholism," M. A. Block. *Medical Times*, September, 1963.

The Illness Called Alcoholism

epidemiology and progress of this group of chronic diseases. Because of the vast variety of patterns in so-called normal behavior and the comparatively slight variations from this so-called normal in the early stage of any of these illnesses, prompt recognition becomes extremely difficult. When, in addition, there is a stigma attached to any of these illnesses, the difficulty of diagnosis is increased because of the denial of the symptoms by the individuals involved, and the refusal of those most closely associated with the patient to accept the existence of the stigmatized condition.[7]

The term "alcoholism" is a general one describing several species of social behavior and conduct associated with the excessive ingestion of alcohol. There are many types of alcoholics, perhaps as many types as there are different types of people. All, however, have one characteristic in common— excessive drinking. In evaluating this condition, which is fairly universal, we see that practically every country in the world has its own predominant type of alcoholic patient. Differences often are the consequences of the drinking customs of a particular country. In our country, many cases of alcoholism are recognized less readily because they do not fit into the observer's preconceived image of the disease. Variations in the patterns of drinking are tremendous. Excessive drinking may be daily or it may be only periodic. This depends on the needs of the individual involved. However, the epidemiology of the disease becomes more difficult to determine because of the difficulty of pinpointing the various patterns. It can only be established after enough studies of normal drinking and other behavioral patterns in the general population, as well as in particular areas, have been made.[8]

In my opinion, and broadly speaking, alcoholism may be defined as the use of alcohol or alcoholic beverages to the ex-

[7] "Epidemiology of Alcoholism," Wardell R. Lipscomb. *Ohio's Health,* 1961.
[8] *The Disease Concept of Alcoholism,* E. M. Jellinek. Hillhouse Press, New Haven, Conn., 1960.

tent of causing any continuing adverse effect upon the individual or his family or community. The malady represents but one segment of a tremendous mental health problem. Alcohol itself is but the agent through which the disease process manifests itself. Without it, there would be no alcoholism. The etiological factors might produce many other behavioral problems, but where the individual takes to the ingestion of alcohol, the result is alcoholism.

The early stages of alcoholism are very difficult to differentiate from normal health, and until excessive drinking becomes manifest to many other people, the disease process is unnoticed. As a rule, manifestations are observed by others before the individual drinker himself recognizes them. However, it is most important that a diagnosis be made at the very earliest stage of the illness. It was for this reason that the term *problem drinking* came into existence. How does this term differ from *excessive drinking?* Excessive drinking may be described as any drinking of alcoholic beverages that produces some untoward results at the point of excess. An individual may ingest alcohol on numerous occasions and have no ill effects. On other occasions, however, his drinking may result in a hangover, staggering, antisocial behavior, physical signs of intoxication, or any one of hundreds of signs that are exhibited when an excessive amount of alcohol has been ingested. Whether or not his drinking has been excessive as far as *volume* is concerned, or even if it is intermittent—if that is his pattern of drinking, then this untoward result becomes a problem and the drinking itself becomes problem drinking.

For a working definition, therefore, we may say that alcoholism is a disease manifested by consistently undesirable results following the ingestion of alcohol. Such consistent adverse effects constitute sufficient evidence of excess on the part of the individual using the agent. This would describe the disease even at its earliest stages. For the individual involved to continue drinking the toxic agent that brings about the adverse effects in spite of the untoward results is only a further manifestation of involvement and of the severity of the disease.

The terms *problem drinking* and *alcoholism* are merely descriptive terms applying to various stages of the same illness. The term *problem drinking* was adopted, in all probability, to appease those individuals who were frightened by the word *alcoholism,* and to whom *problem drinking* seemed more acceptable.

While alcoholism represents a tremendous number of many-faceted conditions, various classifications have been made of the illness. Just as cancer covers a number of different types of growths that have in common the wild proliferation of cells without control, so the term alcoholism covers a number of categories, all characterized by excessive drinking, but with no other characteristics necessarily common to all. In all probability, there are as many types of alcoholics as there are types of individuals and personalities.

E. M. Jellinek divides alcoholics into classifications that explain to some extent the different types of drinking and how they develop. Recognition of these different types may indicate the causes of alcoholism:

> Usually every country has its own predominant type of alcoholism. The alcoholic is less readily recognized because he does not fit into the preconceived notion of what an alcoholic is by the individual who is trying to recognize him. Actually, there are four minor criteria which differentiate the species of which I spoke, and which I will describe. They depend upon 1. psychological dependence, 2. control, 3. progression, and 4. a combination of tissue tolerance and physiological dependence, or so-called craving, characterized by symptoms on withdrawal.[9]

All of the types described by Jellinek are subject to complications and sequelae of excessive alcohol ingestion, but otherwise are divided by him into five major classifications.

[9] *Ibid.*

The first type, which Jellinek labels *Alpha,* demonstrates continued psychological dependence or reliance upon the effect of alcohol for relief of physical or emotional pain. The drinking is undisciplined—but only to the extent that it contravenes the rules of society as to time, occasion, locale, and effect. The Alpha type demonstrates no loss of self-control, no inability to abstain, even though the drinking does disturb interpersonal relationships, the family budget, work, and sometimes nutritional processes. There are no withdrawal signs, no signs of progression, so that the Alpha type of alcoholism is, in truth, more suggestive of a symptom of an underlying illness, usually emotional, than of illness per se. This type may, of course, develop into a later type, the *Gamma,* but it may, on the other hand, fail to progress over a period of many years.

The second type described by Jellinek is termed by him the *Beta.* This is characterized by polyneuropathy, gastritis, cirrhosis, or other of the complications we see in connection with excessive alcohol ingestion. As a rule, no physical or psychological dependence whatever appears. The incentive for drinking is, in most cases, custom in a social group plus poor nutritional habits. The resulting damage is, for the most part, nutritional (deficiency diseases), an impaired budget, diminished job efficiency, and, as is generally the case for alcoholics regardless of type, a life-span curtailment of up to twelve years. In the Beta type, as in the Alpha, no withdrawal symptoms are present. It is true that the Beta type may in time develop into the *Gamma* or the *Delta* type, but the likelihood of such progression is even less than it is for the Alpha.

The *Gamma* type, the most prevalent in our society, is characterized by the acquisition of increased tissue tolerance, adaptive cell metabolism, physical dependence, usually accompanied by withdrawal symptoms or craving, and loss of control. Progression from psychological to physical dependence and behavioral changes likewise help to identify it. This is the type that is most representative of the American-Canadian types of alcoholism.

The *Delta* type displays the first three characteristics of the Gamma and, less markedly, the fourth—loss of control. This type, found most often in countries where wine is an all-purpose beverage, is particularized by inability to abstain. Such drinking is entirely different from ours, for abstinence from it is rare. Hence, many inhabitants of wine-drinking countries are alcoholics without being aware of their condition in the slightest degree. Whereas in the United States we often see a marked increase in the concentration of alcohol in the blood between the hours of four and nine P.M., with little or no increase throughout the morning or early afternoon, in the wine-drinking countries abroad no such extreme fluctuation occurs; the concentration of alcohol is higher than it is here throughout the day and lower than here between four and nine P.M.

It is rare to see a drunken person staggering in the streets in the countries where wine is a staple, even though daylong mild intoxication is a fairly common condition. In addition, there are withdrawal symptoms when all intake of wine is halted, and delirium tremens may develop after four or five days of deprivation. This means that numerous wine-drinkers of the Delta type go through life totally ignorant of their alcoholism unless it is put to the test of withdrawal.

The phenomenon is often observed in hospitals where Delta-type patients are taken for surgery and are deprived of their customary intake of wine for several days. It is not unusual for such patients to go into delirium tremens. The non-abstinence histories in such cases go back, quite obviously, to an overall pattern of drinking that has for centuries been practically prescribed by their society. The pre-alcoholic physiological vulnerability in such cases is low.

The fifth type, which Jellinek labels *Epsilon,* is the so-called periodic alcoholism detected both in this country and abroad. This explosive or fiesta type of drinking is comparable in the United States to "occasional binge" drinking. It is a fairly prevalent indulgence among our people and is characterized by long intervals between bouts. Its periodicity may be marked by a week or two, by one or more months, or even by a year.

There have been many classifications other than Jellinek's sociological classifications. Zwerling [10] tries to differentiate alcoholic types by their psychiatric labels—schizophrenia, schizoid character, paranoid character, sociopathic personality, passive-aggressive personality, anxiety state, obsessive-compulsive character, psycho-physiological reaction, chronic brain syndrome, manic-depressive psychosis. In addition, he lists characteristics of the alcoholic that may be observed apart from the classifications mentioned above: dependency, hostility, depression, or sexual immaturity.

From this classification by Zwerling one can see that alcoholics run the gamut of psychiatric conditions, all of which are characterized, when present in alcoholics, through the ingestion of alcohol. All of these individuals may have the illnesses and the characteristics mentioned above without becoming involved in excessive drinking. The alcoholism in these cases, therefore, can be considered one manifestation of the underlying condition described in the various classifications. Whether one should actually call individuals in Zwerling's classifications "alcoholics" is open to question. Perhaps they should be diagnosed as suffering from one of these conditions complicated by excessive drinking or alcoholism. In these cases the alcoholism would be secondary to the underlying psychiatric condition, and the alcohol addiction would necessarily have to be removed before the underlying psychiatric condition could be treated.

It is not unusual for sick people to have two separate conditions, one complicating the other. It is also not uncommon

---

[10] "Psychiatric Findings in an Interdisciplinary Study of 46 Alcoholic Patients," I. Zwerling. *Quarterly Journal of Studies on Alcohol* 80:543, Sept., 1959.

to find that the occurrence of one disease may be dependent upon the presence of another, preceding disease. In such cases, the two conditions must be considered separately, and the relationship between them taken into consideration in the treatment. In any case, when alcoholism is complicated by an underlying psychiatric condition, even if the psychiatric disease is treated successfully the individual cannot safely go back to any ingestion of alcohol, once the addiction to alcohol has been established. Once the physiological addiction has been established, the ingestion of even a small amount of the addicting drug will initiate the addictive process, the compulsive progress of the addiction will take over, and the addictive drug will be used more and more as a necessity. Therefore the complication of alcoholism with an underlying psychiatric disease makes treatment much more difficult; the prognosis is dependent upon the success of the treatment of the underlying psychiatric condition. Fortunately, this combination of circumstances obtains in only a comparatively small percentage of alcoholics.[11]

Any disease in its earliest stages is extremely difficult to detect. To wait for the patient to recognize his illness is to wait for the disease to become fairly advanced. It is therefore important that we train experts to recognize incipient disease before the patient can do so. The medical profession tries to educate laymen to recognize the early stages of all diseases, but human beings tend to minimize physical as well as mental problems until these interfere with living, because nature so often takes care of milder deviations from health. Hence, many patients do not consult a physician until illness has assumed serious proportions.

The medical profession not only constantly urges people to seek help from experts if there is any suspicion of disease, it also recommends frequent periodic examinations in order that experts in the various health fields can uncover possible illness before the victim himself is aware of any symptom.

[11] *Ibid.*

This is particularly true in the fight against cancer. It should be no less true in the case of alcoholism. Alcoholism, like cancer, covers many disease types, therefore we cannot apply standard measures for all types of alcoholism. Just as each case must be individually treated, so each case must be individually diagnosed. As with cancer, by the time the victim of alcoholism is able to recognize his affliction the malady is already far advanced.

Education is necessary to ensure that the earliest indications of alcoholism can be responsibly established by trained people. Such a diagnosis can be made from accurate information gleaned from the patient or from his family before the patient himself is aware of his pathology. It is never too early to suspect alcoholism in anyone who drinks, but only through acute and exhaustive questioning, through painstaking and honest investigation, is it possible to uncover this illness in its primary stages. Only by removing the stigma attached to this disease can we hope for the cooperation of all the patients who may be suffering from it. Only when we have educated the public, as well, to the importance of this approach shall we have taken any effective strides in the direction of solving the problem.

Taking the patient's history is one of the leading factors in alcoholism case-finding. Medical students and physicians as well as laymen should be taught that a detailed drinking history must be included when taking the history of any illness. Not only must the amount of alcohol be determined, but also the time of drinking and the reasons for doing so. Whenever the slightest indication appears that alcohol is being used by an individual more as a drug than as a beverage, more for a specific result than for a social purpose, we may suspect the existence of alcoholism.

CHAPTER 2

Why People Drink

ALCOHOLIC beverages have been part of man's diet since the beginning of recorded history and may even date back to primitive times. The pleasurable sensations aroused by natural fermentation of fruit juices, a universal phenomenon, doubtless gave rise to drinking and led to the establishment of a flourishing industry.

Today the entire world makes use of alcohol in one form or another, for more or less identical reasons. Almost any type of vegetation can be fermented and later distilled; geography and local agriculture determine the native beverage. If the taste is not in all cases seductive, the pleasant sensation at first induced by it is. So drinking has become a popular indulgence and aid to conviviality wherever custom and mores permit.

Out of fermentation and man's developing sophistication in the management of the forces at his disposal came the process of distillation—the extraction from alcoholic mashes. This is accomplished by means of evaporation and condensation of the concentrated spirits that "step up" otherwise cheerless potions or, swallowed raw, accelerate the advent of the desired sensation. As man became something of a chemist and physicist, among other things, he applied his developing technology to the manufacture of alcohol as a magic drug for the emotions.

Wine-making was a primitive undertaking. The brewing of meads and beers came later, when heat as an outside force was applied. With the invention of the still, brandies and cognacs were created, and fortified wines became possible. As knowledge of the distillation process spread throughout the civilized world, each land's most abundant produce sooner or later was transformed into a corresponding liquor. Where grain and potatoes yield dependable crops, there is whiskey—or vodka, as the case may be—of one type or another. From corn comes bourbon; from sugar cane comes rum; from native fruits and berries, seeds and blossoms, come brandies and cordials of varying types and flavors; from Mexican cacti comes the fiery distillate known as tequila. On tropical islands where the pineapple or the coconut is king, a corresponding alcohol likewise rules supreme. In the Far East, where the staple cereal is rice, both wine and hard liquor flow from that source.

Although the history of the manufacture of alcohol for human consumption is lacking in details, the popularity of the product is a living part of the record of mankind from one era to the next. The literature of almost every people unfailingly reflects widespread use of alcoholic beverages, not only as a stimulant and source of social gaiety, but also in terms of overindulgence and its sometimes tragic consequences. The problem drinker and addict are not strangers to the pages of history.

Because of certain religious prohibitions, there are areas of the world where drinking of alcoholic beverages is forbidden. It is interesting, however, that even in those areas many people drink alcoholic beverages. Traditions and rules exist in all countries, each of which has its own rules for drinking and for the sale of alcoholic beverages. For the most part, these are designed to control the amount people drink,

Why People Drink

since in all areas, without exception, it is recognized that excessive drinking will produce untoward results.

In the United States distilled liquors are the most popular of all forms of alcoholic beverages, the popularity of the individual type varying with the geographic areas of the country. Bourbon is one of the favorite drinks of the South, while in the Northeast, Scotch seems to be more popular. The Midwest and northern parts of the country are said to favor rye. Beer enjoys considerable popularity and is drunk in all parts of the country.[1]

Why do people drink? Why does a beverage which contains a comparatively powerful drug enjoy popular acceptance?

Since time immemorial, drinking has been a part of the ritualistic ceremonies of almost all civilized people. Wine, becauses of its deep, rich, red color, was considered the liquor of life and was compared in its richness and value with blood —in all probability because of the similarity of color. When men pledged loyalty to each other, they often sealed their pledge by cutting the veins of their wrists and mixing their bloods, thus becoming "blood brothers." As men became more civilized, the barbaric custom gave way to pledging loyalty with a glass of wine, the light liquor that resembled blood. Soon the pledge of loyalty and friendship was extended to include such ceremonies as betrothal, marriage, christening, baptism, and even death.[2] In this manner, drinking of an alcoholic beverage became an accepted ritual.

For those who wished relief from the stress of living, the relaxing effect of alcohol gave a pleasant glow, increasing to a kind of carefree feeling as civilization progressed. Cares receded, and the sense of pleasure increased. This social relaxation has come down to us as an accepted tradition.

---

[1] *Young People and Drinking*, Arthur H. Cain, Ph.D., John Day Company, N.Y., 1963.
[2] *To Your Health*. W.H.O. film, Columbia University Educational Films, New York City, Center of Mass Communications of Columbia University Press.

Used in moderation by those in whom drinking can be controlled, this pleasant ritual produces ease and relaxation, which are of great value in the tense world in which we live. It is a social lubricant; it relieves self-consciousness, it loosens the tongue, it encourages congeniality, and it promotes tolerance of defects in others as well as in oneself.

Alcohol belongs in the class with anesthetic drugs, both in its chemical composition and in its effect upon the physiology. By combining with the fatty tissues of the body as well as the brain cells, like ether or chloroform, it produces changes that are anesthetic in character. During the administration of an anesthetic the individual passes through the induction stage and then into activity, when the controls are released, and the same results follow ingestion of alcohol over a period of time. As with other anesthetic agents, there is eventually a period of unconsciousness. If an anesthetic agent is continued in administration for a period beyond safety, the vital centers of respiration and circulation can be paralyzed. The same result comes from the continued ingestion of alcohol beyond the stage of ordinary anesthesia. The vital centers can be just as effectively paralyzed by alcohol as by any other anesthetic agent. Fortunately, we do not see this happen too often, but occasionally we do hear of some individual who, in his anxiety to prove himself capable of downing vast amounts of alcohol, will consume enough at one time to produce the kind of paralyzing effects described. Death results from paralysis of the vital centers, just as it would have if excessive amounts of any anesthetic agent were used.

As a rule, people do not drink in order to anesthetize themselves. They drink only to produce the kind of pleasant relaxation and glow that come from a mild concentration of alcohol in the bloodstream. At this stage of mild concentration—perhaps one part of alcohol in two thousand parts of blood—inhibitions are down, controls are lost or at least reduced, and awareness of unpleasantness and tension is minimized. If the concentration of alcohol remains at that level, comparatively little harm is done to the individual, since at this low concentration of alcohol in the bloodstream the body can easily metabolize the alcohol. For most people no harmful results would ensue, although even at this stage many individuals may be slower in their reflexes or responses and may not think as clearly as they would without the alcohol, but if they are not put to the test no harm is done.

For social occasions alcohol serves a purpose, and if a social lubricant is needed it is one of the more pleasant methods of enjoying good companionship. In small amounts it is not harmful for most people. It must be noted, however, that for a small percentage of people even this low concentration of alcohol can be dangerous, producing untoward results. Just as some persons are peculiarly sensitive to certain chemicals—drugs, foods, or gases that affect others not at all—so there are individuals in whom exposure to even the smallest amount of alcohol will produce tragic results. Usually experience has made these people aware of their sensitivity, and should constitute a warning against the use of alcohol. For these individuals total abstinence is imperative, and to drink even the slightest amount of alcohol in any form is to invite disaster. Why this situation obtains with some and not others is not known, but the facts have been recognized for many years.

There is no hesitancy whatever on the part of most people to abstain from other things that produce such untoward results even when used in small amounts. When it comes to the matter of alcohol, however, the same people display extreme reluctance to abstain. There is a kind of tradition that it is disgraceful not to be able to drink, that it is a sign of weakness of character. The ability to "hold one's liquor" is apparently, in our society, an accomplishment that should excite admiration. The inability to do so denotes a lack of manliness in the eyes of many persons in our society. This is comparable to the admiration accorded the man with big muscles, on the assumption that he is more of a man than someone with less muscular development. In our society, manliness still appears to be associated with physical strength rather than with other attributes of value. The emphasis on these standards in our culture has given an importance to drinking that it little deserves. As a result many people, in spite of their dislike for the beverage and its effect, have attempted to meet society's requirements by downing the necessary number of drinks. Among young people, particularly, drinking represents being "grown-up." In spite of the fact that teen-agers, particularly girls, dislike the taste of alcoholic beverages, they will down the burning liquid or the bitter beer in order to conform to the standards set by those who feel that if they act in what seems to them an adult manner, they achieve adulthood. All too often, unfortunately, they are aided and abetted in this fallacy by well-meaning but ill-informed parents, who think that allowing their children to engage in adult activities makes them adult. To allow the privileges of adulthood to individuals who are not mature only encourages them in their immaturity and leads them to expect more and more privileges without assuming the responsibilities that must go with them.

Why, then, do people drink excessively? Unfortunately, drinking has become so much a part of our culture and society that it is an accepted procedure. People do not usually expect to drink excessively. They do so only to make sure that the pleasant feeling they get from moderate drinking will continue; in fear of the disappearance or diminution of this pleasant sensation, they imbibe more and more, and at a rate faster than the body can metabolize the alcohol. If this continues, the drinking becomes excessive.

Cultural patterns in particular areas have a tremendous effect upon drinking habits. There are cultures where, although drinking is an accepted procedure, excessive drinking or drunkenness is absolutely forbidden. Among Orthodox Jews, for instance, excessive drinking or drunkenness was never tolerated, and anyone who did drink to a point of drunkenness was socially ostracized by his group. In the Jewish tradition anyone who drank too much was betraying his own people, and therefore in this culture we saw no alcoholism. Since drinking of alcohol in excess was not only frowned upon but virtually condemned, young Jews learned very early in their lives that such behavior would not be tolerated. Excessive drinking, therefore, was conscientiously avoided.

As American Jews progressed to the second, and especially, to the third generations, and as they adopted the customs of their chosen country and became Americanized, the same patterns developed among them as among other Americans. We see not only excessive drinking but alcoholism as well. In their newer environment, where excessive drinking is tolerated and where to be drunk does not necessarily mean ostracism, it is socially acceptable in their group to drink excessively at times. The disgrace formerly associated with drunkenness no longer obtains. As the result of this, a small percentage of Jews not only drink excessively, but become alcoholic as well. Whereas their grandparents, equally neurotic, sought some other method of expressing these neuroses, the second and third generation Jews of the United States are demonstrating the same manifestations of neurosis as other Americans.

The reverse picture is found among the Irish who immigrated to the United States around the nineteenth century. The misery and uncertainty of living that they experienced in their own country, where drinking was an accepted thing and quite prevalent, apparently continued after they arrived in their new country. As in Ireland, this led to drinking that was notoriously excessive among the first generation of Irish immigrants, and the rate of alcoholism in that group was extremely high. Their children and grandchildren, however, have become more integrated into the society of the United States, and with the attainment of economic equality have found it less necessary to resort to excessive drinking than their fathers and grandfathers. As a result of this, we see less alcoholism among the Irish of today in the United States than we did a generation ago. Such are the changing patterns of drinking.

For those who drink in what we consider normal fashion, alcohol represents relaxation. However, for those who drink because they are psychologically dependent upon the drug, alcohol becomes a necessity. The individual who cannot face the everyday problems of life and finds that with the ingestion of alcohol these problems become smaller or disappear altogether soon adopts this as one method of handling such frustrating or disagreeable problems. At first this type of psychological dependence means that he can occasionally resort to this drug to help him over the difficult parts of living, but this progresses to dependence upon a drink for every problem that comes along. Eventually he is no longer able to meet these problems at all, and retreats from them by using the drug alcohol. As his life becomes more and more complicated and the problems and frustrations increase, this individual resorts more and more and sinks to greater depths with his drug. Before long, he cannot handle any situation without using alcohol.

For those who are even more unfortunate, there are problems that seem insurmountable. For many, the threshold of suffering is terribly low. The slightest untoward situation will often overwhelm these people. The important objective for these individuals is to deal no longer with these problems, but to find an escape from them; and life itself becomes unbearable. For such unfortunate, sick individuals, the only comfortable state they know is oblivion. Alcohol represents one method of obtaining this oblivion, and since many of these individuals are as frightened of death as they are of living, a compromise is made with the temporary kind of death they experience with excessive drinking.

It is obvious, therefore, that some alcoholics come upon a drug that answers their needs and that they can prescribe for themselves. In other words, a self-medicating process has taken place, whereby the individual seeks to alleviate his suffering with a drug upon which he has become quite dependent. As he uses it more and more, and because of the nature of its chemical effect upon his physiology, he eventually becomes addicted to this drug. Since it affords him the relief he seeks, and since he meets with no criticism for using it, and since it is rarely classified or thought of as a drug by the average individual, including the patient himself, it is not too difficult to become addicted.

A much more sick individual is the one to whom life has become so unbearable that only death seems to be an answer to his problem. Unfortunately, there are many people who have self-destructive tendencies. Many will readily admit that death would be preferable to living, but they have neither the courage nor the means to attempt suicide; the urge to self-destruction is great, but is constantly at odds with the natural instinct of self-preservation. Such people find in alcohol a method of punishing themselves for their guilt in wishing for death, and at the same time of destroying themselves a bit at a time over long periods. When the problems pyramid to the point where life is no longer tolerable, some of these individuals will attempt suicide; but for the most part, with their background and training, they still hope that things will be better and settle for temporary oblivion. This, I think, accounts for the frequency with which alcoholic patients beg for medication to put them to sleep. Many complain that they cannot sleep, although their families volunteer the information that they sleep as much as the average individual. This desire for continual sleep is only another manifestation of the desire for oblivion. It has been my experience with several such patients that after thirty-six hours of continuous sleep under medication, they will again beg for sleep after five or ten minutes of consciousness; even so short a period of facing the realities of living is too painful.

There are many people who have the ability to control the amount of alcohol they drink but who, nevertheless, drink excessively. With these people excessive drinking is a matter of irresponsibility, since they have the control and do not use it. They either exercise poor judgment or lack a sense of responsibility in their actions. Many people who drink do not know their limits, nor can they recognize that they are drinking to excess. Alcohol itself modifies the judgment adversely, so it is no wonder that many people drink excessively without intending to do so. The person with one drink in his system is not the same person as he is with no drink at all. Even one drink will modify his attitude toward drinking, as well as his judgment in general. The individual, therefore, who determines to take one drink may have, after taking that drink, a different attitude about it, since he no longer feels the same as he did when his decision to have only one drink was made. He may now think that he can have a second drink without harm, just as he was sure that he could take the first one without harm.

Some, however, drink compulsively. These people use alcohol to excess not because of lack of judgment, but because of absence of control. Without this control they cannot stop once they have started to drink. These compulsive drinkers are the individuals who are physiologically addicted to the drug alcohol. These are the people who seek in alcohol a complete escape from life.

Many causes of alcoholism have been enumerated, but these are actually only suspicions of causes. The actual cause of the disorder is not known. Many people would like to blame alcohol for alcoholism, but if this were true, everyone who drinks would become alcoholic. Alcohol cannot be considered the cause of alcoholism any more than gasoline can be considered the cause of automobile accidents. Certainly alcoholism could be done away with entirely by prohibiting the use of alcohol, but this would equally be true of automobile accidents, which could be eliminated by prohibiting the sale of gasoline. There is no reason to deprive those who drink normally and in a controlled manner—and they represent the vast majority—of their alcoholic beverages simply because a comparatively small percentage of individuals cannot drink safely. But it is imperative for those who cannot tolerate it that they stop using alcohol completely. There is a small percentage of every population who cannot safely do the same things that most of their friends and neighbors can do. Almost everybody has some limitation, and it is necessary to learn to live with that limitation without imposing it upon his neighbors.

The causes of alcoholism lie not in the agent that brings it about, but in the individual who drinks to excess. Because a fair number of alcoholics are afflicted with alcoholism from the time of their very first drink, and because in others it does not occur until after five to twenty years of drinking, it appears that something exists in the first group that takes five to twenty years to occur in the second. What this is, however, has never been ascertained. Perhaps there is some biochemical change in an individual, or some biochemical condition that exists from birth, that compels him to continue drinking alcohol once he starts, and perhaps this biochemical condition occurs in other individuals only after they have been drinking for long periods.

Many theories have been advanced about the causes of alcoholism. Some theories hold that the hormone glands are responsible for this condition, but no proof has as yet been shown of this. Others believe that the dietary regimen may be responsible, and that the lack of certain elements in the diet may bring about the condition, but this has also never been satisfactorily proved and still remains but a theory. There is general agreement that alcoholism is the result of personality traits in the individual who finds in alcohol, a common drug, a method of making himself feel more comfortable, and that his use of the drug is merely self-medication. As with many other drugs, however, it has been found that this can become more than a habit to such an individual; it can become an addiction.

The reasons for drinking, therefore, are many and varied, and actually lie within the personality of the individual who drinks. When a person drinks he drinks for many reasons, but when he drinks excessively and without control, it is because he wishes to place himself in a state more comfortable than the state he was in before he began to drink. Since alcohol is an anesthetic agent and the individual drinking it excessively wishes to anesthetize himself to the extent where he is not aware of anything unpleasant around him, and since he wishes to be in this state because the state of realistic living is too uncomfortable, then we can say that the cause of alcoholism is the inability of the individual to face the realistic problems of living and deal with them to the best of his ability. The preference for escape into partial or total oblivion by means of an available drug is the most common cause of alcoholism in our society.[3]

[3] "Approaching the Problem of Alcoholism," M. A. Block. *Medical Times*, Sept., 1963.

CHAPTER 3

The Problem as a Public Health Matter

ALCOHOLISM represents but one segment of a tremendous mental health problem. Alcohol itself is but the agent through which the disease process manifests itself; without it there would be no alcoholism. The same etiological factors might produce many other behavioral problems, but for those who resort to alcohol as a drug to meet their particular needs, these etiological factors manifest themselves in excessive drinking and eventual addiction.

In our country, the prevalent type of alcoholism is that in which there is an attempt to escape the realities and problems of living by excessive use of alcohol. Criteria by which the species of alcoholism are differentiated, as was mentioned before, are the presence or absence of psychological dependence, control, progression, and a combination of tissue tolerance and physiological dependence, characterized by symptoms of withdrawal.[1] From the point of view of public health, therefore, efforts should be made to help individuals suffering from this illness to meet the realities of living through education, example, and support. A generalized pro-

[1] *Disease Concept of Alcoholism*, E. M. Jellinek. Hillhouse Press, New Haven, Conn., 1960.

gram must stress the futility of attempting to escape from these realities and of avoiding responsibilities through a readily available and socially acceptable drug.

If the estimate of about five million in this country who suffer from alcoholism is correct, it means that about 6 percent of our adult population, or one out of every fifteen, is afflicted with this illness. Numerically, there are few public health problems that match this in importance. As with any other illness, the earlier it can be detected and treatment instituted, the sooner recovery can be accomplished. Obvious, then, is the tremendous need for everyone to be acquainted with the early signs and symptoms of this illness. Even more important is the necessity of impressing the general public with the fact that it is a prevalent illness, a serious and progressive disease that requires help for its victims at its very earliest manifestations.

For purposes of early diagnosis, it is necessary that the very early signs or even suspicions be accepted as criteria, if we are going to meet this illness as a public health problem. Strictly from a public health viewpoint, we could justify comparative disregard for the present alcoholic population in favor of efforts directed totally at prevention of future alcoholics. The present generation of alcoholics will eventually disappear with time, with or without treatment, and whether they recover or not. We have a responsibility to try to alleviate their suffering, correct their pathology, and, to as great a degree as possible, return them to normal health. However, if we do not take the necessary steps to prevent a future generation from taking their place, we have gained nothing in the overall public health picture. Prevention, then, is the objective, as with any other health problem.

The slightest difficulty with alcohol consistent with drinking, and occurring at any time, should be considered a problem for the person so affected. The term "alcoholism" conjures up in the minds of most people the Skid Row bum. This small percentage of the alcoholic population can hardly be considered typical of alcoholism in the light of our present knowledge. In its early stages, often called problem drinking, alcoholism may be recognized only by the adverse effects upon the drinker, which are consistently present when he drinks. The fact that he does not correspond to the image of the alcoholic in another individual's mind does not mean he is not alcoholic. It can mean that he is in the early stages of a progressive disease that may be as yet unrecognized. Certainly the average layman cannot be relied upon to make a diagnosis, since he does not know the necessary criteria. The patient himself cannot judge accurately, because the very illness itself adversely modifies his judgment. In addition the stigma still attached to the term "alcoholism" encourages denial on the part of the patient. This same stigma will often affect the judgment of the people interested in the patient—family and friends—who would rather deny the facts than apply a term of opprobrium to one they love.

Although there is no indisputable proof that high fat foods cause high cholesteremia or atherosclerosis, there seems to be no criticism attached to the individual who refuses to eat such high fat foods. He is regarded, rather, as a wise person who takes no risks with his health. Even if his actions are based only on a theory, an alcoholic could be in a similar position if we had proper education about alcohol. Certainly everyone who eats excessive amounts of fat will not necessarily suffer from atherosclerosis, but precaution can be respected and not ridiculed, and I need not add that there are many who enjoy high cholesterol foods. The same attitude can be applied to alcohol and its use.

How, then, can we meet so prevalent and serious a problem? Alcoholism represents but one of a serious group of illnesses affecting the behavior of individuals. Its recognition depends not only on the physical or mental state of the individual, but also on the mores and behavioral patterns of the culture in which he lives. The social pressures and customs of the people determine what constitutes average reaction, and in this area there is dire need for further exploration, research, and education. One thing we must acknowledge, however, is that where an individual or his family or society as a whole suffers as a result of a given type of behavior, it constitutes a problem that must be corrected.

In approaching the mental health aspects of alcoholism as a disease, and its prevention, it is essential that a broad educational program be directed at improving mental attitudes toward life generally. This should be conducted on all planes, starting from early youth up through adulthood, in all formal educational spheres. It should include the primary as well as the secondary schools, and the colleges and graduate schools. It is essential that young people be taught to live in a world that is real and not always pleasant, to realize that problems are part of living and must be contended with to the best of their ability.

Prevention must be on many levels. It must include theory and methodology and community mental health approaches. The objective is to reduce impact of stress on individuals where possible, and increase the ability of individuals to cope with stress. It must include education on alcoholism itself as an illness, and patterns of behavior and attitudes of groups toward drinking generally. Not only must the teaching be done by formal methods, but informally by family members, clergymen, police, and court personnel, as well as those persons involved in the so-called caretaker disciplines.

We live in a complex and troubled world. Tensions must be accepted as part of daily living, and should be considered part of normal life. Frustrations must not always be unexpected, and the ability to accept such situations must be part of every individual's training. When adverse situations become overwhelming, all human beings desire to retreat. Such a retreat can be done knowingly and with consciousness of the reasons for such a retreat. To attempt any escape into complete unreality, however, or oblivion itself, is an abnormal response. Under exceptional circumstances—overwhelming grief or tragedy—a period of temporary oblivion through drugs may be justified, but resorting to drugs at the slightest frustration or tension promotes a diminution in the resistance so necessary to overcome the problems of living. Alcohol is one of these drugs, which because of its ready availability and its social acceptance has been used far too often for this purpose. We must recognize that it is but the agent, while the actual etiological factors still reside in the individual using it.

In addition to this aspect of the alcoholism problem, there is another that requires the attention of public health agencies even more. I refer to the communicability of the illness. There is no direct evidence that alcoholism is inherited as such; that is, that it comes down generation to generation through the genes or the chromosomes. But it has been demonstrated that in families where one member is alcoholic, the environment and circumstances become conducive to the production of the same problem in other members of the family. In their method of escaping realities children tend to imitate their parents, even when there is objection to the method used. It is important, then, that education on this aspect be intensified, particularly for those exposed to such communicability.

Another finding that is extremely interesting, and that is a variation of the communicability, is that often the children of an alcoholic parent will become rigidly prejudiced against drinking altogether, and will not drink any alcoholic beverage all his life. This rigidity is carried to a point where drinking is not allowed in the house and is forbidden to the children. As the result of such intense feeling and rigidity, rebellion is very often engendered in the children, who will often drink excessively because of the prohibition in the home, so that in some instances we see the alcoholism skipping a generation and the grandchild of the original alcoholic becoming alcoholic in turn.

In order to prevent such communicability, basic patterns

must be changed. Just as Prohibition engendered a disregard for law and order and it became smart to circumvent the law, proper mass education can engender new attitudes. As was stated previously, in those cultures where excessive drinking is not tolerated and social ostracism is a penalty for violation, very little excessive drinking is seen. By teaching parents that their own behavior is of extreme importance in determining the future of their children, we may be able to convince them that the true sophisticate, if he drinks at all, never does so excessively, and if he cannot control his drinking, knows he must not even start. Early recognition of the indications of problem drinking and speaking freely about them, without prejudice, would remove the stigma for those for whom it would be wiser to abstain.

There is nothing here that should be construed as antialcohol. There are people who are afflicted with certain illnesses for no apparent reason. With some, we can eventually account for the reason. With others we cannot. From a public health viewpoint it is imperative, therefore, that we explore every reasonable avenue to learn as much as we can about the etiology and treatment of alcoholism. Until we can pinpoint the exact cause, however, it is essential that we take whatever measures we know will help us to recognize the problem early and to treat those suffering from it. Beyond that, it is essential that we institute proper measures of prevention of an illness that, without a doubt, can be prevented.

When, through some circumstance or another, the illness does strike, we must be alerted to early case-finding. Many in the public health field are in exceptionally unique positions to serve in this capacity. Physicians, nurses, visiting nurses, public health officers, and all technical personnel must be trained to recognize the early signs of problem drinking or alcoholism. Those in public welfare departments and other social welfare groups also must be alerted to the possibility of this illness in their clients. Industry must cooperate in case-finding and rehabilitation of those in their employ suffering from this disease. The Government has the responsibility of providing the necessary facilities for treatment of those who cannot afford private care. Alcoholism has medical, psychiatric, sociological, and economic aspects, all of which must be considered when attacking the problem. More than any other agency, the Government is equipped to provide and coordinate activities in these areas.

Frequent drinking sprees, drinking the first thing in the morning, time lost from work or duties, the necessity for drinking at definite periods of the day, drinking to gain courage, blackouts or periods of amnesia, criticism of the individual by one's relatives or friends—all constitute the early signs of alcoholism. Whenever alcohol is used as a drug rather than a beverage, to produce certain effects at certain times rather than as a social grace, then the beginning of problem drinking is evident. To get the patient at this stage of the illness means that he can be saved a great deal of trouble. He must be influenced at this time to seek treatment from any of the available public or private resources which stand ready to help him. The tendency on the part of the individual to deny that his drinking is excessive or beyond his control, or even interfering with his life, must be overcome not by scolding or criticism but by education about what constitutes alcoholism and how at its very inception the signs are not too different from those of heavy social drinkers.

Once the disease is diagnosed, then the treatment facilities must be made available to the individual requiring them. Hospital inpatient departments, outpatient clinics, halfway houses, rehabilitation centers, foster homes, and employment opportunities must all be made available to the individual who is to be rehabilitated. This should be part of any public health program, and it is not until all these facilities are made available that a complete program for prevention of the disease can be considered to have been instituted.[2]

[2] "Public Health Aspects of Alcoholism," M. A. Block. *N.Y. State Journal of Medicine,* Vol. 63, No. 2. Jan. 15, 1963.

CHAPTER 4

How Alcohol Affects Humans

ALCOHOLS in the proper concentrations can be considered narcotics or anesthetics.[1] In its way, alcohol can be compared to such anesthetics as ether and chloroform. Narcotics, in concentrations lower than that necessary to induce narcosis, act to produce stimulation of neural structures, and so, in minute doses, may be considered stimulants. Alcohol and other anesthetics, however, though they produce what appears to be stimulation, are rather depressants of the cortical control centers. With the depression of the controls there is an illusion of stimulation or hyperactivity, in much the same way as an automobile without brakes, even though going slowly, gives the illusion of speed because of the lack of control. It is this effect of alcohol, the depression of the cortical control centers, that gives the feeling of stimulation or hyperactivity in the human being after ingestion of sufficient quantities. The same result occurs in the administration of anesthesia when sufficient anesthetic has been administered to inhibit the controls of the cortical centers; the individual under an-

[1] *Some Effects of Alcohols on the Central Nervous System*, R. G. Grennell. Publication No. 47 *American Association for the Advancement of Science*, 1957.

esthesia at this stage becomes hyperactive and sometimes requires restraint until sufficient additional anesthetic agent is given to produce deeper narcosis, which does away with all muscular activity on a controlled level.

The ingestion of alcohol by a human being acts as a mild anesthetic, and in its early stages produces only a mild depression of the cortical centers. This loss of control very often gives the illusion of stimulation to the individual, and produces in increase of his activity beyond that which he normally demonstrates. There is a relaxation of his controls and his awareness so that any cares or troubles he may have seem to dissolve. At the stage of .05 to .1 percent of alcohol in the blood, or from one part of alcohol to two thousand parts of blood to one part of alcohol to one thousand parts of blood, there is this very pleasant glow that is conducive to relaxation and freedom from care, which is the purpose of most social drinking. At this stage, the self-conscious individual loses a great deal of his diffidence, the person with a sense of inferiority will often have a feeling of self-confidence, and those who lack courage will often feel a sense of bravery. It is a pleasant sensation, and one much sought after by the average drinker who finds in this relaxed period a relief from the everyday cares of his workaday world. Alcohol acts as a social lubricant, which makes for freer interrelationships and conversation among people who otherwise might feel strange toward each other.

In the type of alcoholism most prevalent in the United States and Canada, we find a tendency toward exaggeration of this drinking to a point where susceptible people seek to attain a permanent state of the uninhibited, relaxed freedom that relieves them of the cares and responsibilities of their world and allows them to live in this rosy dream world of alcohol. For such as these, such social drinking, continued day after day, will lead them more and more to seek this method of escape from the problems of living, rather than face up to the difficulties of these problems.

The history of the world is replete with episodes and reports of civilizations that, having reached a pinnacle of material wealth and success, have sought only the pleasures of living. Once having assumed the responsibilities and surmounted the obstacles, successful individuals sought the rewards of their industry in the material benefits that accrued to them as a result of their success. With the accumulation of material things that came with success in these civilizations, these people devoted themselves to a pursuit of happiness and carefree living that, now that they were absolved of responsibilities, allowed them to dally for days on end in orgies of irresponsibility. These orgies were usually accompanied by excessive drinking of alcohol, which added to the carefree feeling and irresponsibility of the time. The work and the difficulties of living were taken care of by the conquered people or the slaves over whom the succcessful and wealthy people had complete control.

With the decline of the sense of responsibility, and with the absence of the care that characterized their ascent to the top, came a carelessness about what went on around them and a concentration on enjoyment of the fruits of their victories. Each civilization that enjoyed this level of success and material wealth thought that such conditions would go on forever, and the longer they enjoyed themselves, the more irresponsible and unwary they became. These were the "haves" of their time. The "have-nots," however, the poor people, the slaves, the workers, and those who could not enjoy these orgies, waited only until such time as the irresponsibility and the unwariness of the "haves" reached the point where the "have-nots" could come in and conquer. The "have-nots" in turn went through exactly the same cycle of irresponsibility as their predecessors.

And so the various civilizations of the world rose to great empires and fell in a cycle of such striking similarity that it is a wonder that, with all the intelligence and observation of human beings, nothing had been learned from any civilization by the succeeding one. The excessive drinking of alcoholic beverages throughout the decline of civilizations often serves as an index to the decadence of a civilization.

For those individuals who find that they cannot measure up to the challenges of life, and who cannot admit to themselves that they are inadequate in meeting these challenges, it is much simpler to inflate the ego by drinking alcohol than to face and overcome a feeling of inadequacy in a situation. The assembly-line laborer who is continually criticized by his supervisor cannot answer the criticisms leveled at him when he knows in his heart that they are justified. On his way home, however, he may stop at a local tavern and after a few beers he may tell his supervisor off in no uncertain terms. The supervisor may not be there, but at least it gives the individual laborer the opportunity of venting his spleen—after his courage has been strengthened by a few shots of alcohol.

The self-conscious youth who finds it difficult to say the proper things to the young lady sitting next to him at a party finds a great deal more courage and ability to express himself after a cocktail or two. His remarks may seem inane to the listener, but to him they are the epitome of brilliant repartee.

The inarticulate member of the audience who cannot disagree with the speaker may, after a drink or two, get up and argue vehemently upon a subject he knows nothing about, and the unhappy wife who finds that her marriage is disintegrating and that she can no longer hold the attention of her husband may find that a pint of whiskey when she is alone will help dissolve her troubles. When any of these people, or persons like them, find it easier to take a few drinks than to handle the situation that is giving them trouble, and when this becomes a habit upon which they become dependent, we have the beginning of a dependence on alcohol that might be considered psychological, but which nevertheless has brought about in those individuals the disease known as alcoholism.

When the ingestion of alcohol for any purposes whatever, but particularly for the purposes outlined, continues over long periods of time and in excessive amounts on frequent occasions, then the tissues of the body become tolerant to the drug and develop the necessity for increased dosages to produce the desired effect. After this is continued for a length of time, the tissues actually become dependent upon the presence of the drug in order to function adequately at all. The individual is then physiologically addicted to the drug. The progress of this disease from psychological dependence to physiological dependence is so insidious, so gradual, that the individual involved is the last one to recognize his dependence. Others usually see it in him before he does, and when he is confronted with the possibility, the victim often makes an immediate attempt to deny it. There then follows attempt after attempt to control his drinking, to rationalize his drinking, and a vehement denial on his part that his drinking is excessive.

Where is the line drawn between the heavy social drinker and the problem drinker, or between the problem drinker and the alcoholic? There is no sharp line of demarcation between these classifications, or stages, of alcoholism. There is, rather, a hazy area between the stages in which the individual might be considered in more than one classification simultaneously—heavy social drinker, problem drinker, early alcoholic. Problem drinking is considered an early stage of alcoholism. How, then, does one tell whether one is a problem drinker or an alcoholic?

A problem drinker is exactly what the name implies. Anyone in whom the ingestion of alcohol produces an adverse effect consistent with his drinking, whether it be continuous or intermittent, is a problem drinker. In other words, anyone in whom the ingestion of alcohol produces a problem is a problem drinker. It is of litle consequence whether the problem that ensues is a minor one, such as an argument with one's spouse, or a hangover, or more serious consequences, such as an automobile accident, an arrest for drunkenness, loss of time from one's work, or hospitalization for drunkenness. An extension of that condition is the alcoholic, with whom drinking becomes compulsive; that is, once he starts to drink he cannot stop until he is taken in hand by someone else, or until he is completely anesthetized by the drug. At this stage the individual is an alcoholic. He has lost control over his drinking. He never intends to drink too much, but once started he always does.

Some of the characteristics of behavior in alcoholics that occur in chronological sequence of the disorder are as follows:

> The early phase of behavior in alcoholism consists of frequent excessive drinking, which need not necessarily result in getting drunk. The behavior includes a tendency to take extra drinks in preparation for a party, sneaking drinks during the party, drinking in order to feel at ease with others, drinking in order to feel at ease with the opposite sex, or in order to get up enough courage to dance, blackouts or periods of amnesia during which the behavior of the individual does not seem different to those observing him, but during which time the victim himself has no memory of what went on. These blackouts may vary from seconds to several hours in length.
>
> The second phase, which is the beginning of addiction, is characterized by frequent excessive drinking, loss of control after a few drinks, extravagant behavior characterized by phone calls, particularly long distance calls, taking taxicabs for unreasonably long trips, being exceedingly generous in treating others, and paying for such treats. Reproach by family and friends is also common during this period. Rationalizing his drinking patterns by what he thinks are appropriate alibis, deceiving himself as to the amount he is drinking, lying to himself and others, and excuses for the excessive drinking are also frequent. At this time, also, drunken driving may be one of the characteristics. Another common characteristic at this phase is the humiliation of the spouse in the presence of others. This is particularly true

when there are underlying hostilities between the two. This phase may also consist of solitary drinking on the part of the individual.

The next phase, during which the addiction gets under way, is also characterized by frequent excessive drinking, and also by drinking in the morning, the need for more alcohol in order to produce the same effect that less produced before, antisocial acts, fights, arrest, aggressiveness. At this period the victim begins to lose his friends and uses as an excuse the fact that his friends are no longer interesting. Characteristic here is not only the individual's walking out on his friends, but also his friends walking out on him. During this stage there is considerable resentment against anyone discussing his drinking, he develops unreasonable hostilities toward those with whom he works, begins to resent his employer, unreasonably, and eventually loses his job. At this time he may seek medical or psychiatric advice, and complain of inability to sleep and inability to eat. Very often he will neglect his eating in favor of drinking.

He may at this time also be hospitalized for his drinking problem. At this stage, also, he becomes much less particular about what kind of alcohol he drinks. He may try to go for longer or shorter periods without drinking. He promises himself never to drink again. He promises others that he will not drink. After failure to keep these promises, he may decide to go only on beer, or only on wine, rationalizing that this will not make him alcoholic. He may take to other medications, and ask for pills from his physician or druggist or friends in order to help overcome his nervousness. He begins to neglect his family and his duties. He begins to project his problems, blaming others for his trouble, and feeling sorry for himself. He may go on long binges of drinking, or finally adopt an attitude of "What difference does it make? I may as well continue to drink." [2]

---

[2] "Depth Psychology, Morality, and Alcoholism," by John C. Ford, S.J., A.M., LL.B., S.T.D. Proceedings of the fifth Annual Meeting of the Catholic Theological Society of America. Washington, D.C. June 26-28, 1950.

After the addiction has become complete, the drinking continues without any attempt at control. He finds that it takes less liquor to make him drunk. He begins to have periods of remorse. When unable to get anything in the way of proper drinking alcoholic beverage, he may drink anything that contains alcohol, such as shaving lotion, vanilla extract, even perfume. In this stage he begins to protect his supply so that he will be guaranteed enough alcohol when he needs it. He begins to develop tremors, which are noticeable after a binge; in addition he may have a hangover. His sex urge becomes less potent, although his desire may increase with his drinking. He begins to have vague indeterminate fears of retribution. He becomes resentful of his spouse and his family, and these resentments become quite unreasonable. He may attempt to escape from his problems by moving from one area to another. This is merely a substitution for the escape into alcohol. He may develop convulsions or so-called "rum fits." He may develop delirium tremens or hallucinations. He finds himself unable to rationalize his drinking or to produce sufficient alibis even to satisfy himself. He may attempt to commit suicide in his despair and depression. He may be committed to an institution for his problem, or eventually end up on Skid Row with a definite psychosis due to alcoholism; or he may die.

These are the progressive stages of the disease. It may vary in different individuals, not follow exactly the pattern outlined, but generally speaking, this is the progression the illness takes.

There are a number of questions that have been posed for individuals to answer in order to ascertain whether or not they are alcoholic, such as:

1. Do you take a drink the first thing in the morning?
2. Do you drink alone?
3. Do you feel the necessity for a drink at a definite time of the day?

4. Do you have blackouts or periods of amnesia?
5. Do you go on frequent drinking sprees?
6. Do you miss time from your work or your duties as a result of drinking?

These are not necessarily placed in the order of their importance. Other questions that might be asked are:

7. Do you deny your drinking?
8. Do you have periods of remorse following drinking sprees?
9. Do you start promising not to drink the way you have?
10. Do you begin to lie about your drinking?
11. Do you find yourself beginning to gulp drinks while other people drink slowly?
12. Do you take a drink before going out to a party where you know there will be drinking?
13. Do you space your drinks, or try to space them, and always fail?
14. Do you find excuses for drinking, or excuses for celebrating?
15. Do you feel the necessity for a pick-me-up, which must always be alcoholic?
16. Do you take a drink to settle your nerves?

A very important sign, which I consider extremely indicative, is the reaction to criticism of the victim's drinking by someone who cares about him. If a spouse, a child, or a parent criticizes the drinking of someone in the family, this is a very important point to be considered in the diagnosis of the drinker and it should be heeded by the person involved. Of course, there are those individuals who will criticize any drinking, but I am speaking of people who care about the individual they are criticizing, who see in this individual the tendency to excessive alcohol ingestion, and who see it long before the individual involved may himself recognize his excessive drinking.

How Alcohol Affects Humans

It must be borne in mind that anyone who drinks alcohol may become an alcoholic, even though alcohol is not alone the cause of alcoholism, but merely the agent that brings about the malady. The actual etiological factors are resident in the individual, and not in the alcohol itself. We all recognize that it is the driver behind the wheel who is the cause of an automobile accident, and not the agent—gasoline—that allows the car to run.

There are those alcoholics, of course, who do not drink as a psychological expedient, but whose excessive ingestion of alcohol over long periods of time produces a dependence of the tissues of the body upon the presence of alcohol. Withdrawal of the alcohol brings about the kind of signs and symptoms seen in the chronic alcoholic.

Alcoholism comes about in a most circuitous way, usually without the knowledge of the individual who is becoming addicted. It is incumbent upon everyone who drinks, therefore, to be alert to the early signs of this disease. What is more, it takes a great deal of honesty on the part of each individual to evaluate his own situation when it comes to drinking.

CHAPTER 5

Alcoholism and the Law

ONE cannot legislate against a disease. Nonetheless, many attempts have been made through the years to handle the problem of alcoholism through legal methods. When treatment for mental patients was limited to punishment, the same theory —that such patients were possessed by an evil spirit that could be driven out by beatings or other abuses—was applied to alcoholics. It was thought that punishment would teach them not to drink, thus eliminating the objectionable behavior. Little thought was given to the reasons for their excessive drinking; the only objective was to make them stop. As is usual when such an approach is used, punishment failed to deter those who drank.

In all probability the main reason for invoking the law was for the protection of those who suffered as a result of the drinker's apparent irresponsibility and behavior, not for the protection of the person affected by alcohol. From this viewpoint, any antisocial behavior that adversely affected others was sufficient reason to take the offender into custody. No attempt was made to determine the reasons for such behavior; the offense was deemed deliberate, and punishment was meted out as a deterrent to future offenses. Even the slightest understanding of the compulsive character of alcoholism should expose this fallacy. The term *compulsion* in itself explains why certain persons have no control over their actions, and, thus, why punishment is useless. Only proper treatment will have any effect upon the alcoholic.

An equal and opposite mistake would be to legislate relief for alcoholics. Only a few years ago Congress was considering legislation in which an attempt would be made to include alcoholism among the totally and permanently disabling diseases meriting disability allowances. There is no doubt about the merits of such a law for permanently and totally disabled individuals who cannot be rehabilitated. There is, however, no such thing as a hopeless alcoholic. There is no such thing as an alcoholic who cannot be rehabilitated. This does not mean that there are not people who as a result of alcoholism are eventually totally and permanently disabled, but in such cases we are speaking not of alcoholism *per se* but of complications resulting from excessive drinking and chronic alcoholism. In these cases the diagnosis would not be alcoholism, but rather cirrhosis of the liver, Korsakoff's syndrome, Wernicke's disease, chronic brain deterioration, or other serious organic disturbances. At that time (1955) I gave the following statement to the Senate Committee considering the bill:

> Mr. Chairman and members of the Senate Committee on Finance:
>
> I am Marvin A. Block, M.D., a practicing physician in Buffalo, New York. I am a member of the board of directors of the National Council on Alcoholism and president of the Western New York Committee for Education on Alcoholism.
>
> I am particularly interested in H.R. 7225, from the point of view of patients suffering from the illness in which I specialize—chronic alcoholism. I wish to stress the fact that this illness, alcoholism, which affects so many people, responds favorably to medical treatment.

Alcoholism is the compulsive and uncontrolled drinking of alcohol, interfering with the patient's life, his interpersonal relationships, his ability to earn a livelihood, and to cope with the ordinary problems of life. These patients have a low threshold for suffering and require relief from the ordinary tensions of living. They usually suffer from neuroses characterized by anxieties and immature emotional reactions. They often have feelings of severe inadequacy and inferiority. For the most part, alcoholics seek in drink an escape from the frustrations and problems of everyday living. They are dependent people, in spite of their constant attempts to appear otherwise.

One of the greatest obstacles with which the physician, as well as the family of the patient, must contend is the failure of the individual patient to recognize that he is suffering from an emotional illness and should seek help. Alcoholism alone can rarely, if ever, be considered an illness which is totally and permanently disabling. On the other hand, as with other addictions, recovery depends to a great extent upon the incentive which the patient mobilizes to seek such recovery. Rehabilitation of such patients necessitates not only improvement of their physical health but, of equal importance, a re-education toward assuming responsibility in contending with the adversities of living encountered by us all.

In order to accomplish recovery, proper motivations must be present in each patient. This would apply in any illness. With alcoholics, however, the lack of incentive toward rehabilitation is one of the notoriously adverse symptoms encountered. The symptom is understandable, since alcohol offers escape from responsibility, an escape which so many of these patients seek. Any agent which tends to diminish motivation for recovery would therefore tend to increase the severity of the illness and eventually contribute to the disintegration of the patient. In my opinion, benefits under bill H.R. 7225 would adversely affect patients suffering from alcoholism, since it would discourage them from assuming

Alcoholism and the Law

the responsibility of caring for themselves. These already dependent people might use such benefits to prolong their dependence, increasing the severity of their illness with the proceeds of their disability. Such benefits would be tantamount to subsidizing the illness. It would also provide patients with funds with which to purchase the means of prolonging and intensifying their ailment, thus creating a vicious cycle.

The usual age of alcoholic patients a few years ago was forty-five to fifty-five. This age bracket for alcoholics has now been reduced to a usual thirty-five to forty-five years. From these figures it can be assumed that alcoholism is an illness ordinarily found in the fourth decade of life. To give these patients an opportunity for disability benefits at the age of fifty would afford them very little time for rehabilitation before applying for disability. In any disease which takes years to acquire, very rapid rehabilitation cannot be expected. Incentive for rehabilitation might be discouraged if financial benefit looms on the horizon at so early an age.

Contrary, I believe, to the purpose of the bill, the patient who tries to help himself to recovery receives no benefits. The person who gives up, on the other hand, and accepts his inability to recover, thereby becomes permanently disabled and eligible for benefits. Where treatment for rehabilitation is required, the threat of having benefits withdrawn or not forthcoming militates against the chances of effective recovery and rehabilitation.

From my experience with many of these patients, they may accede to any treatment prescribed. However, with cash benefits available for disability, good responses to such treatment in most cases will not be accomplished. Since there is no specific remedy for aiding these people, much depends upon a strong motivation for recovery. Payment for permanent disability will not provide this type of incentive, but may act in the opposite manner. Many of these people live alone and under substandard conditions. It is characteristic of the illness that they do not eat properly since their primary interest is drinking. Even a small income would be sufficient for them to subsist and yet continue to drink, thus prolonging both the illness and disability. The inevitable complications following prolonged drinking, poor nutrition, and substandard living conditions would expose these people to physical deterioration and other illnesses which come with debilitation. Disability then would be more intense and prolonged.

Certification to total and permanent disability would be very difficult. Alcoholism responds to treatment when such treatment is conscientiously followed. This, of necessity, depends upon the cooperation of the patient. Such cooperation cannot be enforced. Pressure upon physicians to certify to disability would be tremendous. This pressure might be exerted not only by the patients but by their families, who would regard this act as an opportunity to get income for patients who heretofore had been a burden but would not cooperate in seeking help to recovery. Indeed, many of these patients refuse to acknowledge their condition as a serious illness.

In my opinion, further study is necessary to find means of helping these patients to recovery without putting a cash premium on their remaining ill. The neuroses from which these people suffer would only be aggravated to greater complications by any measure which might encourage the patient to remain sick. It must always be borne in mind that alcoholics are dependent people who use alcohol as a crutch to support an unstable personality. To add another crutch in the way of cash benefits will only succeed in making them more dependent.

For those patients unable to work there are usually local agencies where application for financial assistance can be made. These agencies, after thorough investigation, will help indigent people, but also supervise, in most instances, how such money is spent. The patient therefore does not lack for the necessities of life. Social workers in these agencies also recommend methods of rehabilitation and encour-

Alcoholism and the Law

age patients to seek such resources. The natural antipathy of people toward receiving such help and supervision often prompts them to rehabilitation and independence. Benefits from social security, however, where premiums are paid, are looked upon as a right. There would be no supervision of the expenditure of such benefits once they are paid, and no desire, therefore, for rehabilitation. Recovery might mean cessation of benefits and inability to purchase the material to which the patient is addicted. Since addicts of all kinds are known to go to any lengths to obtain the drug or medication to which they are addicted, it cannot be expected that they will act any differently in the case of receiving moneys through disability.[1]

The above statement to some extent illustrates how a good law can be perverted if it is not correctly administered, even allowing for the best of intentions.

Another example of paradoxical administration of the law has to do with driving while under the influence of alcohol. It is a well-known fact, attested to by district attorneys, that in jury trials for drunken driving there is little chance of conviction. *There but for the grace of God go I* is the attitude of most jurors, reflecting the tolerance for drunken behavior in our society. Many judges, however, will convict drunken drivers. The miscarriage of justice in jury trials happens only because drinking is such an acceptable part of our life—even when deaths are involved.

Driving a car has become one of the necessities of life in the United States. Whereas at one time a driver's license was regarded as a privilege conferred upon him by the government, to be revoked at any time if abused, today there are many judges who feel that a driver's license is an individual right, since his living may depend on it. For this reason, the

[1] Hearings before Committee on Finance, United States Senate; Eighty-fourth Congress; Part I, pages 399-401.

prosecution or the vehicle bureau must prove that the individual is not fit to have a driving license.

Welfare rolls can also subsidize the illness alcoholism. All too often families with one or more alcoholics are on the welfare rolls; all too often the alcoholic of the family will spend a large part, if not all, of the welfare check on alcoholic beverages while his wife and children go hungry. Government hospitals, particularly the municipal and county hospitals, have any number of alcoholic patients who, with revolving-door frequency, go in and out as welfare patients, alternately being dried out and returning, a short time later, drunk and ready for the next drying-out period. Sufficient investigation of these cases might reveal many alcoholics who should be carefully supervised before they are allowed to use these welfare resources repeatedly.

Every alcoholic patient is entitled to hospitalization for detoxification if he is sick enough. Acute alcoholic intoxication can be, and often is, a medical emergency. However, to encourage repeated admissions to hospitals for anyone on welfare, or to provide welfare funds for a family where an alcoholic is using the money to support his addiction, is only to subsidize the illness and make those about the alcoholic suffer. Such individuals should be subjected to compulsory treatment for long periods under proper supervision. In many instances it has been found that compulsory treatment produces good results in enough cases to justify it as a routine. Unfortunately, there seems to be too little interest in this phase of the rehabilitation program, and in too many instances the attitude of welfare departments and social workers is to let sleeping dogs lie rather than make more work for such overworked public servants.

In the matter of the driver's license, we find that too many individuals who drive while drunk are not properly examined to determine whether alcoholism exists. Such persons should be subjected to complete physical and psychiatric testing in order to ascertain whether they are alcoholic or irresponsible non-alcoholics who have drunk too much even though they can control their drinking. A person who has control of his drinking and drinks too much commits an irresponsible act and should be punished. But an individual who has no control over his drinking and is not aware of the fact that he is alcoholic is a sick individual and should be treated as such; he should be relieved of his responsibility in this case. Once having pleaded, however, to being an alcoholic, and having had a proper diagnosis and evaluation, he should not be deprived of his license; keeping his license should be contingent on his total sobriety. He should not have to be drunk again for it to be revoked; it should be automatically revoked should he take even one drink, because one drink is dangerous for an alcoholic. He must be on lifelong probation never to drink again. It seems to me that this would be a tremendous deterrent to alcoholics, as well as to those who are not alcoholic and might be tempted to use such a plea to avoid conviction for drunken driving. This approach would make for considerably greater safety on our streets and highways.

The municipal courts of all big cities are crowded with people who are arrested for public intoxication, vagrancy, and other offenses characterized by undesirable behavior and excessive alcohol ingestion. All too often the judge sitting on the bench, sympathetic though he may be to these prisoners, has no choice but to send them to jail. This represents a great loss in time, money, and human life. Were the period of incarceration used for rehabilitation purposes, something could be accomplished; incarceration merely as a punishment helps neither the individual nor his community.

It may be too much to expect that hospitals be erected for the purpose of treating alcoholics, but there is no reason why there should not be some facility where these persons could be detoxified and where an attempt at rehabilitation could be made. There is no reason why traveling teams of physicians, psychiatrists, social workers, and psychiatric social workers could not visit such facilities and provide complete physical examinations and psychiatric evaluations for these individuals in order to determine the extent to which they might be rehabilitated. The most promising ones could be sent to rehabilitation centers, where a good percentage could be returned to normal, healthy living. For those who cannot be so rehabilitated, who do not have the capacity for learning to be independent of alcohol, some facility should be provided on a total custodial basis.

In other parts of this book there are plans offered for the establishment of such facilities. If the plans were followed, judges would have a place to send these unfortunates, and many could be helped. This would save not only the individual and a great deal of manpower, but also millions of dollars for the community which now supports them.

A few years ago I had the opportunity to address the National Association of Municipal Judges in Colorado. The executive Secretary and Treasurer, Mr. Albert B. Logan, had worked for a long time to persuade the municipal court judges to look upon the alcoholic as a sick individual rather than as a criminal offender. Many judges have been successful in handling alcoholics brought before them. Such judges as William H. Burnett of Denver, Colorado, Hyman Feldman of Chicago, Illinois, Ray Harrison of Des Moines, Iowa, and numerous others have shown an understanding of the alcoholic that has brought credit to themselves and considerable benefit to the sick.

The National Association of Municipal Judges has as its objectives:

1) more effective dissemination and exchange of information and knowledge to its members;
2) more efficient and equitable administration of justice in the interest of the individual citizen to whom, more often than not, the municipal court represents a tribunal of original jurisdiction and a last resort;

3) nonpolitical selection of judges on the basis of adequate compensation;
4) improvement of the physical facilities of courtrooms and provision of adequate facilities and personnel for the services expected;
5) promotion of uniform civil and criminal procedures, including uniform traffic code and traffic tickets for stabilization and greater uniformity in sentences and penalties, and for standardization of procedures;
6) survey of the existing facilities, practices and needs of municipal courts on a national scale; and
7) formulation of methods of procedures to decrease congestion of municipal court calendars.

Judge Harrison recommends to those judges who have a "drunk calendar" that they:

1) acquire personal familiarity with A.A. therapy by attending A.A. meetings;
2) secure the cooperation of a number of stable A.A. members;
3) seek cooperation of local medical society and community alcoholism committees;
4) seek counsel of judges experienced in alcoholic rehabilitation programs;
5) confer with the probation officer, jail warden, police chief, budget director, city councils, civic organizations, state alcoholism commission, and hospital superintendents;
6) make the courts the alcoholic's friend rather than his warden.

The National Association of Municipal Judges has had several conferences at which excellent speakers from all over the country have dealt with the problem of alcoholism and how it can be handled by the judge. John Murtagh, Chief Judge of the Municipal Courts of New York City, and others have demonstrated the value of understanding the alcoholic and treating him as a sick person rather than punishing him. Through Murtagh's efforts, many alcoholics in New York City have been rehabilitated.

Judge Frank Sedita of Buffalo did an excellent job when he was on the municipal bench. Later, in his campaign for election as Mayor of Buffalo, he made his rehabilitation program for alcoholics one of the planks of his platform.

Various bar associations have also been interested in this problem. The New York State Bar Association, under the able leadership of the chairman of its Committee on Addiction, Colonel Harold Riegelman, has done a remarkable job in bringing to the attention of its members the importance of looking upon alcoholism as a disease and treating those afflicted with it as patients rather than as miscreants. Colonel Riegelman's report to the Governor and the Health Department of New York State and his activities on behalf of alcoholics in New York State while he was president of the National Council on Alcoholism have resulted in the initiation of a program on alcoholism, to be administered through the Department of Mental Hygiene in New York State. Through his efforts sufficient appropriation was made, not only to increase the educational programs in New York but also to carry out treatment and establish rehabilitation centers and research projects in various parts of the state. Attorneys across the country who in private life have given of their time and effort to help rehabilitate the alcoholic are too numerous to mention. They provide assistance by interesting their state bar associations in alcoholics, and by working with volunteer committees for education and rehabilitation of alcoholics.

In spite of efforts made by enlightened people, there are still many who feel that the alcoholic should be punished. Even relatives of the alcoholic, surprisingly enough, often feel that he should be punished when his actions become obnoxious. It is curious that the spouse of an alcoholic, once the alcoholic's behavior has become too much to handle, should demand that he be punished rather than treated as sick. However, at the time the punishment is to be meted out the spouse often does not wish to be there. Too, it often happens that when it becomes necessary to commit an alcoholic patient for treatment the spouse is unwilling to sign the commitment papers. When questioned, spouses have expressed the belief that the alcoholic would never forgive them for committing him, or her, to an institution. The spouse thereupon requests that the physician do the committing, in which case the nearest of kin must sign the commitment papers. Similarly, when an alcoholic patient misbehaves to the extent that he is actually violating some law and it becomes necessary for the police to interfere, the spouse will often insist that someone else sign the complaint that brings about the arrest.

A complete review of the relationship between alcoholism and the law is necessary if we are to adopt a pattern that will be fair to the community as well as to the alcoholic. There has been too much evasion of this very important area of an illness that, though not necessarily hereditary, is extremely communicable within families. The community has a responsibility not only to those who are well, but also to those who are sick. For too long it has evaded this responsibility to the alcoholic, applying a makeshift arrangement for the sake of conscience rather than the full treatment and research this illness deserves—and requires.

One other point needs discussion: compulsory treatment of individuals suffering from alcoholism. It has long been believed that compelling an individual to undergo treatment would not produce desirable results. Industry, however, in attempting to rehabilitate alcoholic employees, has achieved remarkable success. Here the alcoholic is compelled to accept rehabilitation or lose his job. If it can be done in industry, there is no reason why compulsory treatment of other alcoholics should not result in rehabilitation too. Although many alcoholics are afraid of treatment because they do not know what to expect of it, it usually takes only a short time to convince them that the treatment they so fear involves nothing frightening. Withdrawal from the drug under proper circumstances and surroundings can make rehabilitation not only desirable but pleasant. At present the public looks askance on most alcoholic rehabilitation facilities. This is true not only of the average layman, but often of professional personnel—physicians and nurses included. A change in this attitude would result in a much more pleasant climate for persons being rehabilitated and better effects would be achieved. However, this will require considerable education and understanding, as well as a great deal of money.

Many states are spending large sums in an attempt to achieve this type of rehabilitation. California, New York, Pennsylvania, Michigan, Florida, Colorado, Indiana, Illinois, New Hampshire, Connecticut, Vermont, New Jersey, North Carolina, Georgia, Mississippi, North Dakota, Washington, and Nevada all have programs on alcoholism supported by the government.

In many states, interest in the law and alcoholism has been manifested by leaders in the field. Dr. John Norris of New York, Harold W. Demone, Jr., of Massachusetts, Charles Methvin and Dr. Vernelle Fox of Georgia, Frona McCambridge and Dr. Edward Delehanty of Colorado, Clyde Gooderham of Utah, and Marian Wettrick of Pennsylvania have done much. In Canada, Ontario's excellent program has been under the guidance of David Archibald. A Toronto physician, Dr. Gordon Bell, contributed much there. There are many others in various parts of the country. More on this phase will be found in Chapter 14. All these people have worked under government auspices and with government funds. Of course, there is cooperation between these government-sponsored programs and the lay educational committees and information centers, as well as with the medical societies of the various states and counties.

Unfortunately, there seems to be no law that uniformly meets the requirements of all the states. It would be helpful if such a law could be drawn up, one that would allow for the treatment of the alcoholic patient, both medically and legally, in all states. An attempt to achieve such an end should be made by the medical and legal professions. Until there is greater uniformity of opinion as to the diagnosis of alcoholism and its complications, this may take some time. The laws regarding alcoholism must, of necessity, differ from the laws that apply to other mental health problems. There seem to be sufficient legal grounds governing those individuals diagnosed as psychotic, but no provision has been made for borderline cases that are not necessarily psychotic. The alcoholic falls into a special category. If he is psychotic in addition to being an alcoholic, the same rules that apply to any psychotic apply to him. But often we find alcoholics who have no psychotic tendencies whatever. When these people are not drinking, they are as "normal" as the average individual. A complete change in their personality takes place when they are drinking. It is at this time that they require special consideration, and it is at this time that special laws are required. Further, such laws must be enforced in such a manner that no undesirable stigma will be attached to the individuals involved.

Unfortunately, this stigma still attaches to the term "alcoholic." It would be a difficult task indeed to remove it, but it could be accomplished with the proper approach from the educational and legal viewpoints. An effort should be made by the American Bar Association and the American Medical Association to work jointly toward a satisfactory legal solution to the problem.

CHAPTER 6

Understanding the Alcoholic

PERHAPS the greatest obstacle to helping the patient suffering from alcoholism is the lack of understanding of those around him. Admittedly, it is difficult to label as alcoholic someone you have known for a long time and with whom you have shared a great deal of pleasure—indeed, someone with whom you have drunk. It is even more difficult to label oneself an alcoholic when one can see no difference between one's own drinking and that of so many of one's companions. The slight shadings and differences between the early alcoholic and the heavy social drinker are so vague and so small that differentiation between the two is difficult.

Nevertheless, it is this refusal to take the responsibility of labeling that has contributed to the progress of the disorder in many individuals. Rather than call the attention of someone we know to the possibility that his excessive drinking is alcoholism, we risk the health and happiness of that individual. And we take the same risk ourselves when we refuse to acknowledge that our drinking has become uncontrolled. It is true that in telling an individual he may be drinking excessively we risk his resentment, but to overlook this responsibility when the risk involves someone who is dear to us is to do him a disservice for which we must forever be answerable. The consequences may be calamitous.

The key to removal of these risks lies in the education of everyone on the subject of alcoholism. In times gone by, there were many diseases that were allowed to progress to hopelessness and death because acknowledgment of the presence of such a disease might bring disgrace upon an individual or his family. Not so long ago people suffering from tuberculosis were hidden away or relegated to institutions and never referred to for fear of the disgrace that might ensue from the knowledge that a member of the family was suffering from "consumption." More recently, the term "cancer" was rarely spoken of above a whisper and never acknowledged as having affected anyone near and dear. The stigma attached to these diseases was so great that many who were afflicted, rather than be labeled tubercular or cancerous, would not seek the services of a physician for fear of the label, as a result of which they were allowed to go to termination before medical aid was administered.

The same situation obtains today in many cases of the disease alcoholism. All too often individuals addicted to alcohol refuse to seek help from the medical profession lest their worst fears be confirmed, and they be labeled alcoholic, their families disgraced, and they lose their friends. Even greater is the fear that they will be admonished not to drink, a fate they cannot face. They would rather accept the possibility of chronic illness and death than abstain from alcohol. Because, to many of these people, alcohol has become the answer to any difficult problem, the prospect of trying to do without it is formidable. Many who have in alcohol at last found a way of relieving themselves of the terrible trials and tensions that beset them cannot again face those trials and problems without alcohol.

The vast majority of alcoholics who come to the physician at the behest of family, friends, employer, or clergyman—and it must be admitted that most do not come of their own accord but rather are pressured into seeking help—come not with the idea of seeking relief from their problems or help toward abstinence but with the idea of getting from the expert the assurance that they are not alcoholic. Many of the answers they give to the questions asked by the therapist are aimed at convincing the expert that they are not alcoholic but are simply using alcohol excessively. Denial and prevarication are part of the disease. An evasion of the actual truth is more common than the truth itself. This is not because these people wish to lie, but because they are attempting to protect themselves from the suffering they know will be their lot if the only relief they have found is denied them. When one understands the tragedy of this situation, one has a great deal more understanding and compassion for these sick people.

To illustrate the extent of this desperation we need only observe a common occurrence, one the therapist sees very often. When a patient is so sick that he requires hospitalization in order to withdraw him from his alcohol, the therapist explains to him both the necessity and the advantage of hospitalization. At last, much against his wish in most cases, the patient agrees to go to the hospital. To the surprise of the nurse and very often of the physician, the admitting clerk or the nurse finds a bottle of whiskey in his effects. The patient is aware that he is going into the hospital for the express purpose of being withdrawn from alcohol, and still he brings a bottle of whiskey.

On the surface, this seems to be extremely foolish, evasive, and contrary to his expressed intentions. Careful questioning, however, usually will elicit the fact that the patient is not being perverse, he is not being stubborn or tricky. He has not taken the whiskey into the hospital simply because he likes to drink. He has taken it for fear that at some time the physicians in charge will not give him sufficient drugs to permit him to be comfortable.

Many patients who have been rejected by their families

and by society generally expect to be similarly rejected by the physician to whom they go for help. Unconsciously, they will often test the physician's patience by ignoring his advice, arguing with him, irritating him with unreasonable rationalizations, and in other ways testing his professed acceptance of them as patients. The therapist must understand that such manifestations are part of the illness. Should the therapist allow his emotions to enter into the relationship and become disgusted or lose his temper, the alcoholic will have proved his own point—that here is another person who, not caring, has rejected him. Understanding this phase of the alcoholic patient's unconscious motives will help the therapist avoid falling into a trap. Continued patience with such an alcoholic will eventually yield the desired result.

Society has placed upon the drinking of alcoholic beverages an aura of desirability that most people cannot resist. There would seem to be no opprobrium attached to the diabetic who because of his disease will not eat foods that everyone else eats. When it comes to alcoholic beverages, however, drinkers look askance at nondrinkers. Because of the importance attached to drinking, many people do not want to be placed in a position where they will be conspicuous by their abstinence. Many alcoholics do not actually mind not drinking for a time. What they do mind is feeling conspicuous by their nondrinking. The conspicuousness that they fear exists only in their own minds.

Our American society fears those who do not conform to ordinary standards. The nonconformist is an oddball, a nut, square, and in many instances considered a radical, even a Communist, not because anyone knows anything about his political feelings, but because he does not conform to what society thinks he should do. There is a great need in this country for respect for people who do not conform to the ordinary standards. Though we speak of our desire for freedom, we fear those who insist on having it. Our educational standards have tended to cast suspicion on those who do not conform, rather than encouraging respect for the right to disagree. Here broader education is sorely needed.

Such education should first take place among young people, particularly in the secondary schools and colleges. They must be taught what alcohol is, what its potentials are, and the risks involved in using it. They must be taught, also, that alcohol is a drug that has definite effects which can become habit-forming as well as addictive. Young people must be educated prophylactically in their mental hygiene courses and in their homes so that they will be prepared to meet the problems of living without seeking escape in any drug, particularly in a socially popular one such as alcohol. When this sort of education has been made available on a broad level to all young people, it may be found that there will be an early recognition on the part of each individual of his susceptibility to alcohol as a drug, and if no stigma is attached to abstinence he may be able to refuse to drink rather than risk his health. Young persons must learn to respect the opinions of others, and that those who do not conform may have good reasons for not doing so—that to belong does not necessarily mean to follow blindly. Those who refuse to conform must have the courage not to be influenced by others who may ridicule them. All too often such ridicule is a defense for the scoffer's inability to withstand the pressure to conform.

The education of young people is extremely important and should be carried on not only in schools and at home but in the churches and youth organizations of our country. Prohibition of drinking among young people will not necessarily result in their not drinking. Prohibition has never worked, and where rigid restraints are imposed on young people there is a tendency for them to try what is forbidden just for "kicks." If we give them the correct information on the subject of alcoholism they will grow up to use this knowledge with judgment and discretion. They have done so with other problems, and they can do so with alcohol.

Education of the general public should be undertaken on

a much larger scale than heretofore. There have been exceptionally valuable agencies that have carried on this kind of education. The National Council on Alcoholism, with its affiliates distributed in all our large cities and many of our smaller ones, has done a tremendous job in helping to educate people on the subject of alcoholism. Unfortunately, since alcoholism is not a popular subject, they have had great difficulty financing their educational program. This organization and its affiiliates deserve everyone's support. They are the only lay group in the country carrying on an objective educational program on the subject. Such leaders as Marty Mann, Yvelin Gardner, Brinkley Smithers, Dr. Margaret Bailey, William Ferguson, Lewis F. Presnall, and others of the National Council have given much of their personal time to promoting the kind of program throughout the country that will help people to understand alcoholism as a disease, and to learn what to do about it.

Many schools are in existence throughout the country where the subjects of alcohol and alcoholism are taught, not only to professionals interested from their particular viewpoints, but to laymen. Such institutions as the Rutgers School of Alcohol Studies in New Jersey (formerly the Yale School of Alcohol Studies), the Mississippi School of Alcohol Studies, and the School of Alcohol Studies at the University of Utah are outstanding for the courses they offer. There are also schools in Wisconsin, Indiana, North Carolina, North Dakota, and Colorado, to name a few, which although they may not have a curriculum as complete as those above, nevertheless perform a valuable function in alcohol and alcoholism education. *The Quarterly Journal of Studies on Alcohol,* an outstanding periodical dealing with the subject, now published at the Rutgers School, is an excellent publication devoted to this purpose. Primarily for professional people, it can however be read by laymen and is an invaluable contribution to the field of alcoholism.

Many of the affiliates of the National Council put out their own publications. In addition, the *Observer* of Boston, the papers put out by the Florida State Rehabilitation Program, the Atlanta (Georgia) Program, the Detroit and Michigan Programs, the Cleveland affiliates, the Manitoba affiliate, the Ontario Commission on Alcoholism, the Maryland Department of Health, and many others provide for people interested in the subject various studies related to alcohol and the problems of alcoholism.

For the professional reader, of course, the various journals of medicine from the American Medical Association and the American Psychiatric Association, as well as many other medical and psychiatric journals, carry articles on alcoholism several times during the year. This is in marked contrast to the almost complete absence of such articles before 1945. There has been a further sharp increase in the number of articles on alcoholism published since 1956, when the illness was recognized officially by the American Medical Association.

All of this knowledge, when distributed, contributes to the greater understanding not only of the problem of alcoholism as a sociological phenomenon, but of the individual suffering from the disease. By and large, however, these periodicals and schools reach only a comparatively small percentage of our population. The vast majority, including those suffering from the illness itself, still does not recognize alcoholism as a disease or as the kind of illness in no way the fault of the person afflicted. The alcoholic patient usually has a tremendous sense of guilt and believes that he has brought the illness upon himself. True, when an alcoholic takes a drink he is aggravating his illness, but the drinking itself is only the manifestation of the illness. The illness lies in the craving for drink in an effort to find relief from whatever the pressures are that beset the individual. As with many other illnesses, alcoholic patients feel that they are weak, inferior, and that they do not match up to other individuals. Generally they do not understand that the same type of personality and problem as theirs may have neurotic manifestations other than excessive drinking. But many other neurotic manifestations, which result in excesses of other kinds, such as eating, work, gambling, are not looked upon with the same critical intolerance as alcoholism because they do not visibly affect the behavior of the individual. Not only must alcoholics themselves understand the alcoholic, his problems, and what to do about them, but this understanding must be part of everyone's education.

Why is it, then, that so many people refuse to recognize that they are afflicted with a condition over which they have no control, and for which the only answer is complete and total abstinence? What is so remarkable about a man who once drank and who completely stops drinking? Why should this be a subject for discussion or wonder? When he refuses a drink, why should anyone coax him to take one? Why should anyone even suggest that "just one won't hurt" him? The person who understands anything at all about alcoholism knows that not only can one drink hurt the alcoholic, it can prove disastrous to him. Everyone should appreciate this fact and make no fuss about the person who once drank and now refuses to drink. Why should he be made self-conscious at all? To refrain from drink is his privilege, and it is a terrible responsibility for anyone to question that privilege.

It is this degree of understanding of alcoholism and the alcoholic that, if spread throughout the entire population, with a keen appreciation for the factors involved, will take the opprobrium off the term and allow the alcoholic to mix in society without a feeling of self-consciousness. This understanding must become common knowledge; it must be an accepted fact. When it is, the lot of the alcoholic will be a great deal easier, and the recovery of alcoholics will be much more easily achieved.

CHAPTER 7

Treating the Alcoholic

THE person suffering from alcoholism requires treatment, not only by his physician, but also by everyone with whom he comes in contact. The alcoholic patient does not live in a vacuum, he lives among other people, with whom he deals every day. To those who reject him and do not understand his problem, he represents a threat and an annoyance. Such feelings of rejection are not overlooked by the patient, who will withdraw more and more, and seek greater solace in his drug. It is of the utmost importance that people understand and help the alcoholic, since living among them, he is their responsibility.

It must be clearly understood that the alcoholic is not alcoholic by choice, that although he may seek alcohol over and over again, he does not do so because he wants to be alcoholic. He does so only because it makes him more comfortable. If the patient were made more comfortable by those around him, he would need less alcohol. This places a responsibility upon the laymen who deal with him. They must try to understand him, to help him obtain a certain ease through contact with his fellow men rather than through the use of a drug. Fellow employees, employer, friends, and associates should help rather than reject him.

To coax an alcoholic to have a drink or to reject as incorrect or unlikely the belief that he might be alcoholic does not help him at all. Never try to persuade an individual who is having trouble with alcohol that he is not alcoholic. Nor should one drink in front of an alcoholic when he cannot drink too. This is like eating candy in front of a diabetic child who has been admonished not to partake of such delicacies. No mature, understanding adult would do that, nor would a mature, understanding adult drink in front of an alcoholic if he does not want him to drink also. Even when the patient himself insists that his acquaintance or friend drink, it is wiser not to do so. If one cannot exercise such control with an alcoholic friend, then one had better look into one's own drinking problems.

As a host, never coax someone to drink who has refused a drink. Do not say, "One won't hurt you." One drink for the susceptible person might mean disaster for him and his family. When a drink is refused, there should be no questions asked. To decline is everyone's privilege.

The alcoholic does not want your pity, or your sympathy. He wishes only to have you understand that he has a problem, one no different essentially from many diseases that other people have. He did not choose this one any more than other people have chosen the diseases with which they are afflicted. Neither does he want your prejudice, or your condemnation. If he is a prospective employee and is honest about his problem, he is not asking for special consideration; he is laying his cards on the table and expects a fair judgment from you—not on his ability to drink or not to drink, but on his ability to carry out the duties assigned to him. Bear in mind that he is not necessarily a weak person, but one who has an illness for which he is not responsible.

Relatives have an even greater responsibility to the alcoholic than do other laymen. They must exercise extreme patience and understanding with him. He can be exasperating and irritating, but what he does he does not do out of meanness or spite. He does it because it is part of his illness. The things he says and does that seem to be acts of meanness and sheer cussedness are things over which he has no control, and usually no one is sorrier afterward for what he has done than is the patient himself. This only compounds his sense of guilt, from which, to him, there seems to be no escape, and he drinks more in order to drown his increased suffering. Adverse treatment by his relatives only aggravates the condition and causes him to do again the things he hates to do and that earn him their hatred. Understanding him, sympathizing with him, and helping him to overcome the terrible guilt feelings he has will do more for him than will scolding, haranguing or punishing him.

There is a certain difference between the early alcoholic, or the problem drinker, and the confirmed alcoholic. The problem drinker has a much better opportunity to recover without serious consequences than does the confirmed alcoholic. It is at this early or problem stage that recovery shows the greatest promise. There should be no hesitancy in calling to the attention of such a drinker that his drinking is getting out of hand. It is better for him to stop the condition at this stage than to wait. When a person begins to have problems as a result of his drinking it is time to discuss the matter openly with him and to seek help. His promises not to drink so much in the future usually will be of no avail. Very careful control must be kept, and if this fails total abstinence is the only answer. It is best under such circumstances to arrange one's social life so that drinking does not play an important part in it.

The problem drinker nearly always finds it difficult to believe that he can become alcoholic. He determines over and over not to drink so much, to control himself, to drink only on certain occasions, and he invents plans that are useless. By the time his drinking becomes that serious he is already beyond the bounds of social drinking and should seek help from a professional. If after discussion, however, the problem drinker is able to control his drinking and never let it get out of bounds again, no outside help should be necessary.

The confirmed alcoholic, without a doubt, requires professional help. He cannot go it alone. It is true that under certain circumstances he can be helped by recovered alcoholics, for example, members of Alcoholics Anonymous, but in most cases he requires professional help. He cannot temporize at this stage. It is too late for him to start cutting down or trying to control his drinking. Over and over, the confirmed alcoholic will try to prove that he can go without drinking, or control his drinking, but no one has yet been able to do this. Every alcoholic thinks that he will be the exception. Every alcoholic is sure that by sheer willpower and the application of common sense he will be able to drink like a normal drinker. Each time he fails he produces what he thinks is a good reason for his failure, and he will start again with renewed promises and renewed vigilance. But there is no compromise with abstinence. The alcoholic's only salvation lies in complete abstinence. Let it be said here, categorically, that once a confirmed alcoholic has been labeled as such by a competent judge, he will never be able to drink safely again. Ask any of the millions who have tried.

In all probability hospitalization for such a patient is the best start. This not only will give him complete withdrawal from the drug but will also provide an opportunity for medical experts to test the effects of his excessive drinking and determine whether or not there has been any physical deterioration. There is no doubt that treating him physically, giving him a healthy body again, is a great step toward helping him to abstinence. During the period of hospitalization he may also have the kind of psychiatric evaluation that will determine whether he has an underlying psychiatric problem that has precipitated the excessive drinking, or whether the drinking has masked an underlying psychosis. Once he has recovered physically from these effects, he can go forth with renewed vigor and conduct his life of abstinence under the direction of the professional help available to him, or Alcoholics Anonymous, if he can respond to that program, or a combination of these types of treatment.

Perhaps the most difficult of all alcoholic cases is the terminal one. Treatment of this type of case is discouraging, since the alcoholism has produced such complications, both physically and mentally, that there is very little with which to work. Once the confirmed terminal case has reached this stage there has been such terrible physical damage, as well as mental damage in many cases, that the conditions are irreversible. Such cases as advanced cirrhosis of the liver, hemorrhaging varices of the esophagus, Korsakoff's syndrome, Wernicke's syndrome, and other pathological changes in other parts of the body, once having reached the stage of termination, are considered irreversible. Even if the body can sometimes be kept functioning, the mental deterioration is so rapid and complete that survival leaves but a vegetable. If such cases do survive the ordeal, then they must be placed in custodial institutions for the rest of their lives.

There are many cases that do not reach the terminal stage, but to all intents and purposes the effect of alcohol has produced such damage in the body and mind that the only hope of continuing is under care in a custodial institution. There should be such a custodial institution in every state for such cases. Here, under the care of professional help, these individuals can carry on a type of existence that, though not productive, is no worse than some of the senility cases that we see in state hospitals all over the country. Like vegetables, they serve no particular purpose, but, as long as they live, they can exist in these institutions. It is the prevention of this type of alcoholic patient that must be striven for with concentration on the kind of care required by the problem drinker and the confirmed alcoholic in order to help them avoid reaching such a stage.

CHAPTER 8

Medical Treatment of Alcoholism

MEDICAL treatment has rapidly become one of the prime factors in recovery for alcoholics. Because so many alcoholics have a fear of being faced with any form of psychiatric treatment, a medical approach seems the most acceptable. When there is a general feeling of physical well-being, any type of therapy is less of a threat, and the cooperation of the patient increases.

It is important that the patient be given as healthy a physiological foundation as possible before any type of therapy is applied to his alcohol problem. Newer medications at the therapist's disposal make possible a medical approach with better results and fewer undesirable side effects than previous medications. Medical treatment opens the way for many more practitioners to treat alcoholics than heretofore, because the newer drugs allow greater comfort for the patient, without the lethargy formerly produced. The patient is then more receptive to other types of therapy.

The practicing physician should be equipped with knowledge of the medical treatment for alcoholism. Following is a general medical approach to the problem, arranged in an order that fits within the framework of the practicing physician's experience and knowledge of medicine, physiology, pharmacology, and psychiatry. Special cases and complications may require the aid of experts in various specialties, but for the vast majority of alcoholic patients this outline will serve.

Acute Alcoholic Intoxication

The acute stage of alcoholic intoxication may occur in any individual, whether he is an alcoholic or not. It follows a period of excessive drinking that renders the individual unable to function effectively. The intoxication may vary in degree of intensity as well as duration. Reactions to intoxication by alcohol cover a wide range, depending upon the individual involved. There is a general behavior pattern characteristic of acute alcoholic intoxication, but it varies with the individual's reactions and depends largely upon his emotional response to loss of control. With his control and judgment gone, the individual may respond to various stimuli affecting his interpersonal relationships with his family, friends, employers, and fellow employees in such a way as to result in severe tragedy or unpleasant consequences. When his actions are contrary to law, they may have far-reaching effects. When they are contrary to good judgment, as in the case of automobile accidents, physical harm and even death may result.

The objective of the physician with a patient in this state of acute intoxication is to detoxify him as quickly as possible, so that the effect of the alcohol no longer obtains. It is useless to attempt further remedial measures, such as psychotherapy, while the patient is in the acutely intoxicated state, since there is no judgment present for him to use, nor is there sufficient understanding to make an impression when he is befuddled. This does not mean, however, that recovery during the alcoholic acute stage should not be utilized for the purpose of indoctrination. It is much more effective, however, to wait until the patient's mind has cleared and he can understand the therapist and cooperate with him.

It does not necessarily follow that psychotherapy must be administered only if the patient requests it, for it can be administered without the patient's being aware of it. Many patients emerging from an alcoholic stupor express an intense desire to be returned to the somnolent state. To accede to these wishes would only prolong the period of intoxication, whether from alcohol or from sedative drugs administered by the therapist.

There are times, however, when the patient is physically acutely active and it is necessary to administer drugs as substitutes for the alcohol. These drugs must be given judiciously, and not necessarily at the patient's request. It must be remembered that alcohol acts as an anesthetic agent, with the same effect as any other anesthetic, and that the standard stages of anesthesia may be experienced. Both during induction and as the patient emerges from the anesthetic, he goes through an active phase. With other agents such as nitrous oxide or ether, the stage is much shorter than with alcohol. Since the stage of activity with alcohol is longer than with the other anesthetic agents, it is necessary at times to use sedation to keep such activity from getting out of control.

HOSPITALIZATION

While it is not always necessary to treat the patient suffering from acute alcoholic intoxication in a hospital, beyond a doubt this is the best setting for such treatment. It is of advantage to both the physician and the patient to have the hospital accept such patients. It is in the hospital that the laboratory procedures so often necessary can be carried out quickly and thoroughly. Intravenous therapy is readily available. Emergency measures are possible. Anyone with experience in treating alcoholics will agree that most of them are not very difficult, contrary to the general impression of some personnel. Records confirm that most are no more trouble than other sick people. Further, if the attitude of the hospital toward the acutely ill alcoholic patient is that he is sick and welcome for treatment, he is more cooperative than are many other patients. There are exceptions to this rule, of course. Patients in delirium or those unusually active may cause some difficulty. With the newer methods of treatment, these phases may be passed through so rapidly that they need represent no great problem for the hospital or the physician; no more is required of them than with the patient recovering from an anesthetic after surgery.

There are other advantages in hospitalization of the alcoholic patient during the acute phase. All too frequently the family of the alcoholic is in an unfavorable emotional state during the patient's intoxication. They do not know how to cope with the situation or how to react to his strange behavior. Some, with the best of intentions, continue to give him alcohol. Others, in an attempt to stop his drinking, get into difficulty with the patient, who is suffering emotional reaction as a result of abstinence. In other instances the living conditions and general environment of the alcoholic may be the specific cause for his binge, and if he remains in this environment he continues to be irritated and continues to drink. Removing him from such irritating surroundings is one way of helping him to refrain from drinking. Moreover, his presence in the hospital enables the physician to carry on with laboratory procedures, to change medications without difficulty, to try different approaches, and to control the situation more accurately in other ways. From the point of view of the hospital, especially the teaching hospital, it gives the house staff and nurses an opportunity to deal with such patients and to learn how they react.

None of this must be taken to imply that hospitalization is an absolute necessity for most alcoholic patients. With the proper environment at home and the proper persons to care for the patient, therapy can be carried on elsewhere. Some nursing homes are well equipped but for the most part are not the ideal place to care for the acutely ill alcoholic.

Evaluation of the Patient's Condition

The first step in therapy is a complete physical examination and evaluation of the patient's condition. The smell of alcohol on the breath does not necessarily mean that an apparently intoxicated individual is in a state of acute alcoholic intoxication. Other types of poison, head injuries, or concomitant constitutional diseases may render the patient unconscious, and these must be ruled out before the patient can be said to be acutely intoxicated. Here laboratory procedures and X-rays may be of great value. Hemiplegia, diabetes, insulin shock, concussion, and many other such illnesses give the appearance of acute alcoholic intoxication if the patient with such a condition has also been drinking. Blood concentration tests for alcohol can be very valuable, where there is grave doubt, but will only determine the depth of the alcoholic intoxication. They will not necessarily rule out any additional physical factor.

In most cases of prolonged drinking, dehydration exists. This can be corrected by re-establishing fluid balance. The addition of saline solution and dextrose or fructose will help meet this emergency. Where deficiencies of diet have existed over periods of time, this condition also must be corrected. Nutritional elements and fluids taken orally preclude the necessity for further measures in this respect. However, when there is considerable vomiting, dehydration is usually acute and there is a lack of nutritional as well as mineral elements. This can be corrected by intravenous therapy. A saline solution containing 5 percent of dextrose or fructose may be administered in 1,000 c.c. to 2,000 c.c. doses in the course of twelve to twenty-four hours. This can be repeated every day for three days, if necessary. The addition of an ampule of Vitamin B Complex and ascorbic acid insures an adequate supply of these supplements and will provide the necessary balance of mineral and vitamin content.

Many therapists believe that insulin accelerates the metabolism of alcohol in the body. To accomplish this, 20 to 45 units of regular insulin may be added to the saline solution for intravenous administration. Before administration, however, it is wise to obtain a determination of the blood sugar level to make sure that insulin is not given during a hypoglycemic state. Medicaments employed in acute alcohol intoxication are best classified according to the response of the presenting symptoms to the administration of such medicaments.

Drugs That Stimulate the Central Nervous System and Counteract Depression

If the patient is extremely drowsy or severely depressed as a result of excessive ingestion of alcohol, these states can be counteracted by the administration of caffeine and sodium benzoate, dextroamphetamine (Dexedrine), or amphetamine (Benzedrine). Another drug that has the same effect is methylphenidate hydrochloride (Ritalin); given in dosage of 10 mg., it has been found effective. Still another drug used for the same purpose is pipradrol hydrochloride—alpha-(2-piperidyl) benzhydrol hydrochloride—(Meratran). The dosage of this drug is 2 to 25 mg. daily, depending upon the severity of the narcolepsy or depression. In severe hypotension, ephedrine may be administered subcutaneously, intramuscularly, or intravenously. For patients in the very severely depressed stage, some therapists have advocated the use of pentylenetetrazol (Metrazol), 1 c.c. given directly into the vein. This should be used with caution, as large doses may cause convulsions. These analeptic agents are of value only when the patient is so depressed that he cannot be aroused, or if the pulse is markedly reduced in rate or quality. In most cases where mild stupor is present, if the pulse and respiration are within normal limits the patient will usually rouse from his stupor after the alcohol is metabolized, and there is no necessity for additional drugs. A more recent drug used to counteract depression is meprobamate with benactyzine hydrochloride (Deprol). This drug may be used in 1 mg. doses, and in some cases will prove of benefit in counteracting depression.

DRUGS THAT DEPRESS THE CENTRAL NERVOUS SYSTEM

In treating presenting symptoms such as excitability, restlessness, nausea, vomiting, and hyperacidity, measures are sometimes necessary to control the patient and enable treatment to continue. In the past the use of adrenal cortex extract and the steroids has to some extent simplified the problem of controlling the acutely ill and hyperactive alcoholic, but the recent advent of tranquilizing drugs has been of tremendous value in treating this stage of the illness.

Tranquilizing drugs. The use of tranquilizing drugs has all but revolutionized treatment of the acute alcoholic stage. Such drugs as reserpine, chlorpromazine, meprobamate, promazine hydrochloride, and chlordiazepoxide have proved of immense value in treating the acutely intoxicated patient. The patient not only is given a sense of comfort that enables him to sleep but is also relieved of his nausea and is able to eat much earlier than heretofore. Chlorpromazine is comparatively rapid in its action and can be given intravenously, intramuscularly, or orally in doses ranging from 25 to 100 mg. every four hours. Dosage will depend upon the patient's reaction to the drug. Larger doses are required for some patients than for others. The potentiating characteristics of chlorpromazine must be borne in mind, since the drug increases the sedative effect of the alcohol itself as well as of any other sedative drug that may be given. In most cases, however, no further sedation is required other than administration of chlorpromazine.

Reserpine, which acts more slowly than chlorpromazine, is usually given in doses of from 0.25 mg. to as high as 1 mg. every four hours. Although its action is slower than that of chlorpromazine, the effect of the drug apparently lasts longer. It is well to watch the hypotensive action of this drug when it is administered, although in patients with normal blood pressure levels it rarely has such an effect. Chlorpromazine, on the other hand, particularly when injected intramuscularly, will often give a rather severe hypotensive effect within the first thirty minutes. This possible effect must be watched closely, and the patient must be placed in a supine position to overcome such effect. Reserpine is the refined alkaloid of Rauwolfia serpentina, but the crude drug is also very effective in the treatment of alcoholics. It acts more slowly than reserpine, but its action may last longer. Its tranquilizing effect takes longer to produce, but the patient can be kept on a regimen of smaller doses over longer periods of time. In the acute phase it does not act as rapidly nor is it as effective as chlorpromazine.

Meprobamate (2 methyl-2-n-propyl-1, 3 propanediol dicarbamate), commercially known as Miltown or Equanil, has also been used effectively as a tranquilizer for alcoholics. It has a tranquilizing effect upon the patient, reducing tension and allaying some of the anxieties so common in the alcoholic. It is related to mephenesin (Tolserol), formerly used by many for the treatment of alcoholism. This will be discussed later. Doses of meprobamate vary from 400 mg. given once or twice daily to the same amount given four times a day. For maintenance therapy, dosages are usually smaller, once the condition is stabilized. Habituation and addiction have been noted with this drug, and care should be exercised to prevent such developments. This can be accomplished by changing medications and by not allowing the patient the same drug over long periods of time.

An additional tranquilizing drug, *promazine hydrochloride,* commercially known as Sparine, is also very valuable in the treatment of alcoholism. It is given in doses varying from 25 to 200 mg. three or four times a day, depending upon the reaction of the patient to this drug. It can be given intravenously, intramuscularly, or orally, and has been found to be valuable in the more acutely disturbed patient, bringing about quick sedation and tranquil sleep. The patient awakes refreshed and with a good appetite. The side effects of this drug are much fewer than with chlorpromazine, and for this reason it may be the best drug to use.

Chlordiazepoxide is another tranquilizing drug that has proved very valuable in the treatment of the acute phase as well as the chronic phase of alcoholism. Its trade name is Librium. Given in doses of 25 mg. four times a day, it helps to sedate the patient, make him more comfortable, and relieve the anxieties so often associated with alcoholism. Many therapists feel that chlordiazepoxide is the most appropriate drug in treating the alcoholic. It does not seem to have any of the undesirable side effects associated with some of the other tranquilizing drugs, and therefore can be used with greater safety. Smaller doses of the drug can be of value in less severe cases. In my experience, however, the 25-mg. dose four times a day seems to produce the best effects. Chlordiazepoxide can also be administered parenterally by dissolving prepared crystals in the properly provided diluent. The resultant solution is administered intramuscularly. Preparations must be freshly dissolved in accordance with the instructions.

All of the tranquilizing drugs have some beneficial effect. They produce relaxation without sleep. Their value lies in reducing tension and in allowing the patient to remain aware of his surroundings and available for psychotherapy. There have been some reports made of habituation to some of these drugs. However, such danger can be minimized by changing the drug at frequent intervals. There are some patients, however, who apparently become habituated to anything prescribed. Even placebos seem to offer such opportunities for these patients.

One must always look for the side effects of these tranquilizing drugs. Chlorpromazine has been known to cause severe jaundice, and in many cases severe dermatitis of the allergic type. This can be counteracted by the administration of an adequate antihistaminic such as diphenhydramine hydrochloride (Benadryl), 50 mg. three times a day. The two drugs can be given concomitantly. The antihistaminic is in itself somewhat hypnotic and sedative in action; the combination, therefore, with the chlorpromazine produces adequate rest as well as tranquilization.

The most common side effect of the administration of Rauwolfia serpentina or reserpine is a congestion of the nasal passages and mucous membranes. This can be counteracted by the administration of an antihistaminic. So far there have been no greatly undesirable reactions reported on the use of meprobamate or promazine hydrochloride. With the use of promazine hydrochloride, one case of agranulocytosis has been reported, but investigation indicates that this may be questionable. Although for the most part barbiturates are not recommended for the treatment of the alcoholic, mephobarbital (Mebaral) has been recommended by some as an efficient sedative. As mentioned, meprobamate has been reported by some as being particularly habituating.

Many physicians treating alcoholics use these tranquilizing drugs to the exclusion of other sedation and have obtained good results. With patients in delirium tremens and extreme hyperactivity, larger doses may be necessary.

Adrenal cortex extract. For a long time, the use of the aqueous solution of adrenal cortex extract was popular. This was administered on the theory that the glucose metabolism of the body is altered in the alcoholic and that depleted glycogen stores could be restored to normal by administration of adrenal cortex extract. It was believed that adrenal cortex exhaustion in alcoholics resulted from continued emotional disturbances and produced upsets in the glucose metabolism. The adrenal cortex extract solution is still used intravenously by many and has been found helpful. The dosage varies from 10 to 30 c.c. in 1,000 c.c. of saline solution injected over a period of several hours. Where the adrenals seem to be exhausted to a greater extent and the reaction is more severe, from 10 to 20 c.c. of the aqueous solution can be administered directly into the vein. This method has been found to produce a very quieting effect on the patient, reducing his anxiety and inducing a tranquil sleep. Where the patient is extremely tremulous, from 10 to 50 c.c. of mephenesin aqueous solution may be added. Although the relief from the tremors in these cases is temporary, it does help the agitated patient.

Paraldehyde. Another drug that has enjoyed great popularity for many years among practitioners is paraldehyde. This has long been a favorite in dealing with the acute phase of alcoholism. However, it is little more than an effective hypnotic and renders the patient drowsy even after awakening. Dosages vary from 5 to 25 c.c. orally, or 10 to 15 c.c. intramuscularly, depending upon the size of the patient. When given intramuscularly, great care must be exercised in seeing that the drug is administered deeply into the muscle, since more superficial deposits of this drug will result in necrosis of the tissue. Paraldehyde has definite drawbacks, in that it is habituating, and alcoholics who have been through the acute phase on numerous occasions will request the drug when entering the hospital. The odor it leaves on the breath often makes it unpopular. When there is need to combine this drug with some of the tranquilizing drugs such as chlorpromazine or promazine, it must always be remembered that the chlorpromazine and promazine have a potentiating effect on the sedative, necessitating only a fraction of the ordinary dose of paraldehyde.

Chloral hydrate. Another old favorite used for many years is chloral hydrate. This also has a good sedative and hypnotic effect, but again is one of the drugs that causes the patient to become habituated. The only advantage of this drug is that it makes the patient sleepy. It cannot compare in desirable effects to the newer drugs.

Barbiturates. Barbiturates such as phenobarbital, pentobarbital (Nembutal), amobarbital (Amytal), thiopental (Pentothal), secobarbital (Seconal), and many others of this group have often been used. Today, however, the consensus is that these drugs are neither necessary nor desirable in the treatment of the alcoholic. The habituating properties of these drugs will often lead the addictive alcoholic to switch from alcohol to barbiturates for relief, thus creating a much more complex problem than before. Some therapists contend that mephobarbital, of the barbiturate family, is not as likely to cause habituation as some others of that group. It is generally felt that complete avoidance of barbiturates will in no way deprive the alcoholic and thus eliminate the possibility of his becoming more involved with addiction.

Where sleep is essential and the desired hypnosis is not to be produced by drugs of the tranquilizing group, glutethimide (Doriden) in doses of 0.5 gm. or 1 gm. will often give the desired effect. Doriden has also demonstrated addicting qualities and in large doses can have a toxic effect. It does nevertheless help produce sleep when necessary. Daytime sedation can be produced by smaller doses of the same drug. Habituation or addiction to this drug can lead to serious problems and continuation of its use for any length of time should be discouraged. Ethchlorvynol (Placidyl) and methyprylon (Noludar) have also been used for the same purpose by many therapists, with good results. However, there have been reports of habituation to both Noludar and Placidyl, so that use of these drugs must also be carefully supervised.

DRUGS THAT RELAX THE MUSCLE SYSTEM

Mephenesin and *mephenesin carbamate* (Tolserol) have been recommended for relaxing the muscle system. Although there have been reports of success with these drugs, oral administration has generally not produced the desired results. However, in the severely agitated patient with marked tremor, intravenously given doses of the aqueous solution of mephenesin, varying from 25 to 50 c.c. and injected slowly, have caused dramatic reduction in the tremors. In administering mephenesin intravenously, however, it is important to watch for the occurrence of nystagmus, the appearance of which indicates cessation of administration.

Although tremors will disappear completely under such medication, the effect of the drug does not seem to be very long-lasting, and within a short time the tremors will return. The drug is of value, however, in terminating these coarse tremors when the patient seems unusually agitated. Large doses of the drug administered orally sometimes cause gastric distress, in which case they must be discontinued.

The relationship of mephenesin to the tranquilizer meprobamate may account for the success of the latter with disturbed alcoholics.

Hydroxyzine (Atarax), a product of the tranquilizing group, has been recommended for the purpose of alleviating the tension-anxiety states of alcoholics. Another drug that may be used for control of convulsions, especially in an emergency and with very severe tremors, is curare. Curare also may be administered intravenously. It must be borne in mind, however, that when curare is used paralysis of the muscles of respiration may follow. Great caution must be exerted if the drug is used at all, and then a respiration apparatus should always be at hand.

GLANDULAR AND HORMONAL PRODUCTS

The use of the aqueous solution of adrenal cortex extract has been referred to previously. It is helpful in the acute phase, as described. In severely anxious patients and situations of extreme tension, this can have quieting results and relief from tension when introduced intravenously or intramuscularly. In prolonged cases the value of this drug is questionable. Adrenocorticotropic hormone, however, or corticotropin (ACTH), is valuable in the treatment of delirium tremens; 25 mg. may be given every six hours until six doses have been administered. In many cases this will bring the patient out of his delirium within a very short time.

The alcoholic patient is often found to have some thyroid dysfunction. Where such a condition is suspected, it is recommended that the basal metabolism rate alone not be relied on for the measurement of the thyroid function. The radioactive uptake test is much more reliable for such evaluation and gives a greater indication of thyroid activity than any test used heretofore. The range of thyroid activity in the alcoholic patient is neither greater nor less than that of the non-alcoholic, and the treatment of his case of abnormal thyroid activity can be managed in the same way as with other thyroid patients. Depending on the thyroid activity and the hyperthyroidism, propylthiouracil may be given in 50-mg. doses three times a day, or increased as the case indicates. In the case of hypothyroidism, thyroid extract is prescribed in the same way as with non-alcoholic patients. It has been found that the correction of thyroid dysfunction in alcoholics has resulted in most cases in immediate improvement in the problem of alcoholism. There is no doubt that, in many of such cases, the activity of the thyroid plays an important role and may be the cause of excessive drinking in some patients. Nevertheless, correction of the thyroid condition in these patients does not seem to alter their tolerance for drinking, and, as with other alcoholic patients, they cannot drink with impunity even when the thyroid condition has been corrected.

Other Considerations in Treatment of Acute Alcoholic Intoxication

The dietary regimen of the alcoholic patient in the chronic stage seems to have very little effect on his drinking pattern or on his desire or absence of desire to drink. On general principle, and especially after immediate recovery from the acute phase, a high-carbohydrate, high-protein, and low-fat diet seems to be of greatest value, with a full complement of vitamin and mineral factors. Most patients do not require a special diet except that of the well-balanced regimen that would be recommended for any normal individual.

Another phase of the acute alcoholic intoxication that can be considered a complicating factor is the comatose state. The patient in coma presents the usual problem of differentiation between the coma due to alcohol and the coma caused by other conditions. A complete physical examination is of the utmost importance. Blood and urine studies must be done and differentiation from brain injury, diabetic coma, insulin shock, or cerebral hemorrhage must be made. A blood level of 0.2 to 0.25 percent or above should be present before the patient is considered to be in alcoholic coma, but the presence of such a level does not necessarily mean that the coma is due to alcohol alone. Other possible causes must be ruled out. When it is ascertained that there are no other conditions present, stomach lavage may be done to remove whatever remaining alcohol may be in the stomach. Dextrose, saline solution, and insulin may be administered intravenously to metabolize the alcohol, and caffeine sodium benzoate may be given intramuscularly or intravenously to overcome the comatose state. Where pressure on the brain due to edema is suspected, 50-percent solution of dextrose may be administered intravenously in 25 to 50 c.c. doses. As the patient regains consciousness, treatment for the acute alcoholism can be instituted. Indications of respiratory failure must be looked for and the possibility of infection of the lungs during this period must be considered. If other causes of coma have been eliminated and the respiration and pulse seem to be satisfactory, the natural metabolism of the alcohol by the physiological processes will eventually reduce the concentration in the blood and the patient will regain consciousness, even though no special treatment is instituted. During this time, however, the patient should be closely watched for change in his condition, and treatment should be symptomatic.

Convulsions after several days of abstinence represent another acute problem of alcoholism. The convulsions are epileptiform in character, and a careful history should be taken to rule out the possibility of epilepsy. As with any form of seizure, care should be taken to protect the patient from injuring himself by biting his tongue or otherwise causing injury by falling or striking sharp objects. Electroencephalograms are of value in differentiating these convulsions from true epilepsy. Diphenylhydantoin (Dilantin) sodium in 1½ grain (0.1 gm.) doses three times daily may be given orally where possibility of convulsions is suspected. During the convulsions, if necessary, thiopental sodium or the aqueous solution of mephenesin may be given intravenously. For control of the convulsions, the diphenylhydantoin may be prescribed as indicated. Promazine and chlorpromazine in large doses have also been used successfully to control these convulsions. With the recidivist it is always wise to determine the authenticity of the convulsive seizure. Experience indicates that many recidivists, wise in the hospital procedures, will simulate seizures in order to obtain sedative drugs from which they have been withdrawn.

Treatment of the Alcoholic Not in the Acute Stage

There have been many recommendations for treating the alcoholic who is not in the acute stage, in an effort to prevent him from drinking. There is no doubt that psychotherapy is indicated here. However, it is not always a simple matter to persuade the patient to submit himself to such therapy. Some feel that the alcoholic is the victim of a metabolic disease that can be treated on a dietary regimen. This, however, has never been satisfactorily proved, although claims of such recoveries have been made. Although my experience has been that diet alone does not release the alcoholic patient from his desire to drink, there is no doubt that a feeling of well-being and a healthy physique will make any patient feel better. A sense of well-being, unfortunately, is something that most alcoholics do not have, but they are continually trying to achieve it. It is this lack of comfort that often causes them to seek, in alcohol, relief from their tensions. A well-balanced diet contributes, therefore, to general physical well-being.

Some have suspected hormonal dysfunctions to be the cause of alcoholism. It is possible that glandular abnormality may contribute to a patient's discomfort. However, since alcoholism occurs so frequently where there is no evidence of glandular disturbance, it cannot be considered the cause. Where such abnormal conditions exist, they must be corrected as part of the general treatment, since any disturbance in function can contribute to the discomfort of the patient. It is recognized that the endocrine glands are closely associated with the emotional life of the individual, but a single hormone or group of hormones has not as yet been found to be responsible for alcoholism. But, for the general feeling of well-being desirable for any patient, it is as important that the endocrine system be studied and brought to normal functioning as it is to have a regulated diet. When all of these factors are evaluated and corrected, and good physical health is attained for the patient, any other adverse factors, psychological or emotional, are much more easily regulated. The chances of improving psychological behavior are always much greater when the patient feels physically fit.

Psychotherapy is of tremendous value in the long-term approach to the basic problem of the alcoholic's emotional stability. However, where such psychotherapy is necessary, the problem that confronts the therapist is keeping the patient from resorting to alcohol during such therapy. Chlorpromazine, reserpine, Rauwolfia serpentina, meprobamate, promazine hydrochloride, and chlordiazepoxide can all be used for this purpose. The characteristics of these drugs have already been described, and they can be used during this period of rehabilitation as indicated. Dosages vary, and of course must be much smaller than when used during the acute phase of the illness. Each patient will react differently to these various drugs, and, therefore, the medicaments can be used most effectively by adapting the therapy to what best suits the individual patient. It is sometimes of great advantage to use combinations of these drugs, depending upon the effect on the patient. However, there is a percentage of patients who find it difficult to refrain from alcohol even with these tranquilizing medications. With this type of patient, deterrent therapy is a valuable adjunct.

Deterrent Therapy

Disulfiram [bis (*diethylthiocarbamyl*) disulfide], known as TETD or Antabuse, is a drug designed to keep the alcoholic from drinking. Ingestion of alcohol while under this therapy results in an episode of severe and intense illness, which is so disquieting that knowledge of such a reaction acts as an excellent deterrent. Disulfiram itself has very little effect upon the body. Some patients might complain of fatigue, a slight loss of sex potency, an occasional skin allergy, some headache, some malaise, but generally speaking it is tolerated without any difficulty. Occasionally it causes gastric distress. With the ingestion of the slightest amount of alcohol, however, a succession of symptoms occurs that causes extreme discomfort. Within a few minutes of alcohol ingestion, there is a flushing of the face that extends down over the neck and chest and becomes deeper and deeper until the skin is bright red. This is accompanied by a sensation of great heat, followed by a pounding headache that becomes very severe. The blood pressure rises suddenly with this headache, but within a few minutes there occurs a precipitous drop in the blood pressure, giving the patient a sense of faintness and nausea, sometimes followed by violent vomiting. The patient may break into a cold sweat and he often complains of extreme pain in the precordium, simulating a coronary attack. The discomfort is very severe and may last from one to two or even four hours, depending upon the amount of disulfiram and alcohol that has been ingested. He subsequently falls into a deep sleep which may last for several hours.

When this drug was first used, it was thought necessary that it be administered in a hospital setting. After the patient recovered from the acute intoxication, disulfiram was given and he was subjected to the alcohol test. In this way, he learned what would happen should he drink alcohol while under disulfiram therapy. For some time now, it has been thought unnecessary to subject the patient to this experience. The mere description of what will happen is sufficient for the average patient to understand the risks involved in drinking alcohol while taking this drug. Where doubt does exist and the patient decides to experiment, only a small amount of alcohol is needed to convince him of the effect of disulfiram. It is necessary, however, for the therapist to describe accurately to the patient the risks involved and what will happen, so that there will be no doubt in his mind that drinking alcohol will result in serious consequences. In addition, he is given a card to carry with him, identifying him and his physician, explaining that he is under disulfiram therapy and that no alcohol should be administered should he be found in an unconscious state. The description of this procedure is in most cases quite sufficient to convince the patient of the seriousness of such treatment.

In those cases where the patient does take alcohol while under disulfiram therapy, it is well to know the antidotes that can be used. Recommended measures are putting the patient in shock position and injecting ascorbic acid intravenously. If the patient is unconscious, caffein sodium benzoate may be administered intramuscularly. Dextrose and saline infusions are also recommended, as well as plasma, and oxygen when indicated. A good antihistaminic may be administered intramuscularly or intravenously, and diphenhydramine (Benadryl) hydrochloride has been used this way effectively. Another method of counteracting the effects of the disulfiram-alcohol reaction is the administration of chlorpromazine or promazine intramuscularly in 50 to 100 mg. doses. This usually induces a calming sleep, and the patient will awaken refreshed and without the usual undesirable effects.

Contraindications to disulfiram therapy have been noted. They are cases of severe heart disease, including coronary heart disease, cirrhosis of the liver, epilepsy, drug addiction, psychoses, kidney disease, diabetes, pregnancy, and asthma. Some therapists have used this treatment with all of these types of cases without much difficulty. However, unusual caution must be taken when doing so.

A more recent deterrent used to keep the alcoholic from drinking is *citrated calcium carbimide,* or Temposil. It acts in exactly the same way as disulfiram, but has several advantages. Some of the discomforts found with disulfiram—gastric distress, somnolence, sex impotency, and dermatitis—do not as a rule occur with Temposil. One disadvantage, however, is apparent. While the effect of disulfiram will hold for at least twenty-four hours, or very often longer, citrated calcium carbimide effect lasts a maximum of eighteen hours. This can be a disadvantage if the patient is aware of it, since he may take advantage of the elapsed time to drink. In order to overcome this disadvantage, it may be necessary to prescribe citrated calcium carbimide twice a day.

Over a period of time, a technique can be developed in using this deterrent drug, which can be quite effective. By starting the patient with disulfiram therapy and continuing it for some time, or until such time as there is even the beginning of a bad effect, the patient can then be switched to citrated calcium carbimide with the warning that it produces exactly the same effect as Antabuse. Accustomed to the administration of the one pill a day, the patient does not know of the difference in the duration of the effect, and the single pill will suffice as a deterrent for the full twenty-four-hour period. If the drug is taken in the morning, it will be in effect during his entire working day and he will remain protected even though only one pill is used daily. If there is any doubt, two pills may be used. Due to occasional difficulty, citrated calcium carbimide is not yet on the common market, although it is sold extensively in other parts of the world.

One of the risks in the use of deterrent therapy is the possible occurrence of a psychosis. It was thought that psychoses occurring while this drug was being used were due to the toxicity of the drug itself. However, it is now believed that it is not the drug but the patient's inability to escape into his alcoholic oblivion as an outlet for his emotional instability that precipitates the psychotic episode. It has been found that, with further psychotherapy, these patients have been able to take deterrent therapy again without having any psychotic reaction, even though the dose of disulfiram was exactly the same as before their psychotic episodes. It is wise, therefore, that a psychiatric evaluation be done on the patient before giving deterrent therapy, if severe mental involvement is suspected.

The reaction to alcohol of the patient taking the deterrent drugs is due to the increase of the acetaldehyde content in the blood. In the metabolic breakdown of alcohol into acetaldehyde, acetic acid, carbon dioxide, and water, this process is arrested at the acetaldehyde stage by its contact with these drugs and the subsequent chemical and enzyme reactions. Since acetaldehyde is a very severely toxic agent, the results that follow ingestion of alcohol are due to the increased acetaldehyde concentration in the blood. The same symptoms can be produced by injecting acetaldehyde intravenously.

The deterrent drugs have other uses that have proved of value in the treatment of the alcoholic patient. The original purpose was to guarantee a period of abstinence long enough to practice psychotherapy. They can, however, also be used to determine the degree of sincerity in the patient's willingness to cooperate. After discussion of the effects of alcohol ingestion while under deterrent therapy and the length of time the deterrent drugs affect the body, which may be from twenty-four to seventy-two hours—in rare instances as long as a week—a deterrent tablet may be offered the patient. If he swallows it without hesitation, it is indicative of his motivation and the strength of his incentive to abstain. However, if he demurs, refuses, delays, or in any other way resists taking the pill, it is assurance that he still has many reservations about following through with the rest of his program. The greatest value of deterrent therapy to the patient is the revelation that he can live without drinking. Very often, after long periods of abstinence, he can appreciate how much he has proved this fact to himself. Another not inconsiderate value is the comfort it gives the family that at least for the twenty-four hours following ingestion of the deterrent pill the patient will not drink.

Patients professing a desire to be helped and expressing excellent motivation will sometimes balk at taking the deterrent drug. Such a refusal, when brought to the attention of the patient, will often demonstrate to him how his refusal exhibits a lack of the motivation he professed. To many this comes as a revelation, and after thoughtful consideration they will agree to the deterrent therapy as a means of enforcing their determination to stop drinking.

Conditioned Response Therapy

The conditioned response treatment is based on the theory that the individual patient can be trained to a particular psychological reaction under certain defined situations. This method of therapy has been employed in many areas and reports indicate variable success. In the hands of some therapists, patients respond well to this type of therapy. With others, the success has been questionable. The treatment is carried out by administering to the patient a dose of alcohol to which there has been added some type of emetic, emetine or ipecac. Under controlled conditions, the patient is given the dose of treated alcohol; the ingestion is followed by severe retching and vomiting for some time. The administration is repeated on several occasions. The theory is that after a number of such experiences the patient will automatically refrain from drinking alcohol for fear of the consequences.

This type of therapy must be carried out under controlled circumstances in order to establish the conditioned response. The treatment is usually administered in an institution where the patient can be watched carefully over a given period of time and the administration controlled with a maximum of environmental influence.

Some therapists have substituted the injection of *apo*morphine simultaneously with the ingestion of alcohol.

Hypnosis

Because of its use in psychiatric and psychosomatic problems, hypnosis has been applied by some to the illness of alcoholism. Unfortunately, however, the alcoholic does not necessarily respond to this type of therapy as other patients might. Hypnosis in too many cases may be used by people without the proper background for its effective use. Hypnosis may be used as a diagnostic measure or as an aid in eliciting information. However, merely placing a patient in a hypnotic state and then suggesting that he stop drinking is not enough. Those qualified to use this technique should have a background of psychiatric training and the proper knowledge of psychodynamics.

Care must be exercised when using hypnosis that the excessive drinking might be removed at the cost of substituting another and perhaps worse problem. In most cases, hypnosis has not been successful in treating the alcoholic.

Lysergic Acid

Another type of therapy for the treatment of alcoholics, not as yet proved satisfactorily successful, is the use of lysergic acid, sometimes known as LSD 25. Some therapists find in it encouragement to continue research to determine its value as a therapeutic measure. There is not sufficient evidence, however, to recognize this procedure as one which is generally effective for alcoholic patients.

The reliable and proved methods of treatment are still the ones that so far are generally helpful. While they take a great deal more time and effort on the part of the therapist, they are as yet the safest and best means of accomplishing satisfactory results.

Complications of Chronic Alcoholism

Hallucinosis. Hallucinosis is characterized by auditory or visual hallucination. Usually auditory, they most often occur after the patient has been detoxified. The hallucinations are less severe than those that accompany delirium tremens. Differentiation from delirium tremens is important and can usually be determined by the orientation that is present with hallucinosis and absent with delirium tremens. Sedation with tranquilizing drugs until the phase of hallucinosis has passed is the treatment of choice. However, corticotropin in 25 mg. doses given intramuscularly or intravenously every four hours for six doses has proved effective. The panic and fear associated with delirium tremens is usually not present with this complication.

Recently, azacyclonol (Frenquel) hydrochloride in doses of 20 mg. three or four times a day has also been used for this complication. It is specifically valuable for hallucinosis and has been found to be very effective.

Delirium tremens. Delirium tremens is fairly common and occurs after prolonged drinking. It may also occur upon withdrawal of alcohol after prolonged drinking. The characteristics of this condition are intense excitement, delirium, and coarse tremors. It may be accompanied by convulsions of the *grand mal* type. Present also is marked confusion with disorientation, which differentiates this condition from hallucinosis. Both auditory and visual hallucinations are present as a rule. These halluciations are extremely vivid and often take the form of animals all over the room and the patient. Bizarre combinations of animal bodies and human heads and vice versa are present. Physical findings usually include dilated pupils, flushed skin, subnormal temperatures (unless intercurrent infection is present), and profuse sweating. Minute petechial hemorrhages of the brain may occur during this stage and often give rise to persistent tremors. In spite of the psychiatric manifestations, the treatment of delirium tremens is a completely medical procedure.

Treatment consists of the measures used for patients in the acute alcoholic state. Tranquilizing drugs have been recommended by many therapists, and chlorpromazine, promazine, and chlordiazepoxide have all been used to advantage. They can be given orally, intramuscularly, or, in the case of the first two, intravenously, but in my experience I have found it advantageous to combine them with other sedative drugs when the excitement in the patient is great. Administration of corticotropin in 25 mg. doses at four-hour intervals has also helped in bringing about more rapid recovery. This can be given intramuscularly or intravenously in the dextrose and saline solution. After recovery from the acute delirium, the treatment is continued as in other stages of alcoholism.

Acute gastritis and enteritis. This complication is usually due to chemical irritation of the mucous membrane of the gastrointestinal tract. Mental distress, anxiety, and frustration are usually associated with this irritation. Withdrawal of the alcohol, as well as gastric sedatives and a bland diet, will relieve the symptoms. Drugs used in the usual gastrointestinal cases to reduce motility and soothe the inflamed membranes will also aid in alleviating this condition. The use of chlorpromazine and promazine hydrochloride will often allay the nausea and vomiting that accompany the irritation of the digestive tract membranes. However, it is often also necessary to apply psychotherapy to help relieve the symptoms.

Varices of the esophagus and cardiac end of the stomach. This condition probably occurs much more commonly than is suspected. Its danger lies in the possibility of hemorrhage.

Such signs as vomiting of blood, tarry stools, signs of shock, pallor, low blood count, or low blood pressure, and other obvious evidences of acute hemorrhage must be borne in mind. At the first indication of such signs, immediate treatment should be instituted. The general regimen for acute hemorrhage anywhere may be used here, including complete sedation and quiet for the patient. Intravenous infusions of saline solution may be necessary, as well as transfusion if indicated. Where the hemorrhage continues, use of the Sengstaken or the Patton tube may be indicated. This tube is passed into the stomach and the bulb is inflated to 20 to 40 mm. Hg. The tube is left in place for from twenty to forty-eight hours before deflation. After deflation of the tube, the patient should be observed for twelve hours to make sure that there is no recurrence of the hemorrhage. If no bleeding occurs, the tube may then be removed.

Cirrhosis of the liver. Cirrhosis of the liver is one of the very common complications of chronic alcoholism. While it is now recognized that cirrhosis of the liver is not necessarily due to the action of the alcohol itself, it is nevertheless one of the sequelae associated with chronic alcoholism. It has been established that alcoholism is not the only cause of cirrhosis of the liver but that other conditions responsible for the lack of proper vitamins and minerals and other necessary nutritional elements in the diet are the basic cause of this disease. The liver has proved to be a very hardy organ and can be subjected to a great deal of abuse before the condition becomes irreversible. Administration of the necessary vitamins and minerals and an adequate diet will usually result in the recovery of the liver to its normal function. However, in extreme cases and in cirrhosis of long duration, the destruction may be so severe that complete recovery is impossible. Proper diet, administration of vitamins and minerals, and in some cases injection of liver extract will help support the diseased organ. In some cases surgery has been necessary to establish increased circulation to the liver, in an effort to relieve the portal system. However, in most cases, supportive treatment will be sufficient to correct this condition.

LESS FREQUENT COMPLICATIONS

The less-often-encountered complications of chronic alcoholism are given below:

Pathological intoxication. Pathological intoxication is a severe reaction to the ingestion of alcohol. It is characterized by a precipitous and almost maniacal response to a comparatively small amount of alcohol. It is theorized that in such cases the alcohol acts as a trigger-release mechanism setting off inability of the patient to control his actions. Treatment consists of heavy sedation until the acute phase passes.

Korsakoff's syndrome. Korsakoff's syndrome is characterized by amnesia and confabulation. The treatment consists of supportive measures. Prognosis for recovery in these cases is very poor. Since it is now believed that this complication occurs as a result of inadequate diet, the necessary nutritional elements, vitamins, and minerals must be supplied in sufficient amounts.

Hemorrhagic polioencephalitis, superior (Wernicke's disease). Characteristics of hemorrhagic polioencephalitis, superior (Wernicke's disease), include limited movements of the eyes due to partial paralysis of the eye muscles. Mental changes include intense excitement, convulsions, and clouding of consciousness, which may be severe enough to end in stupor and coma. There are usually pathological reflexes present, with extreme tension of the muscles. Tendon reflexes are absent. Since this complication is also considered to be the result of deficient nutrition, large doses of thiamine, adequate diet, and vitamin and mineral complements are indicated. Not uncommonly, complete restoration fails to occur. Mental confabulation resembling Korsakoff's syndrome is often a residual effect and may remain.

Marchiafava's disease. Marchiafava's disease (primary degeneration of the corpus callosum) was once thought to be due to alcoholism. With only 100 cases reported in the literature, it was finally determined that this complication resulted not from the alcohol but from the metallic impurities found in wine as the result of processing.

Acute lethal alcoholism. Acute lethal alcoholism is due to ingestion of alcohol to a blood concentration sufficient to cause death. It occurs and acts the same as an overdose of anesthetic, producing death by a complete anesthesia of the vital centers of the brain.

SUMMARY AND CONCLUSIONS

In treating the chronic alcoholic, factors other than the medical and psychiatric approach must be taken into consideration. The patient's social environment, religious background, employment or industrial situation, and his relationships with family, friends, fellow employees, and others are pertinent factors. His relationships with his local health department, mental health department, Alcoholics Anonymous, and clergy are additional important contributions to treatment. In the chronic alcoholic, we are dealing not only with a sick individual but with that individual in relationship to his environment. In order to treat him adequately, all of these circumstances must be included.

In treating the chronic alcoholic, the cooperation of the patient is perhaps the greatest single factor, along with the understanding and patience of the attending physician. Such psychotherapy as is necessary can be administered by the average physician who will take the time to understand and help the sick alcoholic. With the advent of the new tranquilizing drugs, the treatment of the acute phase has been greatly simplified. With the use of deterrent drugs (disulfiram and citrated calcium carbimide), the patient can remain without alcohol long enough for the interested physician to help him gain insight into his problem. Helping to give the alcoholic a healthy body so as to maintain optimum physical fitness will in itself make him feel better and more capable of meeting the problems that have induced his illness and probably caused it to continue. The physician has in the alcoholic a challenge from which he cannot retreat. To meet this challenge, he requires knowledge, understanding, and patience. If he will develop and use these qualities, the chances of his success with alcoholic patients will be enhanced and the results will be rewarding.

CHAPTER 9

Effect of Alcohol on the Body*

ALCOHOL is absorbed into the body through the mucous membranes of the gastrointestinal system, starting with the oral cavity, stomach, and intestines. About 20 percent of the alcohol is absorbed from the stomach, and the remaining 80 percent from the intestinal tract. In low concentration, alcohol will stimulate the stomach to secrete its gastric juices; hence its effect as an appetizer. In concentrations of 10 to 20 percent, the irritation produces an inhibition of the secretory action of the stomach. In concentrations of 40 to 50 percent, there is an inflammation of the mucous membranes of the stomach caused by irritation from the chemical itself. Hence, there is the occurrence of gastritis where highly concentrated alcohol is taken into the stomach in large amounts.

Alcohol affects the nervous system as a depressant of the higher brain centers concerned with behavior and speech and memory. It also causes delays in transmitting electrical impulses, which are essential to produce a motor reaction in response to visual stimulation. The early ingestion of alcohol, therefore, produces initial symptoms that result from depres-

* From *Alcohol and Tissues*, by Chester A. Swinyard, M.D., Ph.D. New York, Empire Medical Publishers, 1953.

Effect of Alcohol on the Body

sion of centers concerned with worry and anxiety. As a result, a feeling of expansiveness, exhilaration, vivaciousness, and loss of inhibitions occurs. The person then experiences the so-called "lifted up" feeling.

The next area affected by alcohol is the motor center of the cerebrum and cerebellum. These areas are concerned with coordinated movements, and when they are depressed, movements become increasingly uncoordinated, and reflex movements are significantly slowed.

As the concentration of alcohol continues to rise in the nervous tissue, neurological centers in the midbrain that control eye movement are affected. This results in limitation of eye movement and the appearance of glazed eyes. It may also result in double vision. At the same time, there is interference with coordination of muscles of articulation and speech. There also ensues the staggering gait of intoxication, and as the concentration rises ambulation becomes impossible and the individual lies in an alcoholic stupor.

If the concentration rises to as high as 0.5 to 0.6 percent in the blood, the respiratory and circulatory centers may be so depressed that their activity stops, and death may occur.

Alcohol, therefore, is a continuously acting nervous system depressant. It acts first upon the higher centers of the forebrain, releasing inhibitions normally present, and gives a false sense of stimulation; later, as the concentration rises, it depresses forebrain, midbrain and cerebellar centers for movement; and finally, kills by arresting the activity of the vital centers of the lower part of the brain.

The respiratory system is affected to a much lesser extent by alcohol. It is not until the concentration of alcohol in the blood reaches 0.4 to 0.6 percent that there will be any marked effect upon respiration. At this level it may become very slow and deep, and may finally cease due to paralysis of the respiratory center of the brain. A considerable amount of alcohol is eliminated through the expired air of the lungs, so respiration acts as one of the methods of eliminating alcohol from the system. About 1 percent of alcohol ingested is so excreted, unchanged.

The cardiovascular system, particularly the heart, is not significantly altered until high levels of blood alcohol occur. Then there may be progressive slowing of the heart. Eventually this may cause cardiac arrest, as would any other overdose of an anesthetic agent.

Other parts of the cardiovascular system, particularly the small blood vessels, are dilated by low concentrations of alcohol in the blood. This is particularly true of the superficial vessels in the skin. The vessels of the viscera, or the internal organs, however, are somewhat constricted by these low concentrations. The dilation of the surface vessels causes a feeling of warmth as heat is radiated from the surface of the body, but the constriction of the vessels of the viscera causes the internal temperature of the body to drop, and vital functions become slower, reducing their resistance. This is why the feeling of skin warmth during drinking is a false impression, since the internal temperature has been lowered. The use of alcohol in cold weather to make one feel warm is contraindicated, since internal temperature is reduced and much of the body warmth is lost through the skin radiation.

Alcohol was long thought to be indicated as a medication in heart disease. It was claimed that alcohol dilated the vessels of the heart and therefore could be indicated for therapeutic purposes where heart vessels were constricted or occluded. Many patients benefited. Recent evidence indicates, however, that alcohol does not dilate these vessels; the benefit was derived from its depressive effect upon the brain and the resultant relief from worry and apprehension. In other words, the benefits were those of sedation by a tranquilizing agent.

The excretory system is affected very little by the ingestion of alcohol. There is some increase in the output of urine, but this may not necessarily be due to the alcohol itself, but rather to the dehydration that results and induces the individual to increase the amount of fluid intake from the alcoholic beverage itself.

If there has been any damage to the kidneys due to any disease whatever, however, alcohol is contraindicated. The alcohol itself may directly damage the small units in the kidney that comprise the filtering mechanism to remove water-soluble waste products.

The muscular system is affected by alcohol only to the extent that the controls of the muscles are changed neurologically from the brain. The muscles themselves, however, are affected very little. Any changes in the muscle system are due more to the effect of alcohol upon the nervous system and its failure to deliver to the muscles the properly synchronized and distributed impulses necessary for their normal contractile activity.

The skeletal system, because of the relatively small amount of circulation going to it, is hardly affected at all by the ingestion of alcohol.

The effect of alcohol on the reproductive system has long been the subject of discussion. There has been a fallacious belief that alcohol stimulates sexual desire directly, and acts as an aphrodisiac. Actually, such increased sexual activity results from the removal of inhibition and the loss of control. The ability to perform the sex act successfully decreases progressively as the alcohol in the system increases.

During pregnancy, any alcohol consumed by the mother passes through the placenta and as the alcoholic content in her system becomes higher and higher the alcoholic content of the blood in the fetus also rises. Therefore, an unborn child becomes as intoxicated as the mother.

The numerous erroneous opinions that alcohol itself causes blindness, prematurity, insanity, and stillbirth are untenable. Although it is true that children of alcoholics are more frequently stillborn, premature, or the victims of mental diseases, these effects are indirect, and secondary to the alcoholism. Alcoholic mothers usually consume alcohol rather than a nutritious diet, and may bring about these effects due to malnutrition in the fetus.

It has been a common observation that an alcoholic woman will very often refrain from drinking during a pregnancy.

The endocrine system can be affected to a great extent by the excessive ingestion of alcohol. For a long time it was thought that alcoholism itself might be the result of dysfunction on the part of the endocrine glands. However, more recent studies prove that their dysfunction may be the result of ingestion of large amounts of alcohol rather than the cause of such ingestion. The adrenal gland, particularly, has been the subject of discussion in connection with alcoholism. Once thought to be the cause of alcoholism, because so many alcoholics were found to have poorly functioning adrenal glands, it has been shown by subsequent studies that their poor function is due to the exhaustion of the adrenal glands because of the hyperactivity required of them from tense individuals. These individuals then used alcohol as a tranquilizer to relieve their tensions. Recovery of the glands took place when the tensions were removed by other methods.

We have described the effect of alcohol on the various systems of the body and can see that in moderate or small amounts alcohol has very little effect on the body. It is only when alcohol, an anesthetic drug, is used in great concentration that the systems of the body can be adversely affected. As with any drug, when taken in moderation the natural resources of the body are able to metabolize it and use it without harm. Used in excess, it can cause damage to these tissues. Any signs, therefore, of intoxication by any drug, in this case alcohol, should be regarded as a danger sign. Since alcohol is an addicting drug, an individual who uses it in excess will inevitably suffer further damage, both psychologically and physiologically.

CHAPTER 10

Treating the Abstaining Alcoholic*

MUCH has been written about the alcoholic in the acute stage. There is a plethora of material relating to the pathological complications of excessive drinking, the treatment of the individual who is acutely intoxicated from excessive alcohol ingestion, and the hospital treatment of patients suffering from effects of excessive alcohol ingestion at various stages in the progress of the disease alcoholism.

Comparatively little, however, has been said about the treatment of the patient suffering from alcoholism who has recovered from the acute stage and is in the process of attempting to live his life of complete abstinence. For too long it has been taken for granted that such an individual, having recovered from his acute intoxication, and having experienced its discomfort and the rigors of recovery from that intoxication, should have had enough of a lesson to keep him from drinking in the future. He has been sent from the hospital with the admonition, "Now go forth and drink no more. You should have learned from this bitter experience how horrible this can be." Physicians and hospital personnel, clergy

---

* "Treating The Abstaining Alcoholic" by M. A. Block. *Medical Times*, April, 1962.

and social workers, probation officers and others, as well as members of the family, take it for granted that this will deter the individual from asking for such disagreeable results again.

In attempts to evaluate the attitude of the patient, not enough attention has been given to the individual to ascertain what his attitude is toward his own drinking and his drinking problem. We know that many alcoholics have self-destructive tendencies. We know that many use alcohol as an escape from reality. We know that many alcoholics punish themselves by ingesting alcohol. But not enough attention has been given these attitudes by the average therapist, the family physician, and the people around the patient; not enough effort has been made to aid the alcoholic patient in changing such attitudes, understanding himself and his problems, and modifying his methods of meeting this problem. There are many kinds of alcoholics and they cannot all be treated in the same way.

Jellinek has classified alcoholics into five major groups. Their differentiation depends upon four main criteria: psychological dependence, progression, control, tissue tolerance and physiological dependence or addiction. We must take into account the various types of alcoholics in treating any individual suffering from the illness.

Very often the individual suffering from alcoholism has very poor motivation for giving up drinking. It is much simpler for him to continue, deluding himself that next time he will be able to control the amount. Too often he is scolded for poor judgment, and for not facing the truth of his inability to handle alcohol. His repeated slips are blamed on weakness, stupidity, or self-indulgence.

The physician treating these patients must take time to determine the presence of or absence of sufficient motivation to continue with abstinence. Where such motivation is lacking or of such poor quality as to be of no value, it is the obligation of the physician to supply the incentive. This can only be done by exhaustive investigation and discussion of the problems that face the patient. If there is a physical basis for them, that should have been uncovered and corrected during the hospitalization period or after a complete physical examination and laboratory work.

Once corrected and the patient physically healthy, sufficient explanation must be given him of his need to stop drinking even though he is physically recovered. Where total recovery from the physical ailment is impossible because of some permanent damage to the tissues, or where some irreversible process of disease exists either because of or independently of alcohol ingestion, acceptance of such physical defect must be emphasized.

Many patients find it extremely difficult to accept any physical disability whatever. In this area alone a good deal must be done in the way of therapy. It can be explained that physical difficulties, defects, and disabilities, even though of a permanent nature, are not necessarily progressive, and that chronic illnesses, even though disabling to a certain extent, do not necessarily preclude near-normal activity and living. Adjustment can be made by the patient, if there is sufficient interest shown and explanation given by the therapist.

Deterrent drugs are of great value for those who cannot refrain from drinking long enough to allow necessary psychotherapy to begin, or for those whose physical disabilities become intolerable.

In order to ascertain the type of individual with which we are dealing, we must look back into his history, not only his drinking history but also his personal history—his childhood, his environment, and his family. It is in this information that we may find some basis for the individual's use of a drug to make himself more comfortable, to meet problems, and to overcome his feelings of inadequacy. When one has an intelligent patient who understands the importance of his background in relation to his present condition, explanation and discussion will often help him to understand himself.

With patients lacking this intelligence and understanding, of course, deterrent drugs plus the experience of meeting problems without drinking over long periods of time will help them to continue their abstinence, even after removal of the deterrent drugs.

Actually, the whole program of treating the abstaining alcoholic is a re-educational one. Most of us are conformists, and most of us like to belong to a group. Even if we like to consider ourselves different, we prefer to have this difference lie along lines that are socially acceptable. It is therefore extremely difficult for someone to live in an environment where everyone drinks and be forced to refuse drinks, especially when he has been known as a drinker previously. This self-consciousness has been one of the great factors in slips of alcoholics. Actually, of course, society has done very little to help the alcoholic in this treatment.

Drinking alcoholic beverages has become so prevalent that one is almost forced into drinking by the pressures of social contacts. The abstainer is considered peculiar. He is a nonconformist in a way that, to the drinker, appears too critical. In society nondrinkers are not popular among drinkers. To the abstaining alcoholic, therefore, it is obvious that his social contacts must be modified; he does not feel comfortable among drinkers, and drinkers do not help him to feel comfortable. Although it is well known that members of Alcoholics Anonymous are abstainers, the recovered alcoholic does not wish to associate himself with nondrinkers exclusively in the early stages of recovery, for he feels he is labeled just as much that way as he was when he associated with heavy drinkers. He much prefers to be on a "take it or leave it alone" basis. This is evidenced by the tremendous number of alcoholic patients who request treatment for their problem, not to help them to abstain completely, but to help them to drink normally.

The responsibilities of society toward alcoholism are so many and so vast that we could devote a great deal of time to this alone. Our sense of values, our standards, our status symbols are such that alcohol occupies a place far more important than it deserves. Changes in these attitudes cannot be accomplished in a short time. The ability to drink a great deal of alcohol, the lavishness with which drinks are prepared and offered, the constant refilling of the glasses, the urge to have just one more—all of these must be modified by society. The necessity for drinking must be discouraged.

This is a matter for all educators. Where people wish to drink and no harm results from this drinking, such drinking should be carried out with due regard for propriety. Drunken behavior should not be tolerated. Excessive drinking must be considered gauche. The mark of sophistication in drinking should be a drink or two, and never to appear markedly affected by alcohol. Once we make the standard of drinking such that anyone who shows the effect of alcohol is socially ostracized, it may be considered smart never to drink more than one drink. Unfortunately, at present it is considered smart to drink only if one drinks excessively. Such social attitudes will take generations to modify, but we must start sometime if we are to accomplish this end.

In those societies where drunken behavior is not tolerated, we see very little alcoholism. In societies where drunkenness is tolerated, the rate of alcoholism goes up. All drinking was at one time the prerogative of adults only, but today the age of drinking has dropped lower and lower until we find people not yet out of their childhood or adolescence allowed to drink. And society has accepted this state.

One big factor in helping the alcoholic maintain abstinence is to help him have confidence in himself. It is easy to recognize those whose sense of inadequacy has existed for a long time. For the individual, however, who seems to have confidence in every area other than the ability to refuse a drink it becomes a tremendous problem. Here again the alcoholic is not the only one who bears the responsibility; society is also responsible.

Why does the abstaining alcoholic feel so positive that

everyone is watching what he is drinking or what he is not drinking? It is possible to change this attitude by questioning the patient himself as to what other individuals had been drinking. When he cannot account for the type of beverage others have been drinking he immediately sees the inaccuracy of his statement. This questioning must be done over and over, however, in order to convince him that people have neither the time nor the interest, as a rule, to watch one particular individual.

In educating the abstaining alcoholic to continue his life and meet his problems without alcohol, we must go over the various problems that might confront him. It is impossible, of course, to meet every contingency and discuss it. But, in the case of ordinary problems of living, we must teach the patient to observe those around him who have exactly the same problems but use other methods of meeting them. Emphasis must be laid on the importance of not necessarily solving every problem perfectly. The ability to accept partial solutions, the ability to compromise and adjust must be learned by repetitious discussion. This takes time and understanding on the part of the therapist, but proves extremely valuable to the patient.

From the foregoing it can be seen that this program takes a great deal of time and many visits. All too often the patience of the patient is exhausted quickly. He feels there is no necessity for further treatment now that he has stopped drinking. I think the best way of handling this very common problem is to explain at the very first visit how the program operates, how long it takes, how frequent the visits must be, and what the objectives are, pointing out to the patient that there will come a time before long when he will feel he needs no further treatment. When he begins to demur about coming for treatments, this can be pointed out to him. It will not always change his mind, but at least he will recognize that you have warned him of exactly this.

When the individual is advised in advance that treatment

will continue for many, many months, or even years, he does not expect too much from each visit. The change from visit to visit will be minimal and actually almost undiscernible, but good results can be seen by looking back over long periods of time. The patient should be told that one cannot undo years of training in a short time, nor can training for the future take place in a short time.

The therapist and the patient are not the only ones involved in keeping him abstinent. Everyone who comes in contact with the patient has a part. The cooperation of family, friends, and employer are important. Cooperation can be enlisted from the family by discussing the problem with them and explaining their part in helping the patient remain abstinent. Permission must be obtained from the patient to discuss his problem with friends or with an employer. Denial of this permission gives the physician the opportunity to discuss other problems with the patient.

Where permission is obtained, discussion with the employer is extremely valuable. A great deal of responsibility rests with the doctor, of course, in bringing the matter to the attention of the employer; it is always wise to ascertain his attitude toward the problem before discussing the patient with him. Very few employers, however, will refuse to cooperate.

If the employer is cooperative, there are many ways of helping the patient. Much depends on the patient's position, his work, his contacts on the job, his responsibility, and the part this responsibility plays in his drinking problem. All of these drinking factors must be adequately discussed and treated to the best advantage of the patient.

One problem in treating the abstaining alcoholic that all of us must meet at one time or another is the treatment of the "slip." No matter how well motivated, no matter how well he has learned his lesson, and no matter how conscientious the abstaining alcoholic is, there can and does come a time, very often, when he will drink alcohol. Some will limit this defection to one or two drinks, others will go on drinking until drunk. Almost all of them have a sense of remorse after a slip.

The attitude of the physician in treating this condition, therefore, becomes extremely important. The physician does not sit in judgment on his patient. It is important that he go over very carefully with the patient the circumstances that resulted in the slip; sometimes this experience can prove to be one of the most effective therapeutic factors.

At the same time, the therapist must be careful not to condone the slip, since those individuals who are dependent may accept this attitude as permissiveness. This approach can only be evaluated by the relationship that has existed between the patient and the therapist up to that time. As we are aware, the rapport between the patient and the therapist is extremely important, and there can come a time when this relationship is so close that the patient is practically dependent upon the therapist. In some instances he looks upon the therapist as his parent. When this occurs, it is the physician's responsibility, during treatment, to wean him away so that he becomes less dependent.

The patient must learn to stand on his own feet. When he does slip, he must be encouraged to be honest about the entire matter. Again, there must be repetition of the motivation, the incentives, and the objective. Again, the circumstances of the slip must be described in detail. Very often there are subconscious motivations. These must be explained carefully to the patient.

The usual techniques of psychotherapy brought to bear on emotional and mental problems cannot always be used in treating the abstinent alcoholic. He may not be as verbal as others. Having learned to abstain, he very often feels that further treatment is unnecessary. All too often the alcoholic is convinced that his only problem is drinking, and what lies behind it is of comparatively little importance. He does not always get relief from airing his problems, his anxieties, and tensions. He will often sit for long periods of time in complete silence. He is a rejected individual, and feels rejected. Therefore, the technique of waiting for the patient to speak often does not work with him. Sometimes the therapist must show a warm, cordial, and real interest in him, by talking to him, by asking questions, by prompting him, and by making manifest his actual interest in the patient himself.

We might say here that the physician must actually sell himself to the patient as one who wishes to help him. Unlike most patients coming to a physician, few alcoholics come of their own accord, particularly after they have stopped drinking. Most of the time they seek help from the physician only under pressure from families, friends, employers, or other individuals who insist on their having treatment.

These factors must be borne in mind when treating the patient, especially after a slip. It is not unusual for the slips to occur with greater frequency if the first one is not handled to the best advantage.

Prominent among the factors in maintaining abstinence is the fellowship of Alcoholics Anonymous, described in another chapter. However, we cannot delegate to lay people the treatment of individuals suffering from a severe disease that is properly the business of the physician. It is as important for the physician to continue to treat the abstinent alcoholic until he is fully recovered as it is for him to treat him in his stage of intoxication. To delegate this duty to untrained laymen is like turning over the problem of mental disease to untrained religious people. There is no doubt of the value of faith in the recovery from any illness. However, there are certain techniques of treatment that are essential to the complete recovery of any sick person, which can be learned only by training and understanding of the physiology and psyche of a human being. To depend on faith alone may bring a type of abstinence, but not necessarily a satisfactory recovery.

In a surprising number of cases of alcoholism, there is an

underlying psychosis that the patient has sought to alleviate by drinking. As a result of this self-medication, the patient has become addicted to alcohol and has successfully masked the underlying psychosis. People surrounding him are commonly of the opinion that he is alcoholic without recognizing the fact that there is an underlying psychosis, very often schizophrenia. The psychiatrist will readily recognize this, and of course, in these cases it is the underlying schizophrenia that must be treated.

When the self-medication that the patient has employed is removed, the schizophrenic manifestations become more apparent, and the behavior of the patient becomes bizarre. When disulfiram has been used to withdraw the patient from alcohol, there is a tendency on the part of laymen to attribute the psychosis to the administration of the disulfiram. However, this is not actually the case. What has happened is that the psychosis becomes manifest after the overlying alcoholism has been removed. This must be explained to the patient's family, and the psychosis must be treated. Very often when the schizophrenia is treated successfully—and the type of treatment indicated here rests with the individual psychiatrist—the patient will be able to resume living without the use of alcohol. The response in most cases is most gratifying.

As is the case with many schizophrenes, the treatment very often will not produce the desired results. In these cases, the patient may have to be referred to a mental institution. The same principle applies when the underlying condition is severe depression or any of the other psychoses.

The average family physician is now sufficiently trained in psychiatry to be able to handle the average psychiatric problems that occur in the alcoholic. However, when a psychosis exists, or when some psychiatric complication becomes great enough to be beyond the family physician, a psychiatrist can be consulted for further treatment. The important features in the psychiatric approach to the treatment of the abstaining alcoholic are the re-educational program mentioned above and the psychiatrist's attitude toward the alcoholic. This attitude must be, in so many cases, different from that of other psychiatric patients to achieve good results.

It may be necessary for the psychiatrist to give supportive treatment over long periods of time, and in some cases, even for the rest of the individual's life, to many of the borderline schizophrenic cases who have resorted to alcohol as a method of meeting their problems. This type of supportive therapy may be of great advantage, and is infinitely preferable to commitment to an institution or return to drinking. Many clinics for such supportive therapy have been established for such patients in mental hospitals as well as in general hospitals. These have proved economically sound, keeping the patient productive in his society rather than committing him as a ward of the community.

I doubt if the incidence of psychoses among alcoholics is any higher in percentage than among the general population. However, it is true that the alcoholic psychotic who has become addicted to alcohol may become a much more frustrating problem in treatment than the individual suffering from the same psychotic illness without the overlay of the alcohol. It is for this reason that it is so important that early addiction to alcohol be recognized and treated.

A word of warning is necessary regarding the use of drugs in treating the abstaining alcoholic. I think one must bear in mind always that the alcoholic in many cases is an individual who has become an addict, addicted to the drug alcohol. Such addicts, we all recognize, can become addicted to other drugs as well. We must be very careful, therefore, not to transfer their addiction to other drugs just as detrimental. Barbiturates, particularly, to which the alcoholic can be so easily habituated and then addicted, are frequently used in the medical profession. In my opinion, this is one type of drug that should be avoided.

The tranquilizing drugs are of exceptional value in treating alcoholics, but some of them can also be addictive. (See pages 97-98) This must be watched very carefully. Frequently changing of the drugs, going from one to the other without keeping the patient on any one for too long a time, is one method of avoiding this pitfall. Gradual weaning away from all drugs, however, is the ideal objective, and this should be done as soon as possible without making the patient **too** uncomfortable.

CHAPTER 11

Skid Row
A Socio-Economic and Public Health Problem

For most people the term alcoholic conjures up an image of the Skid Row bum. Statistically, the alcoholics on Skid Row represent but 3 percent of the alcoholic population,[1] but because of the advanced stage of their illness, they are an eyesore and a reproach to the community. The Skid Row alcoholic is frequently in the last stage and at the end point of the disease, and as with other diseases, this represents the most discouraging and revolting picture.

Although only about 50 percent of the homeless men on Skid Row are alcoholics, they have all been lumped together and most people assume that they are all alcoholics. Fifty percent are not alcoholics, but are psychopathic personalities or inadequate individuals who find in the anonymity of Skid Row a way of life that is more satisfactory than living in and facing the problems of the competitive world outside. Here is a refuge where no one asks questions and where their privacy is respected by their fellow men, all of whom feel the same way about their lives. Many efforts have been made to move these people into more desirable quarters, but they

[1] National Opinion Research Center of the University of Chicago, 1958.

eventually gravitate back to the same kind of neighborhood, starting all over again and making a new Skid Row where the old ones had been obliterated. Skid Row is a philosophy and a refuge, and will not be obliterated by those who feel that it is an eyesore.

It is true that most of the denizens would prefer to have a better income and more material blessings, but they usually do not wish to live elsewhere. On Skid Row they feel adequate. Here they feel accepted, whereas in the rest of the world they feel rejected. Here they are not saddled with the responsibilities of wives or children or families or friends. They come and go as they please, and they live only for the present.

Those who are alcoholic seek surcease not only from the outside world, but very often from the very problems of Skid Row itself, and oblivion is theirs for the asking. Those who share desires for alcohol will often share the alcohol itself with each other. Oblivion is purchasable and no criticism is attached to it. They envy no one because they can have anything they like; if not in reality, at least in the dream world achieved through alcohol.

The homeless alcoholic can be defined as a person who has no family or is not in contact with his family, and whose domicile is determined by where he happens to be. If he is employed, it is usually on a day-to-day basis. He has no intimate friends, but only acquaintances in the Skid Row area. Like other alcoholics, the homeless alcoholic drinks alcohol excessively. He may or may not be a compulsive drinker, but in most cases his main interest is to obtain and continue to drink alcohol, with little regard for himself or his surroundings. His excessive drinking may be periodic or continuous. He has the same characteristics, in many instances, as other alcoholics, to which is added homelessness.

All homeless alcoholics cannot be classified into one group. There are as many varieties in this category as in any other of the economic or social strata of society. It is not unusual, however, to find that this individual has arrived at the lowest point of the disease. But the Skid Row alcoholic or the homeless alcoholic was not born in Skid Row. By gradual stages he has reached the status of homelessness and has passed through the various stages of alcoholism until, in a large percentage of cases, he represents the later stage of the disease.

Many of these individuals either have no relatives or have been out of contact with them for so long that their relationship means nothing to them. There are some, however, who still maintain some stability of family situation. In this group there is occasional family contact, if the family lives in the same city or in a nearby area. He does not, however, live with his family. The members of this group often have a good chance for rehabilitation, since constructive family ties still exist, as well as some possible work performance, strong moral concepts, and a sense of individual responsibility and personal integrity not too long lost and possibly capable of reconstruction.

The former group, however, is usually made up of individuals who have drifted into their present way of life from a background that provided few early training patterns. The members of this group may never have learned to accept discipline or constructive life patterns. An attempt at rehabilitation is not an encouraging prospect, since long and arduous work may be necessary to turn them into responsible individuals. However, it is not impossible.

In this chapter we shall describe the various agencies that can contribute toward rehabilitation of the homeless alcoholic. They are arranged in a graduated pattern, beginning with the facility for those most easily rehabilitated and continuing with the facilities for those who are more difficult. Each group will be described in some detail. The ideal plan would be to have all these agencies interlock in their operations, but the plan should also be constructed so that each facility can be operated on an individual basis. The facilities adopted, therefore, would depend upon both the immediate and future needs of a community.[2] Because of the scope required if all agencies were to operate concomitantly, the entire program may have to be approached sectionally. It was with this in mind that the individual agencies have been described in such a way that each can operate on an individual basis.

Since the Skid Row area is usually part of an urban population, it is a part of every large city. Whether we like it or not, it represents an entity with which we must contend. It therefore becames a community responsibility. Such an area can be reduced to proportions so small as to be less of a reproach to the community than it is today. Interest and financial support are necessary. In order to accomplish this in an organized way, the following service facilities are required:

1. *In-hospital service*

This should be a facility in a general hospital where the homeless alcoholic can be restored to as nearly complete physical and mental health as possible. This facility should offer a screening process to determine the proper agency for the individual involved.

Where physical examination reveals organic disease, rehabilitation in that area should be started immediately. A healthy body is a prerequisite for rehabilitation of the alcoholic. The patient need not remain in the hospital until such complete physical rehabilitation is accomplished. His case should be followed up after dismissal to make sure that whatever disease processes were detected will continue to be treated until maximum recovery is obtained. While he is still in the hospital, indoctrination for rehabilitation on physical, mental, and vocational bases should be started. Incentive should be provided for the patient to follow through with his

---

[2] "A Program for the Homeless Alcoholic" by M. A. Block. *Quarterly Journal of Studies on Alcohol*, Vol. 23, No. 4, December, 1962. Rutgers University Center of Alcohol Studies.

treatment after his hospitalization. A voluntary general hospital, or a county or city hospital, usually provides facilities for this. It is desirable, however, that sufficient personnel be utilized to give patients complete care. The hospital can be used as a screening agent to determine subsequent treatment of the patient.

2. *Outpatient clinic*

For patients understanding their problem to be treated on an outpatient basis, the clinic offers a very good opportunity for continued treatment while the patient is gainfully employed. Only the most promising type of individual, one with considerable stability, is a good candidate for the outpatient clinic.

Clinic facilities should be available to these patients after working hours. For this type of patient the chances of rehabilitation are excellent. There should be a sufficient number of such clinics, easily available to certain geographic areas, and officially caring for this type of alcoholic.

3. *Foster homes*

For those individuals who are fairly well integrated but find it impossible to maintain homes of their own, foster homes offer a possible solution. Candidates for this type of facility must be stable enough to continue employment and attend clinics, if necessary. Many families with enough room to house one or more may welcome paying guests. The patient himself, on the other hand, may welcome a family environment to live in for a fair price. For a qualified patient, a family environment in which he can establish rapport and satisfactory social contacts can provide the necessary incentive to continue treatment at a clinic. Satisfactory interpersonal relationships with such a family give a feeling of belonging and engender the sense of responsibility necessary for complete rehabilitation into society. Such foster homes should be supervised by the proper agencies, and attempts should be made to match the patient with the family, and vice versa. Both sides must be investigated to ensure satisfaction. To a great extent, individuals living in foster homes can help to support themselves or earn their keep. Babysitting and helping with the dishes, for instance, will often help give them a feeling of belonging to the family and of being a valuable part of the family group. For those who have lost their families, and who, as a result of discouragement and depression as well as rejection, have taken to excessive drinking, this type of facility represents a very important step in their rehabilitation.

4. *Halfway House*

This type of facility should be used for those individuals who can maintain employment with proper supervision, but who require continuous treatment even during the period of employment. Often they can maintain a good employment situation all day but require supervision at night and a place to live where such treatment can be carried out. A facility like this can also be used for the treatment of alcoholics whose family environment has been one of the contributing factors to their alcoholism. By getting away from a family situation into a supervised institution, the patient can continue to work while under supervision. Once rehabilitated physically and emotionally, he can often return to his family and continue to live happily. This kind of facility has often been used for people referred by domestic relations courts. While the patient is at the facility, the family should also be reeducated in its attitudes toward him.

For the homeless alcoholic the halfway house provides an ideal setting, since it gives him a place to live where he remains under treatment although employed outside. As the patient becomes more advanced in his rehabilitation he can be transferred to a foster home. In the halfway house, however, he has the opportunity of living with people in the same circumstances as himself, and the supervision he obtains varies with his own individual need. The length of time he requires in such a facility also varies, depending on his acceptance of therapy and his response to it. The necessary therapy can be given by psychologists, psychiatric social workers, psychiatrists, or medical men, depending upon the individual involved. Religious training and Alcoholics Anonymous, as well as group therapy, can be employed as indicated. In such a facility, a person who has lost a sense of responsibility has an opportunity to regain it.

The halfway house, as the name implies, is an excellent facility for the homeless individual who through hospitalization has recovered from the acute stage of his illness and must undergo further rehabilitation. Instead of returning to the downtrodden area of Skid Row, he has an opportunity to live in a protected atmosphere, hold a job if he is able, and continue with treatment. If more intensive treatment is required than can be given in the halfway house, he can attend a clinic and still return to this properly supervised facility.

The halfway house can also serve as a facility for those who have been sentenced to jail for excessive drinking or alcoholism. Instead of being turned loose to return to their former Skid Row area, they can be brought to the halfway house, already detoxified, and continue with rehabilitative treatment there. If the rehabilitative treatment is successful, they may be able to get jobs and continue living in a halfway house until they are ready to live independently in society.

5. *Rehabilitation Center*

For the individual in whom alcoholism has advanced to the point where he needs very long periods of intensive therapy, a rehabilitation center can be of great help. Skilled personnel is essential for such long-term therapy. Diagnosis and treatment, both physical and mental, must be carried out. The hospital or infirmary would have to be designed for chronic conditions, with complete supervision and care. In this type of facility the homeless alcoholic with other chronic diseases can be cared for. As a result of long periods of debilitation and dietary indiscretion, many of these patients suffer from a multiplicity of illnesses. It is essential to return them to physical health or as nearly as possible to good health. This often takes a long time.

The patient who qualifies for this facility must be differentiated from the one who qualifies for treatment in the general hospital where only short-term cases should be treated. The patient may remain in the rehabilitation center for months or perhaps years before he can achieve any semblance of physical rehabilitation. During this time, however, selected cases can be treated for psychiatric rehabilitation at the same time they are gaining physical health. Lengthy treatment may be necessary, after which many of these patients can return to living in the outside world.

As their physical health improves, along with intensive psychiatric therapy, it may be possible for a good percentage of such patients to be advanced to the halfway house. It is necessary however that they be given vocational therapy. As they improve they must be taught a trade, if necessary, or some means of earning a living. Even though only a small percentage of these halfway house patients may be rehabilitated fully, this small percentage could prove to be an economically sound investment. With continued improvement, they can move from facility to facility until they become completely integrated into society.

6. *Permanent Supervision*

For those patients who cannot respond to any of the treatments mentioned above, some facility must be provided with a completely sheltered or custodial environment. There are patients who cannot cope with life without adequate support, and they require a pleasant environment in a semi-institutionalized setting where good recreation and lounging facilities are provided. The appearance must be that of a rest home, not a detention home. There may be little likelihood

A Socio-Economic and Public Health Problem

of many of these patients ever leaving such an institution of their own volition, but they are entitled to and should get any necessary assistance. The help for this kind of facility can operate on a volunteer basis. Many patients can help toward its support by working in the institution or on its grounds, and can in this way, to some extent, contribute.

7. State hospitals

In these hospitals the patient who is clearly psychotic can be certified, and in some cases this is absolutely necessary. The state hospital provides facilities for patients who qualify for such treatment. Recovery from the psychosis does not mean that the patient can drink safely again. He must continually abstain from alcohol, but this can be taught him while he is in the hospital.

PERSONNEL

Personnel for all of the facilities mentioned above must be adequately trained, but more than that, they must want to work with this type of patient. Unfortunately, not all people trained in psychiatry and medicine or social work feel this way about alcoholics. It is much more important to have a person who desires to work with such patients than it is to have one, though adequately trained, who dislikes them. Sometimes we find that members of Alcoholics Anonymous, interested volunteers, clergymen, Salvation Army members, and Volunteers of America, some of whom have had no special training in this area, accomplish more with alcoholic patients than do medical men, psychiatrists, or social workers. The reason for this is often that these people are interested and like to deal with such patients. It is important, therefore, that the selection of personnel be made not only on the basis of formal training or certification, but on the basis of sincerity of motivation and understanding of the problem involved.

In the trained disciplines, however, and for screening purposes, it is essential that adequately trained people be employed. It is not necessary than an entire team of all the disciplines be employed in each one of the facilities mentioned. However, one team of medical men, psychiatrists, psychologists, psychiatric social workers, and social workers can be at the service of any one or all the facilities for screening purposes. This same team could also serve the courts when such screening is required for disposition of individual cases. It could also be a traveling team visiting the various facilities for the purpose of diagnosis and consultation in training and therapy. The personnel in each of the facilities could, therefore, have at its service a supervising team that could be available at all times for consultation and direction. The members of other volunteer organizations I have mentioned could also help the team in treating patients and helping them toward rehabilitation.

THE COURT CASE

The homeless alcoholics who appear before the courts represent a unique problem in this entire setup. Disposition could be made of these cases after proper screening by the team mentioned above. In cooperation with the probation department, the individual could be sent to the facility that, in the opinion of the team, is best suited for his benefit. When an individual is assigned to the proper facility a great deal can be done for him.

There is another group that must be taken into consideration. There are many homeless men, even homeless alcoholics, who violate no laws and do not come before the courts. These people will not volunteer to live in or attend any of the facilities mentioned. This is a unique problem, since there is no way of bringing pressure to bear upon them except in terms of education. We must be careful not to impose upon any citizen the wishes of some other citizen when he has violated no law and has in no way trespassed against the public. I feel, however, that many such people can be rehabilitated if proper incentive and motivation is inculcated. For this type I recommend an institution or facility in the home area, the so-called Skid Row area. Here, a small attractive building to which they can repair may be a great help. *No questions asked* should be the rule, with the individual paying his own way to live in comfort and cleanliness. In such a facility, manned by social workers with the help of volunteers of Alcoholics Anonymous and other agencies of this type, many of these people might find an environment that would make them happier and allow them to live self-respecting lives. With a minimum of preaching and a maximum of education, such a facility could become attractive to them. By gradual indoctrination, motivation can be supplied for mental rehabilitation and integration into society.

There is one further point that should be made. Total and complete abstinence is of the utmost importance in rehabilitation for the alcoholic. In the case of the homeless alcoholic it is imperative that such abstinence be maintained if rehabilitation is to be accomplished. There are ways of maintaining this abstinence. One of these is to use Antabuse, which has proven exceptionally effective in thousands of cases. However, supervision in its administration is essential. This drug has been described in detail in the medical treatment of alcoholism, Chapter 8.

Itinerant social workers, working under the direction of a physician, have proved to be of great value in following up the homeless alcoholic or the alcoholic on probation. They can supervise the maintenance of abstinence in foster homes and outside the various domiciliary facilities. They can also follow up cases who do not report as requested. A social worker, equipped with proper transportation and on call, a probation officer, a police officer, or anyone interested in the patient should be available at any time to check on the homeless alcoholic who does not report on time to his proper facility. This worker, under the supervision of a physician, could administer Antabuse and follow up delinquent patients before they have retrogressed too far.

This is a broad outline of a program that I believe covers the entire problem of Skid Row. The financing of these various facilities and the personnel must be arranged. In my opinion, alcoholism represents a public health problem and should be paid for by public health funds. As the individual under care becomes integrated into society and regains his responsibility, further help for him should be sought on a private basis. If the matter is handled adequately, the stigma of immorality now associated with this illness will be removed, and alcoholics will have no hesitancy about consulting their private physicians. As more of such requests are made, more physicians will respond.

Again let me state that each of the facilities described above can be used on an individual basis. I reiterate, this is a community problem and a community responsibility. Only the awareness of the community and its action can do something about a type of alcoholic who has long been neglected, but who has good possibilities for rehabilitation, with the proper approach.

CHAPTER 12

Alcoholics Anonymous

ALCOHOLICS ANONYMOUS is a fellowship of men and women who share their experience, strength, and hope with each other that they may solve their common problem and help others to recover from alcoholism.

The only requirement for membership is a desire to stop drinking. There are no dues or fees for A.A. membership. It is self-supporting through contributions. A.A. is not allied with any sect, denomination, political group, organization, or institution; does not wish to engage in any controversy; neither endorses nor opposes any causes. Its primary cause is to stay sober and help other alcoholics to achieve sobriety.

Thus Alcoholics Anonymous describes itself, no matter what you have heard, what you have seen, or what you think. These statements by Alcoholics Anonymous should be studied very carefully. Unfortunately, through hearsay, misunderstanding, and misrepresentation, many people do not understand what this wonderful, inspiring, and ubiquitous fellowship of Alcoholics Anonymous is. Unfortunately, many of its own members do not understand. Because A.A. is so broad and tolerant, each member makes his own interpretation, and not all are capable of appreciating the significant principles.

The creed of Alcoholics Anonymous includes twelve steps and twelve traditions. Each of these must be studied carefully in order to understand how and why Alcoholics Anonymous operates.

The Twelve Steps:

1. We admitted we were powerless over alcohol... that our lives had become unmanageable.
2. Came to believe that a power greater than ourselves could restore us to sanity.
3. Made a decision to turn our will and our lives over to the care of God AS WE UNDERSTOOD HIM.
4. Made a searching and fearless moral inventory of ourselves.
5. Admitted to God, ourselves, and to another human being the exact nature of our wrongs.
6. Were entirely ready to have God remove all these defects of character.
7. Humbly asked Him to remove our shortcomings.
8. Made a list of all persons we had harmed, and became willing to make amends to them all.
9. Made direct amends to such people wherever possible, except when to do so would injure them or others.
10. Continued to take personal inventory, and when we were wrong, promptly admitted it.
11. Sought through prayer and meditation to improve our conscious contact with God AS WE UNDERSTOOD HIM, praying only for knowledge of His will for us and for the power to carry that out.
12. Having had a spiritual awakening as the result of these steps, we tried to carry this message to alcoholics, and to practice these principles in all our affairs.

A study of these Twelve Steps will give anyone an idea of how the principles of Alcoholics Anonymous can be effective. People suffering from alcoholism are human beings. They have the same failures, the same successes, the same desires, the same antipathies as other human beings. The fact that many people try Alcoholics Anonymous and do not succeed in achieving abstinence is not because of Alcoholics Anonymous, but because of the inability of some individuals to meet the requirements. If one looks over the Twelve Steps of Alcoholics Anonymous, one can see that this is not an easy program to adhere to. It takes a great deal of humility, soul-searching, and maturity to live so demanding a program. In a complex and highly competitive world, this is not easy. The steps could be recommended to anyone, alcoholic or not, and were everyone to adhere to this program, the world would indeed be a better place to live in. Similarly, if everyone were to live his religion, the same results could be achieved.

In order to further understand the fellowship of Alcoholics Anonymous, one must be acquainted with the Twelve Traditions:

1. Our common welfare should come first; personal recovery depends upon A.A. unity.
2. For our group purposes, there is but one authority... a loving God, and He may express Himself in our group conscience. Our leaders are His trusted servants... they do not govern.
3. The only requirement for A.A. membership is a desire to stop drinking.
4. Each group should be autonomous except in matters affecting other groups or A.A. as a whole.
5. Each group has but one primary purpose... to carry its message to the alcoholic who still suffers.
6. An A.A. group ought never endorse, finance, or lend the name to any related facility or outside enterprise, lest problems of money, property and prestige divert us from our primary purpose.
7. Every A.A. group ought to be fully self-supporting, declining outside contributions.

8. Alcoholics Anonymous should remain forever non-professional, but our service centers may employ special workers.

9. A.A. as such ought never be organized; but we may create service boards or committees directly responsible to those they serve.

10. Alcoholics Anonymous has no opinion on outside issues; hence the A.A. name ought never be drawn into public controversy.

11. Our public relations policy is based on attraction rather than promotions; we need always maintain personal anonymity at the level of press, radio and films.

12. Anonymity is the spiritual foundation of all our traditions, ever reminding us to place principles before personalities.

Again, studying these Twelve Traditions, one can understand why Alcoholics Anonymous can be successful. As long as these Traditions are maintained, Alcoholics Anonymous will continue to be successful, since personal ambition, individual enterprise, and material benefits are all precluded by these Traditions.

There is no one method that is universally successful for the alcoholic patient. Some will respond to one method of therapy, some to another. The type of therapy that will succeed with the individual alcoholic cannot be dictated by the therapist; it must be dictated by the patient suffering from the illness. It is for this reason that some people achieve abstinence through a method such as medical or psychiatric therapy, while others do it through Alcoholics Anonymous. It is also the reason why some fail in one type of therapy and succeed in another. The wise therapist exposes his patient to all types of therapy, and follows through with the one that brings about the greatest and best response in his patient. For many patients a combination of several therapies can be more successful than the use of one alone. One thing is certain, however, and that is that the therapy must be tailored to the individual suffering from the illness; the individual must not be forced into the therapy that the therapist chooses to employ. It is in this theory that the value of the objectivity of the therapist lies. It is only with broad experience in all types of therapy that he is able to ascertain, when making his diagnosis and evaluation, which form of therapy may prove most valuable. It is equally true that recovery, to a great extent, depends upon the therapist. Since there are many kinds of therapists, and many different personalities among the various therapists, this is a very important factor to consider.

People who have recovered through the program of Alcoholics Anonymous are often of the opinion that this is the best and only successful method of recovery. This is particularly true if they have been successful in Alcoholics Anonymous after having been unsuccessful with other types of therapy. However, it must be borne in mind here, too, that while it may work for one individual, just the opposite may be true of the next.

Alcoholics Anonymous has achieved phenomenal results with thousands of patients suffering from alcoholism. One of its great values is that, at least among themselves, members of Alcoholics Anonymous feel no stigma from others. Here is one place where the individual, all too often rejected by society, finds acceptance and tolerance for a while. This in itself is enough to make the average alcoholic patient feel much more comfortable. To know that he is among people who are suffering from the same illness, who will not sit in judgment on him, and who will accept him as one of them, in itself gives great comfort to any alcoholic. It is perhaps in this that Alcoholics Anonymous affords its greatest value.

As in any other spiritual approach, the individual who wants to be successful in Alcoholics Anonymous must live and feel its program. To give it lip service is but to delude himself. To be successful in this program, he must experience the spiritual conversion that makes him feel the desire to follow it. Understanding it intellectually is not enough. Following it verbally without the spiritual guidance that it offers, and without the spiritual acceptance that it requires, may lead to a type of abstinence, but not the kind of satisfactory one that brings happiness.

The history of this fellowship goes back to the year 1934.[1] At that time one of its founders was making an extremely unsuccessful attempt to attain sobriety. Bill had been drinking excessively for years, and when he finally decided it might be wise to abstain, he found that abstinence was impossible. He sought help from medical men, but in his opinion was helped very little; the doctors could do nothing for him.

One day, in the midst of one of his drinking bouts, a friend of his who had successfully achieved abstinence told him of his experience in achieving it through religion. Religion was something Bill had long ago abandoned. However, the friend continued to tell him about the type of religion he had found. It was based on the principles laid down in a movement previously recognized as successful—the Oxford Movement, which originated in England. This movement advised people to live according to certain principles, and these were related to Bill by his friend. The steps the friend reported to Bill were:

1. He admitted he was powerless to solve his own problems.
2. He made an examination of his conscience and decided to be honest with himself.
3. He began to take an inventory of his own personal defects, and to admit that they existed.
4. He realized that he had had poor interpersonal relationships previously, and had harmed many people. He decided to visit them and make restitution.

[1] *Hope and Help for the Alcoholic* by Harold W. Lovell, M.D., New York: Doubleday & Co., 1951.

5. Helping others appeared to help him, and so he decided to devote himself to do so without any hope of personal gain.
6. By meditation, he sought for direction from God, and to practice these principles all his life.

Bill could not quite accept this religious approach. He had long ago deserted religion as a way of life. He continued to drink.

After Bill was taken to the hospital for delirium tremens, which he had had many times, his friend called on him again. Just recovered from his binge, Bill was more amenable to the program. He could no longer see any way of improving. Life looked bleak at this point, and he felt he could sink no lower. With this terrible feeling of depression and hopelessness, the formula his friend presented seemed to him to offer at least a possibility. At this stage he felt that the problem was beyond him, and that he could not come back from his low point alone. He had to admit that he was licked, that alcohol had defeated him. With this one admission he already began to feel better. The positive step of admission had had an effect.

As Bill devoted more of his time to the steps his friend had outlined, he began to feel better and better. He could not help but think of others like himself, whose suffering was as deep as his. If he could only help them, he would achieve even more. Bill's physicians tried to help him achieve his goal. Together they all tried to impress upon other alcoholics the very thing that had affected Bill. Bill seemed to improve with the attempts he was making to help others; even though he did not succeed, his efforts seemed to improve his own outlook, and to strengthen his own determination to remain sober. With this sobriety came renewed success in his life and his work.

Bill was a stockbroker, and as his business increased he assumed more and more responsibility. Some time later, on a business trip to Akron, Ohio, he felt himself on the threshold of a tremendous success. This might change the course of his entire career. He looked forward to a successful conclusion of his business there, and was highly encouraged by his prospects.

Unfortunately, the business deal failed to materialize. Bill was tremendously discouraged and depressed. He felt hopelessly defeated, and it occurred to him that he might be helped if he were to drink. In a strange city, he knew no one. The urge to forget his defeat in alcohol became stronger and stronger. If he could only find someone with whom he could work, he might be able to overcome this desire to drink, but where could he locate an alcoholic?

Bill called a number of churches, which were listed in the hotel where he was staying, and asked the ministers if they knew of any alcoholics in their congregations. Many of the clergymen believed that there were no alcoholics in their congregations, but one gave him the name of a woman who might help. She herself was not an alcoholic, he told Bill, but was sympathetic toward them and might know of someone for Bill to visit. The woman gave him the name of a doctor in Akron.

When Bill saw him, Dr. Bob admitted that liquor had become his master. When Bill explained his theory to him, and how it had helped him, Dr. Bob responded favorably. The idea of accepting the fact that he was alcoholic appealed to him, and the two of them sought another alcoholic whom they might help. They found this man in a hospital in Akron, and in this way Alcoholics Anonymous was born. When Bill and Dr. Bob found that it worked for them, and did for the third alcoholic whom they'd found in the hospital, they deduced that perhaps the same program might help others working in groups.

Since that time Alcoholics Anonymous his grown to a fellowship embracing almost three hundred thousand people. It has chapters in practically every community in the United

States, where most of the members reside, but it also has many chapters in other countries of the world. Since there is no way of ascertaining the exact number of members at any particular time, there being no rolls, no dues, and no method of checking on these figures, the number actually represents only an estimate. At any rate, Alcoholics Anonymous has achieved a phenomenal and remarkable success in helping those alcoholics who wish to be helped.

It is important to understand that Alcoholics Anonymous is not a catch-all for everyone suffering from the disease. To be successful in Alcoholics Anonymous, the individual must have an honest desire to achieve abstinence. In fact, this is true no matter what type of therapy the individual may seek. It is axiomatic in the medical profession that the desire to get well is an important factor in the recovery of any patient from any illness.

Unfortunately, there are many individuals who are emotionally incapable of accepting some methods of therapy. These people will be no more successful with Alcoholics Anonymous than they will with many other methods. There are also among alcoholics many people whose mental development precludes them from accepting such a program. These people are much sicker than those who can accept Alcoholics Anonymous. Hoping for success with this program would be expecting too much of them, since they do not have the capacity to understand the steps.

There are some individuals suffering from alcoholism who are so scientifically oriented that they cannot accept the spiritual approach, and require a different method. This must be taken into consideration. On the other hand, A.A. has a tremendous appeal for most people. There is something about the spiritual part that appeals to those who have some religious training. There is also the comfort of being with those who have the same problems. There is no bitterness. There is no criticism. There is no recrimination, such as these people find in the outside world. Fellow members will not flatter them or reassure them about their drinking. They will not help them rationalize their drinking as many of their friends might, or as they themselves might. The people in A.A. are there not only to help the individual, but, even more, to help him help himself.

One must understand that there is no screening process in A.A. There is no way of ascertaining in this fellowship the existence of a physical disease, an underlying mental disorder or psychosis, or any other functional or organic condition that may be contributing to the alcohol addiction. It is imperative, then, in order for A.A. to be most effective with its members, that these conditions be ruled out.

For those individuals who cannot communicate with others about their feelings, and who find it too overwhelming to discuss their problems in a group, it is often advantageous to have medical aid or psychotherapy before they can accept the principles of A.A.

Members of Alcoholics Anonymous assume a tremendous responsibility in helping their fellow alcoholics. Often, in their zeal and in their firm conviction that they can help another person, they are likely to violate the principles they themselves profess by breaking anonymity, by insisting that the new member follow their particular method, and otherwise aggressively frightening the new member. Too often they skip from step one to step twelve without sufficient insight into the other steps.

Such violations are no reflection upon A.A. or the fellowship. They are but manifestations of the inadequacy of any modality that has no method of controlling its members or screening or qualifying new people. Recovery from an illness, regardless of the method, in no way qualifies the recovered patient to treat other patients with the same disease. Individuals vary too much for this to be effective.

In no way is this intended to detract from the value of A.A. and its principles. It is merely to point up the tremendous variation in types of individuals who succumb to the disease and the necessity for further study of its details.

One of the great advantages in A.A. is that the people in Alcoholics Anonymous know what it is to be alcoholic. The old rationalizations, the old excuses, and the old alibis will not work with them. They know the answers because they have been through it. They do not let the neophyte off the hook. They do not excuse him. They bring him face to face with his problem, and insist that he recognize it. All of these steps are important to the individual seeking help.

Alcoholics Anonymous is open to anyone who wishes to join. For those who have friends or relatives who are alcoholic, and who wish to know about A.A., there are open meetings of Alcoholics Anonymous that anyone can attend. This is one way of becoming better acquainted with the program and with the procedure of the group. It is in these meetings that the individual alcoholics learn that "once an alcoholic, always an alcoholic." This comes from the members themselves, and not from non-alcoholics, who, alcoholics very often feel, talk down to them. There is no attempt on the part of these people to feel that they are no longer alcoholic once they have attained abstinence. The principles of the group are such that there is acceptance of certain inevitables, and this in itself is one of the marks of maturity.

For those relatives and friends of alcoholics who cannot understand the problem itself, or whose alcoholic associate will not do anything about his own problem, there is an associate organization of Alcoholics Anonymous called Al-Anon. This group is for the express purpose of educating people who have alcoholics near and dear to them to understand the disease and teach them how to help the alcoholic patient. All too often it is found that a precipitating factor in the drinking problem of the alcoholic is a non-alcoholic spouse or relative. The alcoholic binges are increased or precipitated by the misunderstanding of the non-alcoholic spouse or relative. One of the purposes of Al-Anon is to help this person learn more about alcoholism and how to deal with the alcoholic patient. These groups meet as regularly as do the A.A. groups, and sometimes in conjunction with them. This understanding on the part of the spouse, particularly, can often lead to an improvement in the situation of the alcoholic and to his eventual seeking of help from some source, whether it be Alcoholics Anonymous, the medical profession, or elsewhere.

Al-a-teen, another organization, is a fellowship of teen-age children of alcoholics. The purpose of this fellowship is to help youngsters in their teens whose parents are alcoholic to understand the disease, its implications, its possibilities, and how to cope with it in a parent. To some degree this demands a premature responsibility. On the other hand, it does allow these individuals to understand the implications of alcoholism, and why and how their parents respond under certain circumstances. The abiding faith that Alcoholics Anonymous teaches, helps these young people to maintain a type of stability in the face of the adversity that is brought about by an alcoholic parent. The mere understanding that the alcoholic parent is ill and unable to cope with the problems of living, and has sought in alcohol a refuge from which he cannot withdraw, will often help these youngsters to understand the problem they are up against in helping such a parent. Such understanding will very often lead to the alcoholic parent seeking proper help for his illness.

Alcoholics Anonymous has chapters in any sizable community in the country. The first name in the telephone book is often Alcoholics Anonymous. It represents one of the great resources to which the alcoholic or members of his family can turn for help. It is a distinct asset in the battle against alcoholism.

CHAPTER 13

Women Alcoholics

MOST of us have a tendency when we think of alcoholics to use the pronoun he. Why is it that we feel alcoholism is so much more prevalent among males than females? Perhaps only because over the years we have noticed more male alcoholics than their female counterparts. How accurate, however, is our observation?

Information gathered from various clinics that treat alcoholic patients indicates that the proportion of male to female alcoholics ranges anywhere from five males to one female to eight males to one female. One must remember, however, that these figures are for the most part derived from public clinics, whether independently operated or connected with hospitals. Even though the anonymity of the individual patient is preserved, the clincis themselves are open to the public, and since they do not offer the privacy of individual relationships, women may avoid them. The same proportion of male to female alcoholics does not necessarily hold for the entire alcoholic population. A further study of the places to which the alcoholic patients can apply has revealed different statistics.

It is my opinion that there are as many female as male

problem drinkers and alcoholics. As a private physician engaged in treating alcoholic patients—and 80 percent of my patients suffer from this disease—I have found that this is true. In conferring with other physicians whose practice is largely in the field of alcoholism, I learn that in their private work the same statistics obtain. Why, then, is this not more commonly recognized? Why do not statistics reveal the many female alcoholics? In the tradition of gallantry, we tend to shield the female from stigma. Add to this the fact that the woman alcoholic is much less easily detected, that she is both protected and shielded by her husband and her family, and we may have some understanding of why there appears to have been a general effort to blind ourselves and everyone else to the true facts. It is generally considered bad enough that a man is alcoholic, but society frowns much more on the poor woman addict. Hence, the increased effort to keep her illness a secret.

The male excessive drinker is quickly spotted when he drinks in public, and no one observing him makes any attempt to deny his drunkenness. He is much more careful about his drinking while working, or during his working hours, for fear of being criticized. Besides, during working hours the average worker cannot get to a drink. There are, therefore, long periods of time in which the male alcoholic cannot drink. Should he attempt to do so surreptitiously, his fellow workers, his employer, or anyone with whom he comes in contact at his place of employment would detect the odor on his breath and become suspicious. The housewife, however, has easy access to the bottle on her kitchen shelf, and she is alone whenever she wants to be. Her opportunities to drink in her own home and in complete privacy are boundless. The wife of an alcoholic husband, when she has come to the end of her patience with her unhappiness, will often complain or call for aid for her sick spouse, seek relief in the courts or from a physician, or ask advice of her attorney. The husband of the alcoholic wife, however, is likely to keep his misery a secret for fear disclosure will reflect on his ability to control his wife's behavior.

It has always been a source of surprise that there are so many cases in which a husband prefers to have his wife continue with her addictive behavior rather than seek help and risk bringing the true facts to the attention of his friends, his employer, or his associates. Some husbands have even been known to forbid their wives to seek medical help if in doing so she must admit that her problem is for the most part excessive drinking. Available statistics to the contrary, therefore, I am convinced that addiction to alcohol is fully as common among women as among men.

When this disclosure was published many years ago, it was followed by a deluge of criticism and disbelief. It was thought to be an unchivalrous statement. Sociologists quoted statistics from clinics to prove the disparity in numbers between men and women alcoholics, but no attempt was made to ascertain how many alcoholic patients, men or women, had been treated by private physicians, or had no treatment at all. The opinions quoted at that time were formulated after questioning many physicians who had many patients suffering from alcoholism. My own practice substantiated what all the other private physicians found.

Today, however, there seems to be general agreement that the number of women alcoholics is much nearer that of men than was thought previously. Private physicians still maintain that there are as many women alcoholics in their practices as males. Alcoholics Anonymous reports that there is a tremendous increase in the number of women joining their groups. Clinics themselves now show a reduced ratio, claiming three males to one female. With education of the general public and the gradual removal of the stigma formerly attached to the illness, which nonetheless persists, more women are likely to apply to available clinics for help.

Over the past several years, education about alcoholism has increased to a point where it is a common subject of conversation and is discussed frequently in numerous publications. In many areas, particularly in the large cities, the stigma formerly attached to alcoholism has been reduced sufficiently for women alcoholics to feel less self-conscious about seeking help. Many more women are going to private physicians, many who never before admitted to their doctors that their illness was excessive drinking. More and more women are beginning to recognize the early signs of alcoholism in themselves, and more families are recognizing that it is folly to blind themselves to compulsive excessive drinking by the female members.

Much has been written about the female alcoholic, and many attempts have been made by various writers to differentiate between the alcoholism of the female and that of the male. In my experience there is no difference whatever in the onset nor in the progress of the disease in men and women. It begins and progresses in exactly the same way; the damage, both physically and mentally, is the same; and the emotional and psychiatric etiological factors are very similar.

Naturally, there are physiological differences between men and women and their mental processes may differ as well. There may be different reasons for their drinking, depending on different behavior demands that might cause women to drink more than men. A man in business may find that his financial problems are causing him extreme tension and worry, and he resorts to alcohol for relief; the woman may find that the frustrations of her work at home or difficulty with domestic help sends her for relief to the same source. Although the individual problem in each of these cases may differ, the tensions, frustrations, and anxieties have a similar effect on both sexes.

The question has also been raised about the difference between the woman homemaker and the career woman as being an etiological factor in the difference in the drinking habits. I find no difference between the career woman and the homemaker. We find the same frustrations, anxieties, and tensions, which may arise from different backgrounds but which in the individual produce the same psychological result. Individuals who are well adjusted and have learned how to handle their problems find no necessity for resorting to a drug to escape them. For those who are inadequate and unable to adjust to the problems of living, however, and who find in alcohol their relief from these problems, it seems to make no difference what the problems are from which they seek relief. When an individual woman finds that alcohol helps her when she is tense, ill at ease, frustrated, and unhappy, and then uses alcohol to escape from these feelings, it is of no consequence whatever what the source is of these frustrations, anxieties, and tensions.

When women, either through their own volition or through circumstances beyond their control, are forced to live outside of their spheres as women, they may find themselves in an undesirable position from which they wish escape. Trying to lead men's lives often causes them unhappiness and dissatisfaction. This often leads them to seek relief in alcohol from these unnatural roles. This may also be true of the male alcoholic who finds himself in the unnatural role of trying to perform a woman's functions, a situation that may make him extremely unhappy and that he can tolerate only by resorting to alcohol to make his position more bearable.

Whereas a man's major frustrations may be in the line of economics and interpersonal business relations, a woman may find her greatest problem in her marriage or social environment. Frustrations in both, however, can lead to seeking relief in alcohol. A man may find a routine job boring and without satisfaction, but the same may be said of a woman who finds that homemaking is not to her liking, and, dissatisfied with her position as a glorified domestic, may, like the man, attempt to relieve such frustration by drinking.

In the case of an alcoholic who is sexually maladjusted,

and who resorts to alcohol to cover up these maladjustments, it makes little difference whether the maladjusted individual is male or female. The only significant fact is that the maladjustment exists and that relief from such maladjustment may be sought in alcohol.

The menopausal woman, who often goes into a depression at this time of her life, may find relief from such depression by drinking. Over a period of time, as a result of this excessive drinking, she may become dependent on it, progressing to compulsive drinking, alcoholism, and finally addiction to the drug. This, however, is not unlike the male who begins to feel that he is declining both physically and mentally, is losing his potency and his ability to hold his position in his male world. He may go into a depression that is the counterpart of the female menopause, and may resort to alcohol for the same reasons. If he has drunk alcohol for many years, he may increase the amount he imbibes to relieve himself of these anxieties.

There is, however, one obvious difference between the male and female alcoholic in most of these cases. The female alcoholic is much more difficult to detect. Male alcoholics rarely keep their excessive drinking a secret; there is some protection for them in the double standard. Women, on the other hand, have not only opportunity to drink in secrecy during the day, they can also excite more sympathy from their families. It is not as important for a woman to be alert all the time, and if she is not feeling well she can let her work slide, at least temporarily. Her excuses are more readily accepted by the members of her family than the excuses a male alcoholic might give to an employer. The excuse of not feeling well is used much more often by women, and under the guise of this ill health they have the opportunity of drinking in secret, without detection, for long periods. Few will question the woman alcoholic about her alleged disability. Males, on the other hand, must usually account for their absence from work.

In the United States, for the most part, women occupy a position of privilege and respect. Criticism of women is considered unchivalrous. Motherhood itself is supposed to confer upon women a natural virtue. Women are supposed to be pure, and this notion of perfection, particularly in mothers, has been indoctrinated in children to such an extent that most of them feel that Mother must never be criticized. Therefore any action of a mother that might be considered improper is glossed over and excused. "Mother knows best" might be translated to "Mother is never wrong," or "Mother is always right," and therefore any objectionable behavior on the part of Mother must be overlooked. Under this fiction many women alcoholics have been protected by their husbands and children.

Women have always been considered the bearers of the moral standards and overseers of the intellectual and proper behavior of the family unit. Therefore, the family often blinds itself to the fact that Mother is behaving objectionably or that she might be drunk. They do not realize that this is an illness that is progressive, not merely a behavioral problem. When the condition becomes severe enough, however, everyone is disgusted, and patience is lost totally and precipitously.

Unhappily married women whose social background or mores and training will not allow them to have affairs they desire without the accompaniment of a tremendous sense of guilt will often resort to drinking in order to remove such guilts. When they indulge in sexual escapades under the influence of excessive drinking, their consciences are salved by the excuse that they would never have yielded had they been sober. Such self-delusion is extremely common, and offers the unhappy individuals the opportunity to indulge in affairs without the responsibility they might feel were they sober. Here, again, we see evidence of immaturity, which is so characteristic of the alcoholic, male or female. But, in this area, it is more prevalent among females, to whom such moral transgressions appear to be so much more objectionable than to the male. The double standard, which protected women for a long time, still operates in these instances, resulting not in protection but in feelings of guilt that often lead to drinking.

The alcoholic woman, like the male, very often has an underlying psychotic condition that has been masked by her drinking. It is not unusual for psychotic women, particularly young women who are schizophrenic, to resort to drinking to cover up their psychoses. When it is so covered, they can continue for a long time before either the psychoses or the alcoholism is detected. The alcoholism, simply considered excessive drinking at first, is attributed to poor behavior or immorality. It is not until the alcohol is withdrawn from one of these women that the actual psychosis can be discovered. This type of alcoholic is to be found among many prostitutes in an urban area. Here, inadequate personalities, as well as the split personalities of schizophrenics, are able to carry on with the aid of the mask alcohol provides.

Society as a whole frowns upon the male alcoholic, but it practically condemns the woman with the same disease. For many years, and practically until the last generation, there were certain rules of conduct that protected the woman. The "good" woman never drank and never smoked, nor did a "good" woman ever appear in a public drinking place. Propriety of this sort protected the woman. The odd individual who kicked over the traces and did not conform was considered loose, immoral, or delinquent, and her sisters would not associate with her.

Today, however, women both drink and smoke, and appear in public drinking places. This is considered part of our society and part of our culture. It is accepted by all. Women now have these "rights." Whatever is the privilege of men is equally the privilege of women. The equality and the "togetherness" that is so emphasized in our present-day society includes sharing not only the virtues, to which there is no objection, but also the vices once considered the prerogatives of males. Therefore, protective measures that formerly kept women from drinking excessively have been removed. Her drinking is now accepted, just as the drinking of the male is, and while she is not supposed to drink excessively any more than the male, her drinking is part of our culture. With the safeguard of former values removed, a woman feels no compunction about excessive drinking for relief from problems.

Nonetheless, very often she and her husband and family deny her excessive drinking in the hope that if they deny it, it will disappear. It is only when the disease is far advanced that they begin to feel the seriousness of the condition, and may seek help. By then, the disease is so far advanced that treatment is difficult. The family feels disgraced, and more effort is expended in placating the patient than insisting upon her being properly treated. To send her to a hospital would mean public acknowledgment, and so everyone conspires to keep the matter a secret. It is not until the disease can no longer be a secret to anyone that treatment is instituted. The recovery, therefore, takes a great deal longer than it would have had the illness been acknowledged and treatment for it instituted earlier.

In treating the woman alcoholic, the procedures are exactly the same as for the male. Complete withdrawal is necessary, and a re-educational program must be instituted, teaching the individual to live in the real world and meet her problems. For those with a psychosis, treatment is best carried out in a hospital. The psychosis is in each case treated as though there were no alcohol problem, once the alcohol has been removed. Very often the patients get along very well when they make a satisfactory recovery from these psychoses. However, like all alcoholics, they can never safely return to drinking. The therapy for these individuals should go on for a long time in order to insure stability.

The sexual promiscuity so often associated with the woman

alcoholic is in no way different from the sexual promiscuity of the male, with one exception. Whereas excessive drinking on the part of the male will render him impotent, so that his sexual desire cannot attain fruition, this is not true for the woman alcoholic. Regardless of the amount of alcohol she imbibes, she is still able to carry sexual activities to completion. It is for this reason that more alcoholic women are sexually promiscuous than men. Whereas when men are drunk they very often lose their desire for sexual activity, though present in the earlier stages, or else their ability to perform is impaired. Women, even though they may lose the desire, can still go through with the act.

It is strictly from this physical viewpoint that the woman alcoholic can be considered more promiscuous sexually than the male. As the disease process progresses, and the woman's necessity for alcohol continues, she may resort to greater promiscuity in order to obtain her drinks. As a rule, these circumstances would not apply to men.

With the female alcoholic, therefore, treatment is the same, and success with female alcoholics again will rest on education of the public and the acceptance of alcoholism as a disease with no stigma attached. As soon as this disease is accepted as such, self-consciousness about seeking help on the part of the female alcoholic will disappear. More and more of these unfortunate people will go to proper sources for treatment, and will be aided in their recovery from the illness.

When the refusal of a drink is accepted by everyone, so that the alcoholic can abstain without self-consciousness, many of these patients will become happier and better integrated individuals. While it may be true that a woman can refuse a drink at a social function with greater freedom than a man, it is also true that many women do not enjoy such social functions unless they do drink once they have become addicted to alcohol. Therefore, their self-consciousness is as great as the man's. Along with the advantages gained by women with greater equality between the sexes came the disappearance of some of the so-called disadvantages, which protected women from alcoholism in previous years. The equality has been extended to include her susceptibility and vulnerability to alcoholism.

CHAPTER 14

The Government and Alcoholism

It is incumbent upon the community to be concerned with the rehabilitation of alcoholics. Alcoholism is too widespread to be ignored.

In any public health problem that concerns an entire community, individual government facilities must be involved. Because alcoholism is so often neglected for so long, rehabilitation is a very expensive project. As is the case with many mental health problems, the individuals involved have already exhausted all their economic resources and that of their families before any attempt is made at rehabilitation. Their only refuge, then, is public support, either by voluntary agencies or by the government itself. For many years our mental hospitals, supported by our state and federal governments, were the only places to which these mentally ill patients could resort for care and treatment. Gradually over the years, the government assumed responsibility for caring for them. Not until the value of diagnosing and finding these mental cases early, and treating them individually and collectively was recognized, was anything done by private physicians.

With the advent of the newer biological products and

early diagnosis of mental diseases, people seek help from their private physicians before the disease becomes advanced and have thus been able to be rehabilitated and returned to normal society. The newer methods of treatment have also made it possible for more patients from government-controlled mental hospitals to return to society, rehabilitated and ready to take their places among their fellow men.

The conception of alcoholism as a disease entity is comparatively recent. Even today, because of the stigma and the resultant refusal of sufferers and their families to recognize the need for early treatment, many alcoholics become public charges. The government must then take over if there is to be any treatment at all. The government, therefore, has no choice about assuming responsibility for treatment of alcoholism.

Fortunately, in the past several years the government has recognized that this is more than a custodial problem, and that these people can be rehabilitated if treatment is instituted. At the local level, at the state level, and at the national level, there are now movements afoot to do something about this problem, not only by remedial measures, but through prevention as well.

On the municipal level we find that in many cities the individual governments have sought to help alcoholics by establishing public clinics, inpatient and outpatient treatment centers, and halfway houses and custodial institutions. Local authorities are attempting to commit habitual inebriates to institutions for treatment rather than for punitive measures. In too many areas people who are arrested for chronic intoxication or alcoholism are still being sent to jails and penitentiaries for punishment rather than treatment. Time spent by these people in such institutions is completely wasted, since once released they immediately return to their old habits. There is indeed a crying need to use this time for rehabilitation.

It must be recognized that some of these individuals are

inadequate personalities, psychopaths, and psychotics, and cannot be rehabilitated. For these sick people a custodial institution must be provided to keep them from becoming street nuisances. However, in most cases local governments have not provided such institutions. Occasionally a municipal government is sufficiently enlightened to do this, to the benefit of local citizens at least, if not to the individual patients.

County governments have also seen their responsibility to some extent, and have provided both inpatient and outpatient facilities for the treatment of the chronic alcoholic. County welfare agencies, family service agencies, and other agencies now refer such patients or their families to the facilities provided by the county for help and treatment.

Such facilities exist in only a comparatively small number of counties in the country. Unfortunately, the mistaken belief that the disease is self-induced and that these are worthless individuals has prevented many county governments from proceeding with proper measures. Many citizens are not in favor of spending public funds for this purpose under the mistaken idea that these people do not deserve treatment. Many still feel that punishment is required. In such areas, education must be carried on a great deal longer before the truth will be understood and recognized.

At the state level there is increasing recognition that alcoholism represents not only a health problem and a sociological problem but an economic one as well. It is now recognized that taking care of these people and rehabilitating as many as possible is a good program from an economic as well as a sociological viewpoint. It is estimated that one alcoholic patient rehabilitated into society will pay for ten others who may still require care. This means that if 10 percent of the public charges suffering from alcoholism in any given state can be rehabilitated, the state will be ahead economically. This is indeed a good investment, and most states should consider it carefully.

At most state levels now there is either a commission or a

council or some group that has been appointed by the government to study the problem of alcoholism and institute measures for meeting it. In the last ten years advances have been made, and there is no doubt in anyone's mind that it has paid off. There are still some states, however, that have done nothing about this matter. Here again more education is required, not only of the public but of the legislators as well.

Among the states in the country which have government-sponsored programs, and which form the constituent members of the North American Association of Alcoholism Programs, are Alabama, Arkansas, California, Colorado, Connecticut, District of Columbia, Florida, Georgia, Illinois, Indiana, Kentucky, Louisiana, Maine, Maryland, Massachusetts, Michigan, Minnesota, Montana, Nevada, New Hampshire, New Jersey, New Mexico, New York, North Carolina, North Dakota, Ohio, Oregon, Pennsylvania, Rhode Island, South Carolina, Tennessee, Texas, Utah, Vermont, Virginia, Washington and Wyoming. The provinces of Canada which have similar alcoholism programs, sponsored by their governments, are Alberta, British Columbia, Nova Scotia, Ontario and Saskatchewan.

Mention cannot be made of these programs without including individuals in those states who have contributed so much to the success of their programs on alcoholism. These individuals have not only cooperated with the state commissions or divisions, but also have worked through lay organizations, particularly the constituent affiliates of the National Council on Alcoholism, and have shown an individual interest in promoting help for the victims of the illness. Through their dedicated efforts and energetic cooperation, they have helped many patients suffering from alcoholism to complete recovery and rehabilitation. While all who have worked with the programs are deserving of credit, there are a few outstanding individuals, who should be specifically cited for unusual accomplishment.

In California, Dr. Dudley Porter Miller, who previously had

done the same work in Connecticut, is now continuing his work as head of the department in his new home state. Graydon Dorsch, of Colorado, and Frona McCambridge, of that state, as well as Dr. Edward Delahanty and Mary Delahanty, and Dr. Norbert Shere, deserve special mention. Ernest A. Shepard, who formerly headed the program in Florida, is now in charge of a similar department in Connecticut. In Georgia, not only Charles B. Methvin, Director, but Dr. Vernelle Fox, of Atlanta, stand out as excellent and dedicated workers. The same can be said for Gertrude Nilsson, of Maryland, and W. T. Dixon Gibbs, Executive Director of the Baltimore Council on Alcoholism.

In Massachusetts, Mrs. Elizabeth Whitney, Executive Director of the Boston Council, has carried on an exemplary program for many years. The head of the government program in Massachusetts is Dr. Edward Blacker. In Michigan, Ralph W. Daniel, Executive Director of the State Board of Alcoholism, heads a well organized program. Mrs. Vashti Cain and Ruth Breen, of Mississippi, must be mentioned for the excellent work they are doing in that state. Montana has started a program under Stanley S. Rogers, M.D., with the help of Art S. Baker. Dr. Kenneth Lampert and Walter Custer work with the Educational organization. In Nevada, Grant B. Harris has embarked upon a program which holds very great promise. The Rev. Welles Miller, of Las Vegas, has, on his own initiative, stimulated considerable interest in that area among industrialists and lay people.

James R. McKay launched an excellent program for New Hampshire with the help of Dr. Nathan Brody. Mr. McKay was succeeded in that state by Elmer V. Andrews. In New York State, under the direction of John Butler, the Division of Alcoholism has forged ahead with the able leadership of Dr. John Norris, of Rochester, the Chairman of its Advisory Council. In North Carolina, Dr. Norbert L. Kelly has an excellent state-wide program. Its success owes a great deal also to Dr. Thomas Jones, a dedicated general practitioner, and to Mrs. Robert Garrard, Chairman of the Mental Health Committee of the Women's Auxiliary of the American Medical Association, whose activities have stimulated many in the mental health field.

Terrence J. Boyle, the Director of the Ohio Alcoholism unit, has an excellent state-wide program and has been ably assisted in his state by J. Arthur Hinchliffe, of Columbus, Herman Krimmel of Cleveland, Leonard Simon of Cincinnati, and Dr. James Gorman of Toledo. Oregon's George C. Dimas has done oustanding work in his state for the alcohol studies and rehabilitation section of its Mental Health Division. For several years, Dr. Joseph Adelstein headed the program for Pennsylvania. He was succeeded by Dr. John P. Wells. A tremendous contribution was made in that state by Miss Marian Wettrick, who was in charge of the Division of Behavioral Problems. The Division of Alcoholism in Rhode Island is under the Department of Social Welfare, and its Administrator is Antonio Capone, M.D. Ben Lieberman heads the alcoholism program for the State of Tennessee, which is making great strides. In Texas, Macon W. Freeman is the Executive Director.

Utah's program is headed by Clyde W. Gooderham, Director of the State Board of Alcoholism. Clyde and his wife, Marie, truly dedicated individuals, have not only an excellent program in progress throughout the state, but have organized one of the finest schools on alcohol studies, which is held every June in Salt Lake City. Ably directed by Dr. Ewart Swinyard, and with the blessing of the President of the University, the Gooderhams have accomplished tremendous results with their program.

There is no doubt that the other states mentioned also have excellent programs. It would be impossible to mention in detail all of the accomplishments by the individuals working in the field. I have mentioned only those I am personally acquainted with in the various states. There are, of course, many more people working in the field who deserve credit, but lack of space precludes naming them all here.

In Canada, J. George Strachan, who was the Executive Director for the program in Alberta, and E. D. McRae, of British Columbia, have done remarkable work in the field. In Manitoba, Keith M. Christie is the Executive Director, and in Nova Scotia, Dr. J. M. Snow heads the Alcoholism Research Commission. The Province of Ontario, with its Alcoholism and Drug Addiction Research Foundation, has perhaps one of the best programs on alcoholism and addictions anywhere. Headed by H. David Archibald, a tireless worker in the field, and ably assisted in the area by such people as Dr. John D. Armstrong, Dr. Gordon Bell and others, this group has done an exceptional task in organization and education, as well as research. In Saskatchewan Province, J. P. Metheson heads a Bureau of Alcoholism under its Department of Social Welfare.

In all of these areas, the government has taken steps to treat its alcoholics and prevent alcoholism whenever possible. It is a clear sign of the recognition on the part of the government bodies of their responsibilities in this field, and it augurs well for eventual alleviation of this tremendous public health problem.

At the federal government level, the National Institute of Mental Health and the National Institute of Health have recognized alcoholism as one of the greatest health problems of our time. The National Institute of Mental Health, while under the direction of Robert H. Felix, M.D., has taken important strides to combat alcoholism and has granted money to various groups, not only for the recognition and treatment of alcoholics, but also for research. Its research consultant is Carl L. Anderson, Ph.D. Only recently, Congress appropriated over one million dollars for the National Institute of Mental Health to study what is being done about the problem of alcoholism in the United States, and how measures can be used to combat this illness. This is indeed a tremendous step forward. The money, appropriated for this purpose, is to be used by the group known as the Cooperative Commission on the Study of Alcoholism. This group, appointed by the National Institute of Mental Health, was given the appropriation and commenced working in 1961.

The Cooperative Commission on the Study of Alcoholism, sponsored by the National Institute of Mental Health, is undertaking a five-year study of the entire subject of alcohol problems on this continent.[1] One of its aims will be to make recommendations for coordination and improvement of current efforts toward research, treatment, control, and education in this field. It will also strive to increase the amount and improve the quality of research on alcohol problems by stimulating interest among reputable investigators at major academic centers.

The Scientific Director and research staff of the Commission established their offices July 1, 1961, at the Institute for the Study of Human Problems, Stanford University. Members of the Commission (numbering twenty at present) represent numerous institutions of higher learning in the United States and Canada. They include specialists in biochemistry, biometry, documentation, psychiatry, psychology, and sociology, and representatives of the North American Association of Alcoholism Programs. It is anticipated that specialists in other fields will be added in the future. Because of such diverse membership, the Commission remains independent of individual interests and disciplinary biases. Its work is financed by a $1.1 million grant from NIMH.

The specific objectives of the Commission involve several phases. One initial project will be to survey the wide network of public and private institutions devoted to various aspects of alcoholism—hospitals, clinics, Alcoholics Anonymous, government agencies, medical schools, etc. At the same time the Commission will take a searching look at prevailing attitudes

[1] From the brochure distributed by the Cooperative Commission on the Study of Alcoholism.

and behavior (both individual and social) concerning alcohol. Because alcohol touches nearly all human activity, it must be studied in a broad framework. In considering problems that are directly related to alcohol, attention will be given to a wide range of their ramifications and repercussions within the life of the nation.

Another task will be to survey the vast literature on alcohol problems, evaluating and integrating existing knowledge from various scientific disciplines. As part of this undertaking, the Commission is sponsoring the publication of an Encyclopedia of Problems of Alcohol.[2]

While the Commission will seek to systematize extant knowledge about alcohol, it will also endeavor to determine the many gaps in our knowledge and deal with some of them. It will initiate original research by its own staff in some areas that must be illuminated before recommendations can be made. In other areas, it will stimulate research by outside investigators working at other centers. In the quest for information, the Commission will strive to identify clearly the questions that are being asked by policy-makers, educators, parents, and other segments of the general public, as well as by specialists within the field. Such procedure may lead to a new conceptualization of the problems.

As these various projects move forward, the Commission will publish reports to provide useful information to all interested circles.

Finally, from a synthesis of the preliminary projects there may emanate suggestions on how all existing and potential resources for treatment, research, and education can be most effectively and economically utilized for the management of the problems of alcohol.

It is expected that when the Commission has completed its work we will know a great deal more about what is being done about alcoholism in the United States and Canada, and

[2] This project was abandoned upon the death of Dr. Jellinek in 1964.

about what more can be done toward solving the problem of alcoholism on our continent.

The Department of Health, Education, and Welfare is extremely interested in the subject, and has taken many steps to encourage research. This Department also encourages groups to teach the prevention as well as treatment of the disease. Through its division of Community Health Services, the U.S. Public Health Service now has a program. Dr. William Stewart, Assistant Surgeon General, has been appointed as Chairman of the Committee on Alcoholism to coordinate all of the Department's activities involving alcoholism. In the Bureau of State Services of HEW, Edward S. Sands has been appointed Consultant on Alcoholism in the Division of Health Services.

Courses for physicians, nurses, social workers, hospital administrators, and everyone else interested in the problem of alcoholism are offered by the National Institute of Mental Health in areas where such programs can be instituted. These programs have resulted in education on the subject being offered in all areas of the country, and a tremendous amount of interest has been generated. Great credit is due the people in charge of this department, who have implemented the project.

The North American Association of Alcoholism Programs is an organization composed of people interested in the problem of alcoholism in the United States and Canada. This group meets annually for discussion of the problems that confront people in the various states and provinces who are interested in the programs on alcoholism. It has resulted in great strides in the treatment of the alcoholic patient who comes under the aegis of these various state and provincial governments. An exchange of ideas at these meetings results in increased service as well as research. Although the character and approach of the program may differ in different geographic areas, depending on specific needs, the exchange of ideas is beneficial to all.

The medical profession cooperates with this national association, as well as with all other governmental agencies interested in the problem. Not only do medical men participate in the programs of the various state agencies, but many also serve as consultants for state and federal agencies. Such cooperation has proved to be of tremendous value, and has produced excellent and encouraging results. Inpatient and outpatient facilities are provided in many of the states, and education and information centers in many states operate under this state-controlled body.

One of the more recent developments of the government regarding alcoholism is the help to be given through the 1962 Public Welfare Amendments. A brochure distributed by the Department of Health, Education, and Welfare, reads as follows:

> Recent Federal legislation has strengthened the ability of public welfare agencies to work more effectively with families in which alcoholism is a problem. The 1962 Public Welfare Amendments place major emphasis on the preservation of wholesome family life and the protection of children and adults who are in hazardous circumstances. The new legislation provides public welfare departments with strong weapons in the community effort to overcome many of the social and economic conditions that contribute to alcoholism.
>
> By increasing its share of the cost of a wide range of services from 50 to 75 percent, the Federal Government is now making it possible for public welfare agencies in all States to develop and extend rehabilitative and preventive services in their communities. These are some of the ways the 1962 legislation can help:
>
> Social services can be offered that would minimize, if not prevent, the destructive effects of alcoholism on the family.
>
> More welfare workers can be employed to help alco-

holics learn about and accept the specialized treatment or rehabiltative services available in the community.

Special attention can be given to the problems of the mother who has a tendency to use alcohol to deal with her frustrations and feelings of despair. Her role as mother and homemaker can be strengthened by providing opportunity for healthier emotional outlets.

States are required to make an individal plan for each child receiving assistance under the program of Aid to Families with Dependent Children. The effect of a parent's alcoholism on the welfare of the child is a factor that can be dealt wtih as part of this plan.

Specialized services—day care for children, homemaker service, recreational opportunities for adults and children—can reduce the stress on families.

Guidance can be given to adolescent members of the family. Since attitudes about the use of alcohol and patterns of drinking are often established in adolescence, special attention to the needs of young people might prevent future difficulties. Placement in a suitable school, timely vocational guidance, opportunites for developing hobbies and participating in sports—these are among the counseling services which can be made available to youthful members of a family.

Public assistance recipients who are ill equipped for employment because of inadequate education, lack of motivation, personal appearance and attitude can be helped to prepare for employment under the community work and training program. This program can also be used as an aid in the rehabilitation of an alcoholic person.

For the first time, the Federal Government will help finance the cost of services to former and potential recipients of public assistance as a means of preventing dependency. This could enable States to broaden services to alcoholics and their families.

For the first time also, the Bureau of Family Services in the Welfare Administration has the authority to support demonstration projects in public welfare. The purpose of this legislation is to encourage States to experiment with new and better ways to provide services to recipients. New services for the alcoholic and his family can be developed with such support.

The Federal Government will pay 75 percent of the cost of training personnel in the social services. This should lead to better understanding of the special problems of alcoholism and how to deal with them.

By extending child welfare services to all counties of every State by 1975 (which is required if States wish to continue receiving Federal aid for these programs), more protective services can be given children in their own homes. Additional Federal support will help make it possible for preventive and rehabilitative services to reach all children who need them, regardless of economic circumstances!

But still more needs to be done.

More information is needed about the nature and prevalence of alcoholism in low-income groups.

More needs to be known about the problem of drinking among youths and its connection with juvenile delinquency.

Homemaker services, foster family programs, senior citizen centers, and a variety of volunteer services can alleviate the social isolation of older persons and reduce the hazards of alcoholism among them.

Efforts to prevent alcoholism can be effective only if ever-expanding groups of professional workers and community organizations are directly involved. The prevention of alcoholism must be a major concern of every agency, public and voluntary, in the welfare field. Welfare workers must take as much interest in the prevention of alcoholism as in the prevention of any other social problem.

Alcoholism programs cannot operate in isolation from other health and welfare activities. Coordination is essential. Pooling of resources and personnel may, in many instances, be necessary. Where resources are limited, efforts should be made to ascertain which persons run the greatest risk of alcoholism. Emphasis should be placed on these high risk groups.

It is only through preventive and rehabilitative measures that the incidence and threat of alcoholism can be reduced. The tools for implementing such preventive programs are at hand. They need to be recognized and to be used fully and effectively.[3]

Under the new "War on Poverty" program which has been projected by the Johnson Administration, the Department of Health, Education, and Welfare has proposed a program, which is to be carried out in conjunction with all of its divisions, for alleviating the problems of alcoholism. At the 1964 Annual Meeting of the National Council on Alcoholism, proposals for such a program were outlined by Mr. Wilbur E. Cohen, of the Department of Health, Education and Welfare.

Where private funds are not available, it is the government's responsibility to handle this problem. Without the government, in many areas nothing could be done.

[3] WA Publication No. 3, U.S. Department of Health, Education and Welfare, Washington, D.C., April 1964.

CHAPTER 15

The Medical Profession and Alcoholism

ALCOHOLISM as an illness has been known and recognized for many years. Until comparatively recently, however, the organized medical profession as a whole did very little about it. In the last ten or twelve years there has been a noticeable change in attitude by organized medicine and consequently by individual physicians. Earlier, however, many enlightened physicians who attempted to place alcoholism in its proper perspective as a medical problem met with very little success due to the attitude of the profession as a whole. This attitude may have reflected the attitude of the general public, which looked upon alcoholism more as a moral problem than as a medical one.

Dr. Francis Fronczak, the Commissioner of Health in Buffalo, New York, at the turn of the century, addressed the City Council on the alcoholic problem and stated that in his opinion alcoholism was an illness and not a crime. He recommended that jail sentences be changed to hospitalization for people who habitually drank to excess, so that they could get medical care and proper rehabilitation. However, not much was done about the problem. I am sure that many other physicians met with frustration in those days when they attempted to do something about alcoholism.

In 1948 a prominent physician of Buffalo, New York, Dr. Milton G. Potter, at one time president of his county medical society, having observed the success of Alcoholics Anonymous in rehabilitating alcoholic people, felt that the problem properly belonged within the province of medicine. Through his efforts his county medical society appointed a Committee on Alcoholism. Dr. Potter was chairman. He also helped form a citizen's committee for education on alcoholism to bring the problem before the public.

The purpose of the medical committee was to stimulate interest among physicians in studying alcoholism and urging them to treat alcoholic patients from the medical viewpoint. Dr. Potter, himself a recovered alcoholic, then decided to carry his ideas up through the ranks of the organized medical profession to try to get concerted national action. As a result of his work, a resolution was presented to the House of Delegates of the American Medical Association, at their June, 1950 meeting, establishing a Committee on Problems of Alcoholism in that organization. With the passage of this resolution, it was recommended that the problem be studied by the already existing Committee on Chronic Diseases.

Six months later a new resolution was introduced in the House of Delegates asking that the previous action of the House be rescinded, and that a Special Committee on Problems of Alcoholism be appointed. A year later, in 1951, a Committee on the Problems of Alcoholism was appointed as a Subcommittee of the Chronic Diseases Committee. About ten members were named to this Committee. Since I was a member of that Committee, I know that it never met, because no appropriation was made for its meeting. With no money available, the members of the Committee could not get together.

In 1952, a year after the Committee was appointed, the

Chairman and I were discussing this matter and the inability of the Committee to meet due to lack of funds. We wrote to the American Medical Association and its Chronic Diseases Committee to ascertain what action had been taken regarding the possibility of our Subcommittee meeting. We were informed that the Subcommittee had been disbanded. Although we were members of the Committee, neither of us had ever received notification of dissolution of the Committee. We then asked for action on this problem, and the appointment of a new Committee. In addition, we asked that an appropriation be made so that it could function.

During this time, however, although the medical committee was not able to carry out its work, the lay committee on education on alcoholism was functioning very well. The education committee in our area had become affiliated with the National Committee on Alcoholism, which now bears the name National Council on Alcoholism. The educational campaign in western New York was carried on very energetically and began to bear fruit. As a result of its action, the University of Buffalo Medical School, now the Medical School of the State University of New York at Buffalo, established a Rehabilitation Center for alcoholics. This was located first in the Medical School itself, and later in the Chronic Disease Institute under the auspices of the National Institute of Mental Health and the New York State Health Department, in conjunction with the University of Buffalo, as a tripartite arrangement.

In 1953 we invited the Executive Secretary of the American Medical Association's Committee on Mental Health to visit our facilities and discuss the matter of a Subcommittee on Alcoholism. The American Medical Association decided that the problem of alcoholism properly belonged under the Committee on Mental Health. As a result, a Subcommittee on the Problems of Alcoholism was appointed under the Committee on Mental Health, with the authorization of the House of

Delegates. I was requested to take the chairmanship of this Subcommittee. I accepted the position on the condition that we be given a free hand to act under the Committee on Mental Health and that sufficient funds be allocated for us to meet and operate. These conditions were met and the Committee was appointed. There were representatives from the New England area as well as the Middle Atlantic and the Southwest areas.

Early in 1954, with an adequate annual budget, the Committee began its work. Our first meeting was held in Boston, Massachusetts, on February 6, 1954. Since that time there has been considerable activity. So far, we have had a minimum of two meetings annually. In addition, in cooperation with the Council on Scientific Exhibits, we have built four exhibits on alcoholism at a total cost of several thousand dollars each. These exhibits have met with a wonderful reception wherever they have been sent. They are available for exhibit not only at the meetings of the American Medical Association Conventions, but also for meetings of all state and county medical societies that request them. Health education meetings are also accorded the privilege of using these exhibits.

The Committee on Alcoholism has stimulated interest in the problem in various state medical societies. Whereas before this Committee was formed there were very few state medical societies having committees work on the alcoholism problem, these committees now exist in over forty of the fifty states. Other committees handling the problem bear such titles as Mental Health, Public Health, or Industrial Health. Since we do not study the activities of individual county societies, we have no way of telling how many such committees exist among the county medical organizations.

In 1955 the Committee on Mental Health was raised to council status and became the Council on Mental Health, and the Subcommittee on Alcoholism was thereafter raised to full committee status and became the Committee on Alcoholism of the Council on Mental Health.[1]

In 1956 our Committee began a series of articles in the *Journal* of the American Medical Association, under the auspices of the Mental Health Council. Over a three-month period four articles appeared in the *Journal* dealing with the medical, physiological, psychiatric, and sociological aspects of alcoholism. These papers were written by our Committee members. Thousands of reprints of these articles were distributed throughout the country as requests poured into the American Medical Association headquarters. One order for five thousand copies was received for one of these articles. I mention this only to emphasize the obvious interest on the part of the medical professsion in the problem of alcoholism. It must be borne in mind that these articles are strictly for the medical profession, and writtten on a professional level.

Later that year, at the request of the Committee on Alcoholism and through the Council on Mental Health, the American Medical Association purchased a complete set of the Abstract Archives of the Alcohol Literature. This set of Archives was placed in the headquarters of the American Medical Association in Chicago, and announcement of its purchase appeared in the *Journal*. The number of inquiries on the subject of alcoholism and its various ramifications was so enormous as a result of this announcement that the staff found itself swamped with requests and fell months behind in answering. Any doubts in our minds of the medical professsion's interest in alcoholism were now dispelled. It was necessary that we send one of our staff to Yale University to learn how to operate the Archives files more efficiently. Even so, it took months before the first avalanche of inquiries was answered.

---

[1] To 1962: Selden Bacon, Ph.D.—Rutgers Univ.; Robert Fleming, M.D.—Boston, Mass.; Harold Himwich, M.D.—Galesburg, Ill.; Jackson A. Smith, M.D.—Chicago, Ill.; Marvin A. Block, M.D., Chairman.

In 1963: Robert Fleming, M.D.; E. M. Jellinek, D.Sc. (deceased); Harold Himwich, M.D.; H. Thomas McGuire—New Castle, Del.; Marvin A. Block, M.D., Chairman.

While the number of requests has diminished somewhat since that initial announcement, it appears that this is not due to lack of interest, but rather to the fact that the availability of these Archives has not been sufficiently publicized. A subsequent announcement brought another wave of inquiries. Actually, we have purposely postponed such additional publicity because of staff limitations. However, it will be called to the attention of the profession regularly in the future, and as our staff increases it will be continually put before them.

Later in 1956 a resolution was brought before the House of Delegates of the A.M.A., urging all general hospitals throughout the country to admit alcoholic patients to their general medical floors. This resolution had been approved by the Council on Mental Health and the Board of Trustees. It was imperative that if physicians in training were to understand the problem, patients with the diagnosis of acute or chronic alcoholism must be admitted to general hospitals without prejudice. The resolution was unanimously passed by the House of Delegates. This represented a tremendous victory. The largest medical organization in the world had now recognized alcoholism as an illness that warrants admission to general hospitals for people suffering from it. Since then the resolution has been forwarded to the Council on Education and Hospitals as well as the Joint Commission on Accreditation of Hospitals. The purpose of this action is to promote education on alcoholism among hospital staffs and resident staffs so that patients suffering from this disease can be properly treated when they are admitted. I am informed that in 1957 a similar resolution was adopted by the Board of Trustees of the American Hospital Association.

In 1957 the Committee on Alcoholism prepared for publication a manual for the use of medical practitioners. This manual on alcoholism consists of the four articles printed in the *Journal,* the guest editorial on alcoholism that appeared in the *Journal,* the announcement and instructions for use of the Abstract Archives of the Alcohol Literature, and other pertinent material useful to practitioners in treating alcoholic patients. In addition, the Committee has also produced a directory of rehabilitation resources, listed by states, for those interested in the alcoholic patient. This directory and the manual, an eighty-seven-page booklet, as well as individual reprints of the articles are all available at national headquarters. The Committee received 20,000 advance requests for the Manual on Alcoholism before it was printed. In 1962 the manual was revised and brought up-to-date and it is now available at A.M.A. headquarters.

The Committee has made a survey of the teaching on alcoholism in medical schools, in cooperation with the A.M.A. Council on Education and Hospitals, and with the Association of American Medical Colleges. We arranged for a study of what the Committee feels is necessary in the way of education for medical students on the subject of alcoholism. The results will be forwarded to the American Association of Medical Colleges for its perusal and comment. In 1960, a curriculum for teaching the subject in medical schools was completed. This was accepted by the Council on Education and Hospitals of the A.M.A. and the Association of American Medical Colleges. It has been distributed to every medical school in the country, and copies are available at A.M.A. headquarters.

In addition, we are making a survey of the laws that relate to alcoholism of the various states. This study is being carried on in cooperation with the Legal Department of the American Medical Association. In all probability, we shall enlist the aid of bar associations at state levels and at the national level as well. We hope eventually to formulate a uniform law regarding the handling of alcoholics and the proper legal disposition of such cases. We hope to publish a directory of the state laws relating to alcoholism, so that any physician can find out from a legal viewpoint what his responsibilities and obligations are toward alcoholic patients.

The Committee on Alcoholism has approached Blue Cross

headquarters regarding its attitude about the payment of hospitalization expenses for patients suffering from alcoholism. This is a tremendous undertaking, since various Blue Cross corporations have their own regulations on this matter. We hope that by publishing information about those corporations who do pay hospital benefits for alcoholism we will be able to induce all Blue Cross corporations to pay for such hospitalization. As of today, about 65 percent of all Blue Cross corporations pay for alcoholism in some way.

I have already mentioned that the Joint Commission on Accreditation of Hospitals has received the resolution on hospitalization of alcoholics that was passed by the House of Delegates in 1956. This Commission is studying the problem from the viewpoint of implementing the ideas that were incorporated in that resolution as they relate to qualifications of hospitals for teaching purposes.

All the steps enumerated are part of the 18-point program that our Committee adopted and presented to the Council on Mental Health in 1954. This 18-point program is available to anyone who requests it. It outlines the proposed activities of the Committee on Alcoholism for the future as well as some of the work we have already accomplished. For those who are interested, this program can serve as a model for state programs, since the same activities that have been carried on at the national level can be done by state medical societies.

The Committee on Alcoholism throughout the past several years has attempted to direct the education of the medical profession regarding the subject of alcoholism. In 1954 a conference of mental health repersentatives of all the state medical societies was held in Chicago, under the auspices of the Mental Health Council. The conference was devoted to the problem of alcoholism, and discussions took place at the headquarters of the American Medical Association, where thirty-six state medical societies were represented. Various aspects of the problem were discussed and the state representatives were urged to carry back to their societies a message promoting interest in and education on alcoholism.

In 1956 another such conference was held, at which sixty-five representatives from forty-one states were present. These were mental health representatives from the state medical societies. Alcoholism, of course, was not the only subject discussed. At this particular conference in 1956, the program was divided into four parts: Child Psychiatry, Hypnosis, Tranquilizing Drugs, and Hospital Treatment of Alcoholics. The conferences were conducted as workshops, and the numbers representing the various states were divided into these four groups and given their choice as to which subjects or workshops they wished to attend. It was surprising to find that of the four workshops mentioned, the subject Hospital Treatment of Alcoholics drew about twice as many people as any of the other three. I mention this only to illustrate the increased interest in the treatment of alcoholics in this country.

In 1958 a similar conference was held, at which several subjects were treated. I attended the workshop on Mental Health Problems in Industry. It was not surprising to find that the problem of alcoholism attracted considerable discussion in this particular workshop. It was agreed by most of the people there that alcoholism was one of the mental health problems most often encountered in industry. At the end of the conference, the representative of the Women's Auxiliary of the A.M.A. and its Mental Health Committee, Mrs. Elizabeth Margulis, suggested that as its project for 1958 the Auxiliary consider the excessive drinker and automobile driving. While this may not necessarily refer to alcoholism, excessive drinking must also be considered in this project. Again, this is mentioned only to illustrate the increased interest on the part of the medical profession, the wives of physicians, and the public, on the subject of excessive drinking and alcoholism.

In 1957 the Mental Health Council permitted our Committee on Alcoholism to provide a new service to physicians.

The Medical Profession and Alcoholism

It authorized us to hold institutes on alcoholism for any state medical society that requested it. We were given authority to hold as many as three of such institutes annually. To date we have held many such meetings, one in San Francisco for the California State Medical Society, one in Galesburg, Illinois, for the Illinois State Medical Society, and several county societies from adjoining states and areas. Another was held for the State of Colorado and one for the State of Arizona. All of these institutes were considered outstanding successes, judging from the responses of the physicians attending. Not only are the talks given at these institutes instructive to physicians, but the discusssions following are stimulating and provocative. These meetings give the doctors an opportunity to voice their opinions, to relate their experiences, and to exchange ideas on treating this problem from the physician's viewpoint.

But the organized profession itself can be of very little help unless the individual physician recognizes his responsibilities in his own community to the patient suffering from alcoholism. One thing is clear. He can no longer avoid this issue. He can no longer neglect these patients. He cannot pass the buck. He must treat them. There are methods, and satisfactory ones, of doing this. There is sufficient evidence that good results can be obtained. True, we cannot promise cures, since a cure would imply that the patient might be able to drink normally again. However, complete recovery can be attained by the patient with the help of his physician, and it is to this end that the doctor must work. Properly trained in the medical approach to this problem, and with sufficient psychiatric orientation, with which every modern physician today is equipped, he can achieve very satisfactory results with most patients.

It must be recognized, however, that there is no single specific treatment for this sickness. There is no antibiotic or chemical miracle drug that will do away with the illness. The physician must spend sufficient time with his patient, rehabilitate him physically, and help him mature emotionally. This cannot be done with shotgun prescriptions or pills. It requires time, patience, and investigation. The physician must study this illness as he does other illnesses, its etiological factors, its background, and its history. He must do complete physical examinations. He must perform necessary laboratory tests. He must make definite evaluations, and he must pursue the therapeutic programs with thoroughness and understanding.

Postgraduate courses on the problems of alcohol are available; if they do not exist in a physician's area, he must request or organize such courses. The Committee on Alcoholism of the American Medical Association stands ready to help him in these matters. If he will request of his state medical society or his county medical society that such courses be given and such education be made available, they in turn, can request help from our Committee and we will be more than happy to supply them with information—or actual teaching facilities, if necessary.

In 1961 the Committee on Alcoholism, in cooperation with the Committee on Medico-Legal Problems and the Committee on Legal Aspects of Automobile Injuries of the American Medical Association, cooperated in drawing up a statement for the use of the Council on Safety of the Department of Health, Education, and Welfare, relative to drinking and the ingestion of alcohol. This statement was presented to the Safety Council with the objective of establishing authoritative standards for levels of alcohol concentration in the blood, in reference to drivers and their ability to drive.

In 1960 the American Medical Association, by action of its House of Delegates, unanimously adopted a resolution that 0.1 percent of alcohol in the blood should be the level of concentration that indicates that the subject is under the influence of alcohol, and that anyone with a concentration of 0.1 percent and above should be considered under the influence of alcohol, and therefore liable in any driving accident. This adoption of a standardized concentration will be a big help in determining legal measures to be taken for drivers with alcohol in their blood. The joint statement made by the three committees was in confirmation of this act from a technical viewpoint.

In 1962 the Committee on Alcoholism of the American Medical Association built its first exhibit on alcoholism for the public. This very elaborate presentation portrays to the layman the incidence, prevalence, and communicability of alcoholism. It also shows the early signs the layman can look for and so recognize the early stages of problem drinking and alcoholism. The exhibit carries other educational material in the way of visual and audio aids to educate the public regarding the problem as a public health measure and as a disorder of the individual. It emphasizes the part played by the members of the family and the community in aiding to combat this prevalent illness.

Because of the similarity of the problems of alcoholism and narcotic addiction, the American Medical Association in 1964 decided to combine the work of the committees devoted to these two subjects. A new committee, called the Committee on Alcoholism and Addictions, was formed to handle the two problems.[2] The work on the alcoholism program continues in the same way with this committee.

These are some of the measures that have been taken up by the medical profession as an organization in attempting to meet the challenge of alcoholism as a disease in the United States. However, the physician has a greater duty than to act with his organization. He must also act as an individual.

In addition, the physician must serve as a a case-finder. As with other diseases, the answer to this problem lies in prevention rather than in therapy. Therapy must be provided

[2] Dale C. Cameron, M.D., Washington, D.C., Chairman; Lindsay E. Beaton, M.D., Tucson, Ariz.; Marvin A. Block, M.D., Buffalo, N.Y.; Edward R. Bloomquist, M.D., Glendale, Calif.; Henry Brill, M.D., Albany, N.Y.; Herbert A. Raskin, M.D., Detroit, Mich.; Maurice H. Seevers, M.D., Ann Arbor, Mich.

for those patients who are presently suffering from alcoholism, but prevention of this illness is the eventual solution to the problem. It is important, therefore, that the physician be a case-finder. It is important, also, that his history of any patient include a detailed history of his drinking patterns. The slightest indication of trouble as a result of drinking should alert the astute physician to the possibility that here is a potential alcoholic. By instituting proper prophylactic measures, by careful advice, many cases of alcoholism can be prevented. Just as the competent physician will look upon hemoptysis as a possible sign of tuberculosis, gastric distress as a possible forerunner of peptic ulcer, glycosuria as a possibility of diabetes, so he must look upon trouble as a result of drinking as an indication of a possible case of alcoholism. It is never too early to detect these signs.

Not only the practicing physician, but other medical agencies must be used to combat the problem of alcoholism. Not the least of these is the general hospital. The general hospital should accept these patients as sick people who deserve and require their attention. Acute alcoholic intoxication can be, and often is, a medical emergency.

Hospital personnel should be instructed about treating these patients. This is especially important for the nurse. The nurse has three professional capacities in her community. First, she too is a case-finder. This is especially true of the district nurse. She, more than anyone else, perhaps, can detect the early signs and symptoms of alcoholism in members of the families she visits. A timely warning can prevent a great deal of grief for such a family. I need not add that in her actual nursing service she can also be of tremendous help.

The attitude of the nurse in treating the sick alcoholic is one of the greatest therapeutic aids. Her sympathetic approach and her understanding of his problem can be the turning point in his motivation. Often the patient will confide in the nurse many things that he cannot or will not tell his physician. Such information conveyed to the doctor can

The Medical Profession and Alcoholism

in many cases help the physician to understand the problems that beset the patient, and he can then put the patient's mind at rest or open an avenue for proper discussion. The nurse's sympathetic understanding of the emotional problems underlying this illness can be a great therapeutic aid.

The third area in which the nurse can be of great value is in her role as an educator in the community. The nurse must take sufficient interest in the community problems to engage in activity with the lay groups for education on alcoholism, as well as in professional groups.

Where all of the facilities that can be provided are pressed for by the physician and the ancillary professions, and where there is sufficient understanding of the problem on the part of all these people, enough interest can be stimulated in others to learn more about this important problem. If there is more interest, more facilities for research will be provided. As a result of more research, more knowledge will be forthcoming. As is true of many medical problems in the past, increased research and the resultant knowledge will eventually lead to the answers. With more attention focused properly, and with sufficient work, an eventual solution must be reached.

CHAPTER 16

Alcoholism and Industry

INDUSTRY has had to be concerned with many of its employees' problems over the years. As unionization grew, more and more demands were made upon management to provide services of all kinds for employees in industry. Among these services were hospitalization, medical services, workmen's compensation benefits, disability benefits, and other welfare programs that would lead to increased health and efficiency for people in industry.

In recent years, rehabilitation of injured individuals has been one of the problems that industry had to face and solve. As a result of various forms of taxation and legislation, industry has also been partially responsible for the care of dependents of disabled employees. Even where the employee himself makes some contribution in taxes, industry must also make its contribution. The contributions vary with national laws, state laws, the customs of the community in which the industry operates, and the personalities in management and labor unions.

This is true of alcoholism as well as other diseases. The extent and variation of the programs industry employs in helping alcoholics is so great that it runs the gamut from punishment or inattention to complete care and rehabilitation. How far an industry will go in care and rehabilitation depends a great deal on the individuals at its head and on the understanding of both management and union.

At a conference held by the Mental Health Council in Chicago a few years ago to discuss the problems of mental health in industry, there was general agreement that of all the causes of absenteeism, alcoholism represented the greatest percentage of absences due to illness. Monday morning absenteeism, so common in industry, was found to be, to a great extent, due to the excessive use of alcohol over the weekend.

Of the estimated five million alcoholics in this country, it is considered that two million are employed in industry.[1] This represents about three percent of all the job-holders in the country. According to statistics, the alcoholic loses on the average of two days per year more than the average worker as a result of his illness. His absenteeism is estimated at about twenty-two days each year. This means that, in the United States, forty-four million working days or three hundred and fifty-two million working hours are lost to industry each year as a result of this one illness among its employees.

A conservative cost attributable to alcoholism each year is one billion dollars. About half is accountable to lost time, absenteeism, lowered productivity, accidents, and inefficiency. The remaining amount includes twenty-five million dollars for custodial care in institutions of various sorts for alcoholics or in correctional institutions; about twenty million dollars spent by voluntary agencies caring for the families of alcoholics; a like amount spent by public agencies for the same purpose; a hundred and twenty-five million dollars for accidents as the result of alcoholism; thirty million dollars for care of alcoholics in general hospitals, and many millions spent in futile treatments for the disease when the patient or his family decide to take care of the matter without pro-

[1] "Alcoholism in Industry," M. A. Block, *American Association of Industrial Nurses' Journal*, April, 1959.

fessional help. Another startling statistic is that the alcoholic on the average dies twelve years earlier than the nonalcoholic.

It is not easy to detect the alcoholic in industry. Many such employees have been with their firms for a long time. Many are valued employees whose services cannot be estimated in money by their employers. Since most people do not develop this disease in a short time, many efficient workers do not show signs of deterioration until they have been in the employ of a firm for ten or fifteen years or longer. By then they represent tremendous investments by their organizations. This is particularly true among skilled workers.

How, then, can we detect these patients? There are several indications of excessive drinking. The most common, of course, is absenteeism, particularly the Monday morning absenteeism known to all industrial physicians and nurses. Tardiness on other days may be another sign. Carelessness on the job, after having been good workers over long periods of time, sometimes indicates trouble. There are often, of course, other emotional problems that may bring about the same symptoms, but the appearance of these symptoms should be sufficient reason for interested investigation.

Personality changes in the individual should be closely watched and investigated. Evidence of undue tensions or a change from the previous norm in working pace may also be considered indicative. Physical irregularities or temperamental outbursts where none appeared before may be a clue to trouble. Reports of unusual drinking behavior off the job should be investigated for accuracy. Growing domestic, financial, or community problems in an individual who had not had such problems previously may indicate the beginning of a drinking problem.

Almost everyone is familiar with the physical manifestations of excessive drinking—bloodshot eyes, flushed face, florid skin, carelessness in personal appearance, staggering when intoxication is acute, trembling hands, and so on. All these are physical manifestations of a hangover or too much alcohol the past day or so. The work begins to suffer, and further deteriorates as time goes on. At times the employee drinks during working hours; resentment at having this called to his attention is extremely symptomatic. Unexplained disappearance from the post often occurs at odd times. Reports of accidents and fights while off duty are suspicious, especially if frequent. Antagonism, rationalization, projection of blame on fellow workers or on tools, and argumentativeness are all indications of irritability that might result from alcoholism.

In industry it is essential that whatever information is gleaned from the patient or his associates be confidential. The patient should be interviewed alone, and preferably by the medical department. It goes without saying that the interviewer must be one who understands the problem and the disease. He must not sit in judgment; his attitude must be sympathetic; there must be a desire to help. Criticism, censure, scolding, haranguing, have never helped the alcoholic. Telling him to stop drinking is like telling an anxious person to stop worrying. He does not drink because he likes it; he can't help it. Therefore, an understanding of the problem of the individual and of his disorder is extremely important in handling these situations. Since it is a medical problem, it should be handled by medical personnel. However, the understanding of the problem should be taught to all supervisory personnel, of both management and unions, since a complete understanding of this illness by all parties involved will help the individual suffering from it. It must always be borne in mind that alcoholism is a treatable disease, and that recovery is possible for all alcoholics. However, it does take the cooperation not only of the patient, but also of his family, his employer, and his fellow workers.

These are some of the principles involved in detection and handling of the alcoholic in industry. Proof that the proper approach is successful lies in the fact that many industries have adopted programs for this illness among their employees, and have been extremely successful in saving the employee, the job, and money for the company. Allis-Chalmers reduced its discharge of alcoholics from 94 percent to 8 percent by means of a comprehensive program. Eastman Kodak has done a remarkable job through its medical department. Consolidated Edison, in New York, maintains a clinic completely staffed for the care and treatment of its alcoholic employees. Their percentage of success is extremely high. Western Electric Company, DuPont, and Commonwealth Edison of Chicago are all firms that have instituted programs for alcoholic employees with remarkable success. The same may be said for American Telephone, Standard Oil of New Jersey, and General Motors.

The methods used by these companies vary. Some rely on their medical departments, some maintain separate clinics for the employee, and others have found considerable success with groups of Alcoholics Anonymous. Many have been quite successful by simply interviewing the individual involved and referring him to proper community resources or individual physicians for advice and treatment. Unions have taken a tremendous interest in this problem, and the first conference on alcoholism by a union was held in western New York in March, 1957. At that time the suggestion was made by members that the union itself might establish a clinic for treatment of alcoholic members.

Medical departments of industries should be properly briefed about alcoholism and staffed by personnel who can interview these people and guide them to treatment. Private physicians, clinics, Alcoholics Anonymous, and other agencies all stand ready to help not only the individual but any industry willing to cooperate.

Since alcoholism has been recognized by the American Medical Association as an illness that properly falls within the purview of medical practice, large industries are beginning to recognize that they must contend with the problem and that it will be to their advantage to seek out and help the alcoholic employee. The cooperation of unions has benefited the individual, the union, and the industry. In one case an individual who was discharged from his job because of alcoholism sought help from his union when he recovered. The union took issue with the employer who had discharged this person because he was sick, and the case was held for arbitration. During the arbitration proceedings a medical witness was called to testify as to the illness from which the discharged employee suffered and his success in treating him. As a result, the employer was found remiss in not sending the sick employee through the regular medical channels of the industry for the necessary care and rehabilitation. The employee was reinstated with full pay from the date of discharge, and performed his work successfully.

Dealing with the problem of alcoholism is not only the responsibility of large industries. It is also the responsibility of smaller industries with comparatively few employees. The loss to small industry can be just as great proportionately. It must be conceded, however, that smaller industries cannot maintain medical departments comparable to those of larger industry, but this should in no way prevent them from caring for the alcoholic patient. Because it is a source of sensitivity, the problem of alcoholism has been avoided by small industries and, to a great extent, misunderstood by both labor and management in these smaller plants. For a long time laborers and executives alike have asserted that a man's drinking patterns or habits are a personal matter, his business alone.

This attitude is so prevalent that until fairly recently, the entire subject was carefully avoided. Though excessive drinking was sometimes obvious to the point of common in-plant gossip, the problem was seldom accepted as a medical one, and as a rule was summarily handled by foremen or other supervisors. Time off or outright firing were the everyday remedies.

What about the problem for small industry? How can the average employer cope with this problem? He may not have a full-fledged medical department. He may only employ a part-time doctor, or only have a doctor on call when needed. The problem of alcoholism, nevertheless, can exist among his employees in precisely the same ratio that it is present in a large enterprise, and there is no reason why these people should be deprived of adequate protection and care. There are ways in which the problem can be dealt with effectively.

One way of handling the problem in small industry is for several employers to cooperate. In an area where a community educational group or alcoholism information center exists, such an agency can be engaged to serve in the development of a cooperative clinical facility, or several small enterprises can join forces to establish a clinic of their own if they so desire. Where no educational group exists, one can be formed. Application to the National Council on Alcoholism will immediately bring help in forming such an agency.

The physicians of the area are as a rule happy to offer professional advice. Other sources of cooperative assistance are the county medical society and various organizations of industrial physicians with full and responsible access to the experiences of larger industry dealing with the problem of alcoholism. Finally, there are the part-time physicians who care for the other medical problems of small industry in the area. These doctors need only the encouragement of the employer group they serve.

Alcoholics Anonymous has chapters in practically every populated section of the country. A request addressed to the local A.A. chapter would not be ignored. One or more A.A. members employed by local small industry can always be counted on for help. It is simply a case of bringing the problem into the open.

The single most important factor is successful promotion of constructive local interest, and this lies in the attitude of the industries themselves, small as well as large. Here again, the stigma presently attached to alcoholism must be removed. All moral overtones must be deleted before the problem can be approached, to overcome difficulties like individual lack of confidence, fear that detection will lead inevitably to loss of job and would become a matter of public knowledge. Until each patient's confidence is fully restored by his employer and complete assurance is given that recovery from an illness is the only problem that concerns either the patient or his employer, no effective beginning can be made.

Patients suffering from alcoholism use alcohol not as a pleasure-giving beverage, but as a drug promising relief. With no help from the outside, and with a terrible fear of being discovered, they suffer in what they think is secrecy, and gradually go downhill as the increased fear of discovery and all it entails leads to increased drinking. They need help and assurance from those from whom it would be most valuable—from their employers and fellow workers.

If the stigma were removed, the sense of shame that the alcoholic feels would be gone and he would be moved to seek the help he requires. Understanding, sound advice, and adequate care would arrest the progress of his disease and he would know again the comfort and mental poise that would restore him to sound mental health. At his work, his productivity and job efficiency would return, would improve, and would be maintained in a normal upward curve.

Employees must be encouraged to consult with the medical staff without fear of reprisals. Cooperation with private physicians must be urged. Sufferers must have full confidence the industrial physician will keep their confidence and will help them as with any other disease, with no reflection on them because their illness happens to be alcoholism. Consultation between the industrial physician and management should be frequent and complete, so that management itself will understand the seriousness of this malady and the value of rehabilitating employees suffering from it.

Private physicians and their patients must be assured that all discussions of alcoholic cases between them and the industry's medical department will secure the employer's full cooperation, and that discharge or censure will not result.

Industrial personnel, no less than mechanical equipment, represents a tremendous financial investment. This is particularly true of employees who have been with a company for a considerable length of time, and who have developed unusual skills of great value to their employers. When such a valuable employee becomes ill, management is for the most part extremely patient in waiting for him to recover and return to his job. Even when chronic diseases periodically render such individuals incapacitated for extended periods, patience is manifested by management until the patient recovers.

This, however, is not true when the patient is suffering from alcoholism. Because this appears to some management people to be a self-induced problem, such patients are too often summarily discharged after no more than a word of warning not to drink again. This treatment of the alcoholic patient is tantamount to telling a patient with a diseased gallbladder that the next time he has an attack he will be fired, and that he, therefore, should be careful not to have another attack.

Alcoholism is a chronic sickness with which anyone can be afflicted. It has periods of remission and periods of exacerbation, as do many other chronic diseases. There are good recoveries that last for long periods of time, and there are some recoveries of shorter duration. Alcoholism is a malady that has frequent or infrequent relapses, or none at all, depending upon many conditions. Unfortunately, the very employer who criticizes the alcoholic often constitutes an etiological factor in the relapse of the individual whom he is criticizing.

If I were a stockholder in a company, I would be deeply interested in how well my investment was being protected by the management of that company. Capital expenditures for valuable machinery would ge much of my attention, if I felt that such equipment were being carelessly handled. I would want to know what happens when an expensive machine begins to lose its efficiency. Does the management dispose of it completely, or is some effort made to have it overhauled by competent technicians and put back into good working condition at minimum expense? Were I to discover that a still valuable machine was discarded and replaced with a costly new one simply because management failed to recognize the possibility of repairing it at a fraction of the cost of replacement, I would feel that my industrial investment was being seriously threatened.

Some companies have found it profitable to assume responsibility for treatment of alcoholics on their payroll. Others equally interested may not undertake the treatment but will advise that treatment be instituted and will cooperate with the sick person so that a maximum of help can be given.

While we know there is no such thing as a cure, which would imply a return to normal drinking, complete recovery and restoration to previous health and efficiency is possible through total abstinence and the establishment of the motivation necessary to maintain that abstinence. Every medical department has a responsibility to acquaint itself with the measures recommended for treating the alcoholic, for detecting early symptoms of the disease before the victim loses too much of his efficiency, and for taking proper steps to see that treatment is instituted in time for the patient to make a good recovery.

Perhaps the most difficult type of problem to be faced is to convince managers of the wisdom of taking the steps described, particularly when a management executive is personally involved. As a defensive measure, and as a further escape from facing his own problem, many managers will insist upon discharging all alcoholic employees. They are too close a reminder of his own sickness, and he prefers to avoid being confronted with his problem in another when he himself can or will do very little about it. These are the people who are most likely to be impatient. Once they have made a recovery themselves, however, they become much more patient with other victims of the illness.

While alcoholism represents a risk and a danger to any industry because of the possibility of accidents that might occur as a result of an alcoholic's carelessness or uncertainty when drinking, it does not necessarily follow that the alcoholic must be careless in this manner. It is often true that because he knows his problem he will be unduly careful even though he is drinking, and will avoid many risks he otherwise might take. Very often the fear of detection makes these sick individuals extremely cautious once they have been drinking, especially on the job. By and large, however, sufficient alcohol may result in recklessness or accidental miscalculations. Such accidents can be costly to the employee as well as to the employer.

In the transportation industry, the risk and eventual loss due to alcoholism goes beyond the patient or his family and his employer, and involves risk to fellow workers and other innocent people. Where judgment is rendered faulty or inaccurate because of alcoholism, grave danger may arise for people with whom the alcoholic works. This can occur with other emotional or mental problems as well. Excessive drinking, however, is tolerated much too long by far too many.

The risk of using alcoholic employees on railroads, bus lines, trucking lines, and airlines can be of far greater importance to the public than in other industries, where the risk may be only to the employer, the employee, and fellow employees. In the transportation industry we are always confronted with the necessity of putting our lives in the hands of individuals about whom we know nothing at all. When that railroad engineer or conductor, bus driver, truck driver, or airline pilot undertakes to guide his vehicle filled with innocent passengers, it is of the utmost importance that that man, that employee of that industry, be at his top efficiency, both mentally and physically.

Great responsibility rests upon the employer, upon the

medical departments of these industries, and on industrial and private physicians. Alcoholic bus drivers, locomotive engineers, truck drivers, or airplane pilots expose countless people to the danger of injury or death. This is true, of course, in all cases of excessive drinking, even if it has not progressed to the compulsive drinking of alcoholism.

Many workers in the field of alcoholism are aware that in the transportation industry positions of authority and responsibility are held by alcoholics. There is evidence that in some areas this is recognized by the management, and steps have been taken to aid these people. Some companies take elaborate precautions to detect excessive drinking among their employees. Some have established rehabilitation facilities. But it may be assumed that many alcoholic employees are working in positions of responsibility without the knowledge of their superiors, though often the facts may be known to some fellow employees, to a private physician, or occasionally to supervisory personnel.

When the facts are known to the patient's personal physician, privileged communication prevents him from reporting them without his patient's consent. How far shall the physician go in respecting this confidence where the safety of the public is at stake? When fellow employees are aware of it, the information is often suppressed in the mistaken notion that it protects the afflicted employee. It might prevent immediate discovery, but at what cost, at what risk?

Alcoholics are subject to emotional tensions like anyone else, and in certain circumstances may resort to drinking. Since there is no specific cure available for this disease, alcoholics cannot ever drink safely under any circumstances. They are perpetually susceptible, and with this susceptibility they endanger the safety of others for whom they are immediately responsible.

Alcoholism is not common in all transportation industries. However, the employment of one alcoholic pilot on a passenger plane can be a much greater risk than the employment of many such people as truck drivers. Some transportation industries are more careful than others about taking precautions against their employees working while under the influence of alcohol. The Committee on Aviation Medicine of the American Medical Association states that precautions in cases of airplane pilots are said to be quite exhaustive. Railroads, bus companies, and trucking lines also have stringent rules regarding drinking by employees. Does this mean, then, that there are no alcoholics employed in these industries as pilots, engineers, or drivers? As a matter of fact, we know that such individuals *are* employed by these industries, and are working without their employers' knowledge that they are suffering from this illness. In spite of all precautions, these alcoholics are still working in these industries. Even when employers have been notified, there are instances where nothing was done to remove these employees from the responsible positions they occupy.

In some instances, warnings that have been given to the medical departments about some of these employees have been completely ignored. Each employer thinks that this does not exist in his organization, but I have been told, for example, by one railroad engineer, that the cab of the engine in which he works has contained as much as a case of beer, and that the fireman and the engineer and the conductor of the train all drank freely of this beverage while working. It was shocking to hear these revelations *from an alcoholic engineer.*

In considering this problem, we are not speaking of drinking per se *but of alcoholism, an emotional illness that makes its victims compulsive drinkers.* Some patients have been known to circumvent all ordinary precautionary measures, and they are resourceful in avoiding detection. Where precautionary measures are taken, it is the responsibility of the medical department of these industries to instigate and follow through on the detection of such employees. The work should not be delegated to employees whose training has not been in this field. The signs and symptoms to be recognized are not necessarily the obvious ones of excessive drinking, or of drinking at all, but of the emotional problems underlying compulsive drinking. Diagnosis of this emotional problem can be made only by trained medical personnel.

It is not suggested that any person be deprived of employment because of an emotional illness. It is imperative, however, that those in charge of passenger carriers be carefully observed, examined, and screened to ascertain whether such a problem exists. Those found to be affected should be transferred from a position of direct public safety responsibility until recovery is assured. Signs of emotional instability in personnel always should be reported to the proper medical authorities for investigation. Any indication of alcoholism should be considered legitimate reason for suspension or transfer to a position not directly responsible for public safety. The treatment of such emotional instability in such cases as only temporary behavioral problems is a form of negligence.

Examinations and history-taking by medical departments of all transportation industries should be complete and exhaustive. Consent should be given for withdrawal of blood samples for alcohol content at any time. Such measures may be unpopular, but they are necessary. The common carriers should be made completely responsible for seeing that the public is protected.

It is obvious that automobile drivers who drink excessively are a risk on the road. Knowingly to allow drinkers to drive passenger buses, pilot planes, drive trucks, or operate trains is much more reprehensible.

One could enumerate individual industries and go into details about the various risks to the individual, his employer, his fellow workmen, his family, and the public that might result because of alcoholism. Carelessness in many industries, for instance, on an automobile assembly line, or among inspectors in many industries, could easily result in danger to the public as well as to individuals close to the drinker. In all of these matters, it is extremely important that the alcoholic be treated and rehabilitated so that these risks can be removed.

Alcoholism represents a health problem that cannot be ignored. With one out of every fifteen adults in our country afflicted, it can hardly be considered a minor problem. In industry it is eventually paid for by every individual consumer in the country. To eradicate alcoholism from industry would help to bring down prices of all commodities and make living safer and happier for all of us.

CHAPTER 17

The Teacher and Alcoholism

IN my opinion the solution to the problem of alcoholism will lie not in the recovery of the present-day alcoholic, but in the prevention of the disease in future generations. After many years of teaching at the graduate level, I believe that if alcoholism had been explained properly in the secondary schools, I would not have to teach so much about it to graduate students. The problem can first be sufficiently appreciated in the secondary schools. In the primary grades children are a little young to understand the implications of alcoholism. At that level, the properties, qualities, and effects of alcohol can be taught to a certain extent, and at least the groundwork can be laid, but the actual understanding of the mental problems involved, the emotional complications, and the matter of addiction to drugs can best be started at the secondary school level.

For many years teaching was attempted in the classrooms of the secondary schools by various experts in the field of alcoholism. The success was proportionate to the numbers of students the individual expert could reach. With a limited number of instructors, not enough students could be reached, in our opinion, and it seemed obvious that other methods would be more advantageous. One of these was to teach the teachers. This type of teaching proved to be very successful. We were agreeably surprised to find how many students had learned about alcoholism and how much they had learned. In many instances, we learned how far they had outstripped the teachers, because very often the students were more interested in alcoholism than their teachers, because of experience in their own home with relatives, parents, and other members of the immediate or distant family.

Such interest serves as an incentive toward research on the problem. More and more inquiries come from high school students who are writing theses, compositions, and articles on the subject of alcoholism. This is becoming so common, especially in the colleges, that much of the literature of the educational committees is distributed to college students writing their theses on alcoholism. In the high schools, it has become quite a subject for discussion and a favorite one for original research and reporting. As is to be expected, students exposed to the subject of alcoholism through education were much more interested in further research than those who did not have this kind of exposure. This is not unlike what happens in the medical profession, where we find that physicians who have attended lectures on alcoholism become interested in the subject, and thereafter show a great deal more interest in treating such patients and pursuing the subject than those who have not been exposed to such education. Of course, the greatest stimulus to the doctor is the patient or patients who come to him repeatedly asking for information and help in the matter of alcoholism. When there are enough such requests, he decides that he had better learn something about the subject so that he can at least answer the questions.

This is, to some extent, also true of the teaching profession. In spite of the fact that alcoholism is today a subject of great interest, and one that occupies considerable space in various publications, newspapers, magazines, and so on, there are still many teachers who, through their own prejudices, have avoided the subject when teaching. When the student begins to ask questions, however, the teacher finds it necessary to learn something about the subject so that he or she can answer such students intelligently.

A few points must be considered, particularly for the teacher. First, we must consider why education on this subject in the secondary schools is important at all. We cannot avoid the fact that drinking is a part of our culture. Not only is it an accepted part of our culture, but there are many pressures brought to bear so that it is often thought to be necessary either to drink or at least to accept the idea of drinking. Such advertising as "men of distinction," whether we like it or not, does have an effect on youngsters who read advertisements in magazines. The young high school girl buying a dress is exposed to the term "cocktail dress." It may be just a term, but to her it means something, and if she doesn't know what a cocktail is by then, she certainly is going to try to find out. Little things like these are bound to make students conscious of alcohol, even if up to that time they had not been exposed to it. According to statistics, most youngsters have already tasted their first drink of an alcoholic beverage before they have been in their teens very long. Actually, therefore, by the time most students have reached their second or third year of secondary school, they have already tasted alcohol and have an idea of what it is like. Since this is a fact, and since so many of these students do drink, whether we approve of it or not, it is important that they be taught a sense of responsibility about it.

First, we must recognize that alcohol is a drug. Regardless of whether it is taken with that in mind or not, it does have the effect of a drug, and a very effective drug it is. If it were not for the unpleasant effects and excessive use, it might even be considered an ideal drug. It is therefore necessary to teach anyone who is going to use this drug, no matter how innocuous it may seem, the responsibility that must go with handling so dangerous an agent. Anything in excess can be dangerous, even the comparatively innocent aspirin tablet; even that must be taken with a sense of responsibility. The Purdue Opinion Poll, which sampled 3,000 ninth- to twelfth-graders in all parts of the country, found that while only a small percentage of the student population approved of drinking, an average of 45 percent of the boys and 27 percent of the girls "sometimes drank." This poll was conducted by the Purdue Opinion Poll for Young People, Division of Educational Research, Purdue University, Lafayette, Indiana, in 1949. Other surveys have produced similar findings.

Unfortunately, up to a short time ago most of the teaching about alcoholism in secondary schools was based on laws that were passed in the latter half of the nineteenth century. During the eighteen hundreds the idea of prohibition swept across the country. This was about the time that the Prohibitionist Party was born, the W.C.T.U. was formed, and the Anti-Saloon League came into existence. Whether or not there was justification for these organizations is not up to us to decide at this time. However, most of the laws concerning the use of alcohol and teaching about it in the public schools were passed at that time. The teachers were on the whole required to teach their students that alcohol and the drinking of alcohol were evil. Under this heading of evil also went smoking and the use of other agents that had varying amounts and various types of drugs. This included tea and coffee, to some extent. Actually, the only thing that was recommended that could be drunk with impunity was milk. Even milk has come under careful scrutiny recently because of its fat content and its possible effect on cholesterol concentration in the blood.

In the past, teaching about alcoholism in the secondary schools has been not an error in commission but one of omission. I think there was omission of certain important facts in the teaching. In the last few years there has been marked improvement in this area and also considerable pressure to bring such teaching up to date so that students will get the scientific truth about alcohol and alcoholism.

Excessive drinking as a social problem was rarely mentioned in curricula up to a few years ago. I think this is one of the first aspects to be explained to the students. This need not be emphasized as alcoholism, because it is not always that, but perhaps it can be shown in a discussion of the drunken driver, whose drinking may not necessarily be a manifestation of alcoholism, but is an example of the need for a sense of responsibility in drinking.

Another conspicuous failure was the omission of known scientific facts. Much of the teaching on alcoholism in past years was a reflection of the emotional reaction of the people who were teaching it. This did not always reflect the scientific truth. Today, actual scientific facts are being publicized so that the student has an opportunity to use his own judgment. As with any other subject, if the truth is taught and the child is given a sense of responsibility, his own judgment will serve him well. The tremendous number of untruths and half-truths he so often hears confuse him, and he cannot use his judgment. It is very confusing to tell a student that drinking is evil, only to have him go home to his parents, whom he loves and who love him, and see them drinking, apparently with no ill effects. Regardless of what he has been told by his teacher, he is bound to be confused. There will be a conflict in his own mind, not only about the drinking but about his parents. This is certainly not a desirable effect and does not reflect credit on such teaching. When any conflict is generated in the mind of a student, he becomes ambivalent about the various factors involved, which results in confusion and loss of confidence in those who are teaching. A teacher in whom the student has no confidence is not effective for that student.

Another conspicuous omission was in the statistics about the rate of absorption of alcohol. All sorts of stories were told to young people. Many books relate terrific damage and destruction as the result of ingestion of alcohol. There is no tremendous destruction of the body as the result of drinking alcohol. Actually, if there is destruction it is not the result of the alcohol, necessarily, but may be due to side effects of improper nutrition and lack of nutritional elements. Teaching that alcohol itself is destructive to the tissues, therefore, is not factual. Although it could possibly be damaging in very excessive amounts, this must be specifically stated; and it can also be true of many other things we eat and drink.

Most of the teaching up to a few years ago dealt with drinking rather than excessive drinking. Here, too, confusion is caused to students who see people drinking with no apparent ill effects. The resultant conflicts, intensified by repeated observation, can cause unhappiness among students, especially when the confusion continues to the point where they cannot exercise proper judgment. They want to believe what they hear from their teachers, but their personal experiences contradict what they have heard. This affects the student's attitude not only toward the value of instruction about alcohol, but also toward the rest of his subjects. The entire educational system is actually on trial when truths, as they are scientifically known, are not properly taught.

Another flagrant omission is not mentioning the fact that drinking is a psychological phenomenon as well as a physiological one. This is very important. The young person must be taught that alcohol is a drug, and that though all drugs are not necessarily evil, many can be habituating. We all know of many people who cannot be civil in the morning until they have had a cup of coffee; they require a certain amount of caffeine before they can function adequately. As far as drinking is concerned, the psychological phenomenon must be emphasized as well as the physiological one. We must always keep in mind that unless the teacher can be objective about alcohol, his or her own prejudices may enter into the subject. Even with some objectivity, an emotional reaction may creep through. If one teacher refers to alcohol as a stimulant, and another refers to it as a sedative, the actual scientific facts being ignored, there will be conflicts in the students' minds.

When discussing drinking with students, we must be very careful to differentiate between the different types of drinking. There are people who drink because they are sick. There are also people whose drinking is a sickness. There are many people who drink without any undesirable results. There are some who cannot drink without having undesirable results. There is a percentage of the population who are mentally sick, and in whom drinking to excess is only a symptom of an underlying mental illness. In such cases, excessive drinking is only secondary to the underlying mental illness, but the student must understand this. On the other hand, there are some people where the drinking itself becomes an illness and the results of such excess are a complication of this illness.

We rarely see in teaching manuals or in curricula a reference to community responsibility about the care of people who suffer from excessive drinking. This is another omission that is to be regretted. The necessity for community responsibility for people too ill to care for themselves must be taught to and understood by students. They must be made conscious of the fact that there is such a segment of the population, and that they are entitled to the same type of treatment as other sick people, people suffering from poliomyelitis, cerebral palsy, multiple sclerosis, and many other diseases, which often must be a community responsibility. Alcoholism must be included. Schools are a major force in attitude education, and it is the attitude that determines how such problems are handled. Textbooks must be scientifically correct and teacher training must be proper and complete. The attitudes of the teachers themselves must be improved and made consistent with the proper curricula.

Students are unusually curious about alcohol and alcoholism. They ask many questions to which they are entitled to correct answers, as far as we know them. What are some of the common questions that are brought up by students, and that teachers must answer? One of the very common ones is whether or not alcohol is a stimulant. How does it act? There are reasons why many uninformed people believe that alcohol is a stimulant. Actually, however, it is no more stimulating than is ether or chloroform or any of the anesthetic agents. The apparent increase in activity the individual manifests at certain stages of alcohol ingestion is comparable to the early stages of induction of anesthesia. We know, for instance, that ether is a very powerful anesthetic agent and can reduce the patient to complete coma and even death. However, in the early stages of ether anesthesia the patient will become hyperactive. This is because in the early stages of anesthesia the cerebral cortex is depressed first, and the cerebral cortex is in charge of control. Therefore, when the controls are depressed, there is an increase of activity. Then, as the rest of the brain is anesthetized, the patient becomes sedated and then inactive.

Alcohol acts in exactly the same manner. In its first stages, when the concentration of alcohol in the blood is low, the control centers of the cerebral cortex are anesthetized and the patient is without control. As the result of this, there is an increase in activity. This is not stimulation—it is the removal of the brakes, a depression of the controls. Alcohol is a depressant, a narcotic agent.

Another favorite question is whether or not alcohol is a food. Alcohol does provide calories and is an energy-producing agent. It provides these calories, but it has no nutritional value, since it cannot participate in rebuilding tissue. Therefore alcohol may be said to produce energy, but it has no rebuilding qualities, it has no ability to provide the necessary nutrient elements—fats, carbohydrates, protein, or any of the vitamins and minerals necessary to qualify a substance as food.

Does alcohol overcome fatigue? In the same way that it may be said to stimulate. Actually, it does not overcome fatigue, but there is a depression of the consciousness of fatigue; since the controls are lost, judgment is depressed, and therefore the consciousness of fatigue is gone. If the fatigue is due to a lack of calories or energy-producing substance, then alcohol can supply these calories very readily and does give available energy quickly, but it does not overcome the feeling of fatigue if the fatigue is actual.

Is alcohol fattening? Only in that energy required for work can be made up by the calories provided by the alcohol, and therefore other foods taken in can be stored to provide added weight. If no food is taken, no matter how much alcohol is ingested, there would be no weight gain since there is no tissue-rebuilding. In order to gain weight the necessary nutritional elements must be supplied—that is, carbohydrates, proteins and fats—none of which is in alcohol.

Another common question is that which comes up about the effect of drinking on athletes. Of course, most of us know that alcohol cannot benefit athletes, since there is a loss and diminution of the reflexes and the reactions of various kinds. Actually, because it is an anesthetic agent, it is detrimental to athletes.

One of the most common and curiosity-arousing questions that comes up is the effect of alcohol on sex. The effect is best described by Shakespeare in the quotation, "It enhances the desire but decreases the performance." Since alcohol depresses the powers of judgment, drinking may release inhibitions that create desires that are better controlled when not drinking. In most cases, however, excessive drinking will produce impotence, and most people who drink excessively experience a diminution in sexual powers rather than an increase. As far as sexual behavior is concerned, it is well known that alcohol reduces the inhibitions of individuals and removes the controls. The individual becomes careless and will often do things under the influence of alcohol that he would not do if his judgment were not impaired. Therefore, impairment of the judgment by alcohol may cause sexual behavior that would not occur were he not exposed to the loss of control that alcohol brings about.

Does alcohol have any medicinal value? Some physicians have maintained that alcohol is a very effective therapeutic agent. I suppose in years gone by alcohol had some value in therapy, and was used to some advantage, since many other drugs were not yet available. There are many physicians who still feel that alcohol is a valuable drug, and it is true that it can be used to some advantage in a few instances. But in my experience, there has been no condition where alcohol could not be superseded by some other drug, with greater benefit to the patient. Under certain circumstances, particularly during senility and in the older age groups, I think that alcohol can be used to the benefit of the patient; but again I believe that other drugs are of as great or greater value. Many claim that alcohol is a vasodilator, dilating the vessels and beneficial where circulation is insufficient. Research workers have found, however, that this is not necessarily so. The vasodilation may be limited to the superficial vessels, and there is no effect on the deeper vessels at all.

I do not mean to imply that alcohol cannot be used. Where properly indicated and properly tolerated, it, like many other drugs, can be used to advantage under certain circumstances.

Students are very often taught that cirrhosis of the liver results from ingestion of alcohol. It must be clearly stated that cirrhosis of the liver is not necessarily the result of ingestion of alcohol, and that even in those cases where there is excessive use of alcohol, it is not necessarily the use of alcohol itself that produces this condition, but rather the lack of other nutritional elements—minerals and vitamins—that occurs so often in cases of alcoholism. Alcoholics, we know, very often do not eat properly or do not eat at all, and the absence of the necessary nutritional elements and of minerals and vitamins is what causes the cirrhosis in these cases. Truthfully, we do not know exactly what causes cirrhosis of the liver, since it is often seen in cases for which there appears to be no sufficient cause. The liver serves so many purposes and has so many functions that we are only now beginning to understand how little we know of this wonderful organ. We do know, however, that its proper function is necessary to good emotional and mental health, as well as to physical health. More and more we find that the functioning of the liver is critical in all matters of health. This particular organ offers a vast field for research, and I am afraid we have not yet gone far enough to determine all the possibilities. It has been ascertained almost conclusively, however, that cirrhosis, when it does occur, is probably due to a lack of certain vitamins, minerals, and other nutritional elements necessary to the health of this organ. Such facts as are known must be properly taught to the students.

Ulcers of the stomach is another subject that often comes up for discussion when alcohol is discussed. It is generally conceded now that the ulcer, gastric or duodenal, and alcoholism have the very same kind of emotional background. At one time it was thought that alcohol aggravates an ulcer condition. Actually, from the local viewpoint, this may be true. On the other hand, there have been alcoholic patients with ulcers, and the ulcers disappear when they drink; and when they are deprived of alcohol, the ulcer returns.

I am sure this is related to the emotional life of the individual. Certainly we know that emotions affect the secreting mechanisms of the stomach lining. We also know that under certain emotional conditions ulcers occur. I do not recommend, of course, that people with ulcers drink alcohol; what I do recommend is that the emotional problems underlying both excessive drinking and peptic ulcers be uncovered and resolved in therapy. Alcohol, used as a sedative drug, relieves the emotional tensions so common to many ulcer patients. The effect on the ulcer may be beneficial, but the patient may be kept dependent upon alcohol, the drug. It is, therefore, more advantageous to treat such patients with other tension-relieving drugs. If the teacher understands these basic facts, sufficient explanation can be given to the student so that he will understand.

Many years ago alcohol was used frequently in the treatment of respiratory diseases—pneumonia, for instance. However, today it is rarely used in treating such cases, since we have many more effective drugs for this purpose.

Another intriguing question is, "Is alcohol habit-forming?" For a long time this has been a subject of controversy. Does the patient become habituated, or addicted? There is still much discussion, but most people who do research in the field lean toward the opinion that alcoholism is a real addiction. There is a physiological change in the cells of the body as the result of prolonged excessive drinking. This addiction is manifested by what happens when an alcoholic stops drinking. Withdrawal of alcohol causes real physiological changes in the cells, giving rise to severe signs and symptoms known as withdrawal signs. I think it can now be stated that alcohol is genuinely an addictive drug.

The matter of heredity and alcohol always crops up in discussions with students. The illness alcoholism is not hereditary; that is, it does not come down in the genes and the chromosomes. However, the various home conditions that result from alcoholism in one or more parents can lead to neurotic temperament in the children, which could result in alcoholism. The disease itself, however, is not hereditary. The neurosis may not necessarily manifest itself as alcoholism, but it is possible, because children very often imitate their parents. It is very possible that such neurotic children will seek the same methods of escape from tension as their parents did, even though during childhood they objected to their parents' behavior.

Can alcoholism be cured? Most young people want to know the answer to this question. As far as we are able to say now, there is no cure for alcoholism. There can be a complete recovery from the disease, but a cure would mean that the individual could drink safely without drinking excessively.

This, in the light of our present-day knowledge, is impossible. However, as long as the alcoholic does not drink at all, he can have a complete recovery and live a long and healthy life. One of the most difficult obstacles for the alcoholic patient to surmount is the fact that he cannot drink with safety. Each of us has a private opinion of himself, a self-image that is an improvement on reality. It is something of a letdown to realize that we are not all that we thought we were, to admit that we are not perfect. For the alcoholic, accepting the fact that there is something that he cannot do that other people can do is very difficult. We all want to do the things we are not supposed to do, and for the alcoholic the thing he is not supposed to do is drink. However, acceptance of the inevitable is a mark of maturity, and this is something that the immature alcoholic must learn.

It is very important that students learn that there is a successful treatment for the alcoholic. Despite the many educational programs available, many people do not appreciate this fact and do not know that complete recovery is both possible and frequent.

There are definite medications and nutritional agents for restoring the alcoholic to physical health. After his physical health has been restored, emotional rehabilitation must take place. He must be taught to accept the fact that he cannot drink alcohol, much as the person with a severe allergy must learn to get along without certain foods to which he is sensitive, or as the diabetic must learn to limit his diet. This acceptance of the inevitable is necessary for the attainment of maturity. There must be public programs and clinics and information centers to which patients can be referred, and students must learn about these places. They must take part in community life so that they can be informed about the location and efficiency of these agencies. There is always Alcoholics Anonymous, ever present, ever willing to help; there are clergymen who are always ready to aid people in need; there are good friends and understanding people; there are mature acquaintances; *and* of course there is the family doctor. All of these people and agencies are sources of help for people suffering from alcoholism. The person suffering from alcoholism or any other disease should consult his physician, and of course the student should be taught to have confidence in the physician.

Above all, the student should be advised that research is of the utmost importance, as is true of any illness where the solution has not been completely attained.

Interest must be stimulated in these young people and their curiosity aroused, so that they can be spurred to greater discussion and greater research in this field. More education must be carried on in law enforcement agencies and among health authorities about excessive drinking and alcoholism. The subject is an excellent one for discussion groups. Last, but not least, the community general hospital must, as a center for treatment and rehabilitation of people suffering from this illness, be concerned with the education of youth on the subject.

Teaching about alcoholism in the public schools must follow a well-planned curriculum. The planning of such a curriculum is of the utmost importance and should involve considerable organization on the part of the faculty. There must be a meeting of minds among teachers of other subjects when it comes to the teaching about alcohol. The subject may come up in any number of courses—in literature, biology, the social sciences, hygiene, and many other courses—and the teachers of all these courses must be in agreement on how to approach it. There must be no conflict in their minds, for this would be communicated to the students. The extent to which each of these courses will emphasize the problem of alcohol or excessive drinking must also be determined, and all aspects must be explained to the entire faculty so that there will be no dissension about the scientific facts. Regular conferences among faculty members for discussion of the subject are desirable. The general purposes of the program should be clear to each individual teacher, so that he can make his proper contribution to the entire program. All teachers should know why the schools must assume responsibility for teaching the subject as a public health problem. Public awareness of alcoholism is increasing, and it is the responsibility of the secondary schools to discuss and teach this subject as it does any other interesting current problem. Legislation is being passed all over the country dealing with alcoholism, and unless the teacher keeps up with the facts, he is going to find himself in an embarrassing situation when bright young students come up with questions.

There are some general factors that must be taken into consideration in such a program. One is the attitude of the community generally about the secondary schools in the area. The mores of drinking in the particular community must be considered. To what extent are there temperance forces, and what is their activity in the particular community? What is the influence of advertising upon the children in the area, and what is the character of the control of liquor sales in the community? All such factors are important, and all must be taken into consideration in preparing programs for various parts of the country, of the state, and of the city. Controls in the sale of alcohol in a large metropolitan area may vary from one part of the city to another.

Geographical areas make considerable difference in the teaching of this subject. Several studies made in different parts of the country have revealed differences in attitudes among young people toward drinking. In highly urbanized and industrialized Nassau County in New York State, for instance, as many as 86 per cent of 1000 high school students reported they sometimes used alcoholic beverages, the majority with parental permission.[1] In Racine County, Wisconsin, another largely urban community but with a relatively more stable population, about two-thirds of the students ques-

[1] Hofstra College—Use of Alcoholic Beverages Among High School Students. Mrs. John S. Sheppard Foundation, Inc., New York City, 1954.

tioned had occasionally done some drinking,[2] and in a third study in Kansas, which included over twenty rural counties, only about half the students had ever taken an alcoholic drink.[3]

Both the sale of alcohol and the drinking of alcoholic beverages by students are important. Violations of existing laws are all too common. The degree of consciousness of young people of criticism of those who violate these laws sometimes plays an important part in their interpersonal relationships. Many young girls hesitate to go out with boys who drink, and they hesitate to drink themselves, but they are afraid to refuse or criticize for fear of being ostracized socially by the people of their own group. Subtle techniques must be used by teachers in introducing these subjects and bringing about changes where undesirable conditions exist.

Individual localities must be considered, and each teacher must take into consideration his or her own locality when discussing the subject of drinking. Local drinking customs, proximity of bars and cocktail lounges, attitudes of parents, civic groups in local areas all must be considered. The customs and beliefs of the parents are particularly important, and a teacher must acquaint himself or herself with these when discussing the subject with his students.

Instructions must be related to the students and their needs. The facts must be presented as fully and as truthfully as possible, and there must be free discussion. Although at the high school level it may be almost impossible to avoid being pedagogical, while at the college level it is better not to be too didactic, I think the important thing in both instances is to be provocative in one's questions and allow for wide-open discussion. It is healthy to have students disagree on a

[2] University of Wisconsin—Attitudes of High School Students Toward Alcoholic Beverages. Mrs. John S. Sheppard Foundation, Inc., New York City, 1956.
[3] University of Kansas—Attitudes of High School Students Toward Alcoholic Beverages—Mrs. John S. Sheppard Foundation, Inc., New York City, 1956.

subject like alcoholism; disagreement gives rise to creative discussion in the classroom.

I need not emphasize the importance of not moralizing, and of sticking to the facts. One must be objective but not too objective, for this is not a cold subject. There is much emotionality in discussing drinking and alcoholism, but one must not become too emotional about it either. There is a certain happy medium that a teacher can reach and then allow the children to do the discussing. It is important to try to be specific in terminology so that there will be no confusion among the students; the teacher, of course, must be familiar with the correct terminology. Drinking is not alcoholism, nor does it necessarily lead to alcoholism, and the teacher must not let his personal feelings get into the discussion.

One popular way of bringing the subject of alcoholism to secondary school students is to have outside speakers. When such a speaker has scientific facts and knows the subject from many aspects, this can be valuable. When the speaker, however, is a recovered alcoholic and just gives a history of his drinking experiences and how he recovered by "reforming" or "seeing the light," the value of such a presentation is questionable. When he is a prohibitionist and against drinking as a moral principle, his bias must color his presentation.

Teachers who have prejudices regarding drinking can rarely present the subject objectively. They can only convey the prejudices.

We live in a society where drinking is acceptable. Even though one out of 15 or 16 adults is afflicted with alcoholism, we must be aware that most people who drink have no difficulty. The minority who do must learn to live without it. This is true of many people who are ill, and in order to maintain their well-being, must forego many things which others have. Alcohol is not a necessity of life, and abstinence entails little sacrifice if recovery can be effected. When the stigma is removed, this will be much easier for the patient.

When discussing drinking or alcoholism with students, the instability of youth must be emphasized when compared with drinking by older people. Students must be impressed with the fact that alcohol is a drug, and that its popularity can be attributed to its druglike effect of removing control. The self-consciousness which so many young people feel can be overcome by better methods than the use of a drug. Here is where the teacher plays a big part.

The desire to be grown up and escape from emotional problems, two of the reasons why students drink, can be overcome by methods which should be conveyed by the teacher. Often these problems are beyond the scope of the teacher. Professional care should then be recommended. These problems are most often encountered at the secondary school level.

As important as anything is the attitude of the student toward those already afflicted with problem drinking. The teacher has an obligation to develop in these students the proper attitude and understanding of such sick people. The students' interest must be stimulated not only in the individuals as sick people, but in the problem itself as one with which they can help. Presented properly, more young people will become interested in research into this area, to which they may in the future contribute toward its solution.

CHAPTER 18

The Hospital and Alcoholism*

In recent years the hospital has become more and more important as a community center for health problems. In the public mind a hospital building—the institution itself, is the hub of activity for the care of the sick. The attending physicians, nursing personnel, and administrative officers are, to most people, the authorities on all health problems in the community.

The hospital is looked upon as the center for learning about health and disease. Hospitals are the laboratories of medical schools, where the results of didactic teaching and the lessons learned by students are applied, tested, and measured. Within its walls are housed medical and surgical patients for whom all medical knowledge can be brought to bear to alleviate their maladies. It is no wonder, then, that the hospital occupies an important position of leadership. With this position, however, goes a peculiar and definite responsibility on the part of attending physicians and other personnel. It is a responsibility that requires initiative, courage, and conviction.

* "The Hospital's Place in a Program on Alcoholism," by M. A. Block. *Ohio's Health,* Winter Edition, December 1958.

Because of its unusual position, therefore, the hospital must be especially careful of its attitude toward disease. A patient who is sick requires care, regardless of the type of illness. Because the disorder carries some connotations of opprobrium, or because in the past it had moral implications, is no reason for a hospital to discriminate against the patient. In the case of alcoholism, therefore, either acute or chronic, the hospital must accept as its responsibility the treatment of human suffering in this illness. Acute alcoholic intoxication can be, and often is, a medical emergency. Like any other medical emergency, the proper place for treatment is the general hospital. Any acute intoxication, regardless of the agents responsible, can have disastrous results if proper care is not administered. Regardless, then, of the agent that brings about the acute intoxication, necessary procedures, both diagnostic and laboratory, must be employed and relief must be given where indicated.

There is a fallacious opinion prevalent that the care of the acutely ill alcoholic patient requires some special facility or equipment. This is not true. Any acutely intoxicated individual must have adequate diagnosis and then treatment. The odor of alcohol on the breath is not always indicative of acute alcoholic intoxication. Particularly if the patient is unconscious and can give no history, it is extremely important that a differential diagnosis be made to determine the exact cause of unconsciousness. All too often the odor on the breath may be a diagnostic point that can mask many other serious conditions, such as diabetic coma, cerebral hemorrhage, concussion, or fracture of the skull. These more serious diagnoses may be missed if assumptions are made on the basis of the odor of alcohol.

All the necessary tests for differentiation can be made in a general hospital more easily and more effectively than anywhere else, and an unconscious patient is entitled to all the indicated measures for an accurate diagnosis. On many occasions, reports have appeared in the press of individuals who have died in custodial care because it was taken for granted that their condition was due to acute alcoholic intoxication. Autopsies in such cases have often revealed that other conditions were the cause of death. Had proper diagnostic measures been taken, many of these lives would no doubt have been saved. In the light of our present knowledge, such errors of omission are inexcusable.

Care of the acutely intoxicated individual is only one phase of the proper and complete treatment of the alcoholic in a hospital. The available facilities must be utilized for supportive therapy after the patient recovers from the acute phase. Such therapeutic measures are often necessary just to restore the patient's good physical health. Proper diet and the necessary vitamin and mineral elements must be administered during convalescence. The patient must learn how to conduct himself in the future in order to retain his physical health.

Prolonged drinking, characteristic of alcoholic patients, often has devastating effects on individual organs of the body. Adequate therapeutic measures for restoring these organs to normal health must be instituted, and the patient must be instructed on how to continue such a regimen after leaving the hospital. Hospital dietitians can often be of great value here. It is extremely common to find many physical complications associated with chronic alcoholism. These complications often reduce the patient's physical efficiency. The patient must be taught about this impairment in his body and how to adjust his living to insure maximum rehabilitation of the affected organs.

In the past it was the custom of many hospitals to dismiss the patient once he recovered from his acute intoxication. This only resulted in his return within a short time. Such a revolving-door plan is not consistent with good therapy. The patient must be indoctrinated with proper motivation for continuation of therapy after he has left the hospital, and this is the responsibility of his attending physician. However, the social service department, the nursing personnel, and the others associated in the treatment of the patient, all have their place in stimulating such motivation. Where the patient has a private physician, it is imperative that he return to him for follow-up treatment. Where the private physician is not available or the patient cannot afford private care, it is the hospital's responsibility to provide adequate outpatient facilities.

The clinic in a general hospital serves to rehabilitate the patient and help him take his place as a responsible member of society. It not only follows up its patients after hospitalization, but also serves as an outpatient facility for those sick alcoholics who do not require inpatient care. It is now recognized that the most important treatment for the chronic alcoholic comes *after* the acute phase of his illness. Then he is sober and capable of responding to the medical and psychiatric treatment so necessary for successful rehabilitation.

Many general hospitals have avoided their responsibilities to care for alcoholics. Many have refused to admit patients with a diagnosis of acute alcoholism. A few are controlled by by-laws that specifically prohibit such admissions. It is difficult to understand a general hospital discriminating against any sick person, and it is strangely significant that many such hospitals have resorted to subterfuge for selected patients suffering from alcoholism. They are admitted on the basis of other diagnoses upon the insistence of the attending physician or someone with power and prestige in the institution. Neither subterfuge nor discrimination should be condoned in any general hospital that serves the community. To mask the diagnosis is to mask the truth and encourage patients thus admitted in their self-delusion. It postpones the day of recognition by the patient of the serious nature of his illness. Even though a patient requests it, it is a disservice to accede to such a request.

Alcoholism is not the only disease that carries a stigma; many others were thus labeled in the past. With public education, however, and public acceptance of the fact that these illnesses were serious, it was found that nothing could be gained by avoiding the issue. Gradually, the stigma disappeared, and today many of these diseases are accepted without the slightest remembrance of stigma. Alcoholism is said to affect one out of every fifteen adults in our country, and such prevalence is too great to be ignored. We cannot hope to solve so enormous a problem if responsible leaders insist on evading it.

The American Medical Association, at its meeting in Seattle, Washington, in 1956, passed a resolution urging all general hospitals in the country to admit physicians' patients suffering from alcoholism. Its House of Delegates passed this resolution unanimously. This was a tremendous stride in the recognition of alcoholism as an illness that properly falls within the purview of medical practice. It properly places a responsibility on the physician and the general hospital.

A short time later the American Hospital Association passed a similar resolution, urging the same procedure in the case of alcoholic patients. Is this not significant? Is it not impressive that these two great national organizations regard the proper approach to this problem as important? Anyone with considerable experience caring for patients suffering from alcoholism will readily attest that these patients, when accepted, are as tractable and cooperative as most patients in a hospital. Poor behavior on the part of the alcoholic patient is often an expression of resentment against the discrimination he feels, rather than a result of the illness itself.

There are many maladies in which an unexpected or unpleasant event may result in a situation that requires extra attention for the patient. Psychoses following parturition are not uncommon. Delirium tremens following surgery is not a rare occurrence. Post-anesthetic excitement can hardly be called a rarity in any hospital. Temporary and often inconvenient hyperactivity on the part of an alcoholic may occur in a small number of cases but, like the other conditions mentioned, is temporary, usually of short duration and without incident if proper treatment is instituted. Other conditions, such as diseases of the brain and the nervous system, may at times necessitate more than ordinary nursing care. When this occurs, the close attention of an extra attendent may be required. This may occasionally happen with the alcoholic patient also, but certainly not with any more frequency than in other patients.

Like other human beings, physicians are often subject to the same prejudices that affect the general public. Many people feel that alcoholism is a self-induced disease, but most concede that the alcoholic does not wish to be an alcoholic any more than the diabetic wishes to be a diabetic, or the coronary patient wishes to have heart trouble. The fact is that he is an extremely sick person who seeks relief from his inner tensions and problems through the most available method he knows.

Unfortunately, we usually do not see the alcoholic patient until his therapeutic disorder is fairly well advanced. It is not surprising, therefore, that the learning process may be more difficult for him. However, if by constant vigilance we were to detect these cases earlier, much of this difficulty might be obviated. As with other diseases, the earlier it is detected, the better the recovery rate.

In a hospital setting, with proper history-taking and examination regardless of the admission diagnosis, many such cases could be detected sooner. A proper history will often reveal early problem drinking long before it is recognized by the patient. To call his attention to this threat before it becomes a serious problem is to do him a tremendous service and spare him a great deal of trouble. Recognition of the early stage of this illness would bring to everyone's attention the necessity for treatment.

The physician plays a key role in the attitude of the hospital toward the problem of alcoholism. No institution can function without trained personnel. In the hospital, it is the physician to whom the other employees look for guidance and leadership. His attitude toward the disease will determine the attitude of other hospital personnel toward that disease. In this day of specialization, not all physicians are particularly interested in alcoholism. However, there is no patient who provides the challenge to medicine that the alcoholic does. As a public health problem, alcoholism ranks third. With such a great percentage of the population afflicted with this illness, it is probable that every physician sees many of these patients frequently.

It is the obligation of every doctor, when he detects anything that suggests a disease, to so advise his patient. The physician who detects in his patient the possibility of trouble with drinking should see that the patient is directed to the proper source for care. Every doctor should have a working knowledge of the symptomatology of alcoholism. If he does not treat such patients, he should refer them to someone who does.

Actually, it is the physician's duty to accept alcoholism as an illness and to see that the patient gets proper care. For many years, alcoholism has been a frustrating problem. Today, with the new modern drugs and techniques, the doctor no longer need feel this frustration. Medical literature abounds with articles on the subject of proper methods of treatment. The satisfaction derived from success with such a patient is extremely rewarding. Any physician will find it well worth his effort to devote the time and energy necessary to care for these people.

How and where can a doctor learn to take care of alcoholic patients? There is no doubt that the hospital is the best place for instruction in the clinical aspects of any disease, but how can such instruction on alcoholism be carried out if these patients are not admitted to the hospital? This factor alone should determine the hospital's attitude toward the alcoholic patient. A good general hospital would not consider omitting from its curriculum for its house officers or nurses any disease that affects five million people in our country. For many years, nevertheless, interns and residents have completed their training periods without having had sufficient instruction in the diagnosis and treatment of alcoholism. Now that this subject has been brought out into the open, these very men find themselves severely handicapped when the alcoholic patient presents himself for care. Never having had the oppportunity to treat these patients during their hospital training days, the physicians feel inadequate when alcoholic patients appear. We cannot afford to let more young physicians go into practice without this training.

When the general hospital accepts these patients and they are on the medical floors along with other medical diseases, interns and residents will have an opportunity to make adequate diagnoses and to follow through on treatment. Such training will serve them well when they go into private practice. It is important, however, that the attitude of the attending staff toward these patients be one that is conducive to proper training of house officers. If the attending staff is prejudiced about this disease, such an attitude will communicate itself to the men in training. If, on the other hand, the attending staff takes an interest in these patients and shows the same energy in treating them as in treating others, the desired attitude on the part of interns, residents, and nursing personnel is assured.

A few years of such training in general hospitals and the term *alcoholism* will no longer carry the stigma it had in the past. With the stigma removed, more physicians will become interested, not only in the diagnosis and treatment of alcoholism, but also in research into its etiology and prevention. Once the medical profession applies itself diligently, a solution is usually found. So it will be with alcoholism when interest is great enough.

The problem of alcoholism is an enormous one. It will not disappear of itself. Combating it requires the concerted efforts of all those interested. For a long time the physician and the hospital have allowed others to care for alcoholics. Lay people have undertaken to help these sick people as best they could. Without a background of medical knowledge or therapy, they have succeeded admirably. It is high time now for the physician to recognize his responsibility in this area.

Both the American Medical Association and the American Hospital Association have recognized this challenge and have urged hospitals to do the same. It is a challenge from which they cannot retreat.

CHAPTER 19

Necessary Components for an Effective Program on Alcoholism

PROGRAMS for education on alcoholism and its diagnosis and treatment have sprung up all over the world. For a complete program certain components are essential.

First, there must be the incentive for such a program among people of the area. They must be made aware not only of the existence of alcoholism as a problem in their community, but also of what can be done about it to remedy, if not eradicate the problem. The educational program requires personnel acquainted with the subject, help from the communication media, and central headquarters where information can be obtained. This headquarters should be known as an information center and must be staffed by competent, capable, and informed personnel. At its head should be a director able to organize and direct the staff. He must be a personable individual with the ability to make contacts with the proper individuals and groups in both management and labor, with educational leaders in the area, with law enforcement officers at all levels, with medical organizations as well as individual doctors, with law organizations as well as individual lawyers, with individual clergymen and clerical organizations, and with hospital administrators and board members of hospitals.

Choosing a director is very important. He must be well trained and knowledgeable as well as diplomatic and personable.

Under him should be an educational director, one who understands alcoholism and is able to impart this knowledge to others, articulately and objectively, particularly from the point of view of public health and sociology. He should have sufficient knowledge of the various approaches, the early signs of alcoholism, and what can be done for the alcoholic, to answer questions intelligently and to refer the individual questioner to the correct source for more information. The educational director should be able to carry on his work in the schools, introducing students to the subject of alcoholism and stimulating them to learn more about it and to do further research on the subject.

The information center should also include counselors trained in alcoholism and endowed with objectivity and a professional background in the psychological and sociological aspects of the disease. They should have some previous training with individual alcoholics to ensure that their counseling will benefit the patient and his family.

In this particular instance, recovered alcoholics can very often be of value. It is desirable, however, that they receive training about all disciplines and their application to the rehabilitation of the alcoholic.

In addition, the information center should have clerical help and telephone operators. These people should be understanding and patient and be able to answer questions on the telephone. They should be sufficiently personable to interest the questioner in further inquiries at the information center.

The Educational Program

Education on alcoholism must have a broad base in the formal educational system. Textbooks on health and hygiene should be reviewed periodically to make sure that information about alcoholism is up to date. The subject can be included in many courses in the secondary schools, such as zoology, physical education, psychology, and sex education. Audio-visual aids should be made available to teachers in all schools. In such courses as literature and art, the mores and drinking habits of various geographical areas and periods in history can be studied with a view to comparing civilizations and their drinking patterns.

UNIVERSITIES AND COLLEGES

In graduate schools the subject must be introduced in medicine and dentistry, nursing, law, social work, sociology, graduate education, and business administration. After graduation these students will find that alcoholism is a problem with which they must contend. Knowledge of the subject will help them not only in their personal affairs, but also in dealing with others.

A. *School of Medicine and Dentistry*

In the first year there is ample opportunity for introducing and discussing the subject in such courses as anatomy, physiology, biochemistry, and psychiatry. In the second year the subject can again be considered in psychiatry, physical diagnosis and history-taking, pathology, and neurology. In the third year preventive medicine and public health, medicine and psychiatry, and clinical work in the wards can introduce the student to actual patients suffering from alcoholism; and in the fourth year, in both inpatient and outpatient facilities, complete care of the alcoholic can be given over to the student. By the time he graduates he will have a working knowledge of the subject and its treatment. We are not recommending teaching about alcoholism as a subject per se, but rather teaching about it in all courses where it applies. Since it is a psychiatric, medical, sociological, and economic problem, it is best included in all those courses. A curriculum that has been drawn up by the American Medical Association is available to those interested.

B. *School of Law*

It is extremely important that the law student learn to differentiate between drunkenness and alcoholism. The responsibilities of law enforcement agencies to sick people and knowledge about committing individuals suffering from mental illness are all necessary for a complete education in this school.

C. *School of Social Work*

Understanding about alcoholism is essential for future social workers. They should become familiar with case-finding methods, methods of referral, the value of facilities like the hospital, the outpatient clinic, private physicians, the halfway house, rehabilitation centers, Alcoholics Anonymous, information centers, etc.

D. *School of Sociology*

Alcoholism is one of the sociological problems of our day. The extent and incidence of the disease, its communicability and prevalence, its impact on society, and methods of correction are all points that must be taught in schools of sociology.

E. *Business Administration*

Mental health is an asset in business. Dealing with the sick executive suffering from alcoholism, dealing with the sick employee suffering from alcoholism, the place of the medical department in industry, the place of Alcoholics Anonymous in the medical department in industry—all of these are subjects that can be taught in the school of business administration. Since alcoholism is one of the big problems that confront industry, it is to the advantage of the students in a school of business administration to learn as much about it as possible.

Labor groups are also studied in the school of business administration, and classes should be held for future union officers and stewards. The value of cooperation with management in handling the alcoholic worker, and the value of Alcoholics Anonymous in the union itself, can also be taught here.

Law Enforcement Agencies and Legislators

Members of law enforcement agencies on the municipal, county, state, and federal level should also receive education. It is important that they be able to differentiate between the acute alcoholic and other acute toxic conditions, that they learn that if there is any doubt medical help should be sought. The value of hospitalization versus incarceration should be stressed. Education for law enforcement agencies should also apply to judges, lawyers, and legislators. Since a tremendous percentage of domestic relations cases involve alcohol, it is important that judges and lawyers understand the effects of alcohol and can differentiate between the irresponsible drunken individual and the sick alcoholic. It is also important that lawyers learn the difference between the arbitrary legal level of drunkenness and actual drunkenness, and the varying tolerance in individuals for blood alcohol levels.

Legislators in particular should have as much education as possible about alcoholism in order to help bring about proper legal procedures and laws relating to drunkenness and alcoholism. It is essential that they learn that sickness requires treatment and not punishment.

The Clergy

Another group which requires considerable indoctrination on the subject of alcoholism is the clergy. Unfortunately, there are many clergymen who look upon alcoholism as a moral problem. A training course in psychology or psychiatric orientation would enable this group of intelligent people to understand more clearly the psychiatric and physical components of alcoholism and how they affect the individual. There is no doubt that their attitude of morality may to some extent help many of the people involved with this illness. On the other hand, it is not a moral problem alone, and the other factors should be studied in detail. Clergymen should understand both the nature of the problem and the individual alcoholic: the nature of alcohol as a drug, how it acts, and why the alcoholic drinks. He should understand very clearly the difference between the irresponsible drinker who can control his drinking and the sick, compulsive drinker who has no control over his drinking.

HOSPITAL ADMINISTRATORS
AND BOARD MEMBERS OF HOSPITALS

Too many in this group do not accept the tremendous responsibility that rests with them. These people must be taught that the alcoholic can be a patient who cooperates if treated properly. They must also explore the problem of segregation of alcoholics in a hospital. It is their duty to see to it that hospital personnel are properly educated, that nurses, nurses' aids, and orderlies know something about the problem, and that interns and residents are trained in the field of alcoholism. If they do this, the problem of the alcoholic will be no greater in their institutions than any other illness.

THE NURSING SCHOOL

The nursing school is very important to the problem of alcoholism. There should be complete courses on this subject. This is up to the hospital administrators and board members as well as the medical staff of each hospital. Training should be given in the training school. There should also be lectures and forums for graduates, and postgraduate training consisting of forums, lectures, and ward work, which should be given just as it is to others in the medical profession.

THE GOVERNMENT DEPARTMENTS

The department of health, mental hygiene, hospitals, education, social welfare, and labor, and all personnel attached to these departments should have some knowledge of the problem of alcoholism from a sociological as well as from a health viewpoint. It is important that these departments be kept independent of pressure groups, since this is a controversial and emotionally charged subject, and that they have sufficient consultation with experts in the field to keep their programs on as high a scientific level as possible.

Communications Personnel

The ignorance of press, radio, and TV personnel and newspaper and magazine writers on the subject of alcoholism is astounding. Of course, there are some who are very well-informed and whose works are outstanding. On the whole, however, communciations personnel seem to have a very poor understanding of alcoholism. They do not appear to know the difference between drunkenness and alcoholism. There is also a tendency for many of them to think of the alcoholic as a comical person, or that alcoholism is funny.

Nothing could be farther from the truth. Education of these people is extremely important so that the proper information can be given to the general public. Communications personnel are in a unique position to offer great service to these ill people, who need understanding. Before they can do it, however, they must understand something of the illness itself. Any educational program should include special courses for communcations people.

Other necessary components of a good program on alcoholism are hospital outpatient clinics, halfway houses, hostels, foster homes, rehabilitation centers, and state mental hospitals, all of which are described in more detail in other sections of this book.

Personnel in all facilities mentioned must be adequately trained. They must like and understand alcoholics. They must be objective about these people, and not sit in judgment on them. The personnel must include internists, general practitioners, psychiatrists, social workers, psychiatric social workers, psychologists, clerical help, health educators, sociologists. In addition, there must also be policemen for special areas, Alcoholics Anonymous members, lay people who have an understanding of the problem, volunteers of the proper personality and approach whose mere presence can help these people.

In addition to the facilities mentioned, any complete program must include research. This covers such vast territory that it is impossible to go into detail. But wherever a complete program is in existence, research studies should be made, whether on the prevalence of alcoholism in the particular area or the number of times the patients return to the clinic or whether there are more females than males in the alcoholic population, or on any other aspect of the problem. The more knowledge that we can gather, the greater will be our chance of meeting the challenge it represents.

CHAPTER 20

The Nurse

THE nurse is in a unique position to understand and help the patient suffering from alcoholism. Perhaps, by virtue of her training and because she is a woman, she has more compassion for sick people than anyone else in the professions.

Once she is graduated, the nurse has a choice of becoming a private duty nurse, a floor nurse working in an institution, a public health nurse, an industrial nurse, or of entering any one of a dozen branches of the nursing profession, where she may function efficiently and well. As a student nurse, however, she is exposed to many influences and one of these is the alcoholic patient. It is at this time that she can learn about the illness and the patient suffering from it.

As a student nurse she can be, to a great extent, a therapeutic agent. This function can continue when she has her RN and is taking care of such patients. There are many points that may be helpful to her under these circumstances, whether she becomes a private nurse, a floor nurse, an industrial nurse, or a public health nurse.

First, she must learn that she is dealing with a sick person who has an insidious disease that is very difficult to detect. The nurse must be extremely diplomatic in broaching this subject to laymen. This is particularly true for the public health nurse, who comes in contact with alcoholics in families where she is visiting, or with members of a family in which there is an alcoholic. The greatest subtlety must be used if the subject is not brought up by the alcoholic himself or by one of the members of the family, and the nurse must exert considerable objectivity in the discussion. She must always be sympathetic, and never sit in judgment on either the individual or the family with which the alcoholic is associated.

If a visiting nurse suspects alcoholism in one member of a family, she must be able to converse with the other members in order to verify her opinions. She must decide from their replies how reliable their information is. She must also be able to detect any defensive measures used to protect the sick person—by the family or by the patient himself. Very often discrepancies in the history received from the patient as compared with those of the family are an indication of the severity of the illness.

The visiting nurse must be convincing when she evaluates the alcoholic to his family and explains the seriousness of the disease. She must be able to discuss the addictive qualities of alcohol and how insidious the addiction can be. Without attempting to preach, she must be able to impart to them the importance of abstinence, and must do so without giving the impression that she is a blue-nose or a teetotaler. Her own emotional involvement with the problem of drinking must be set aside in the interests of the objectivity necessary in any illness. Where there is doubt expressed about the possibility of alcoholism, she must suggest a test of abstinence in such a manner that both the family and the individual concerned are willing to follow through just to prove the point for themselves. Asking the patient to abstain for one month as a method of determining whether or not he is dependent upon alcohol may be a very good test.

Since the criteria for alcoholism, discussed elsewhere in this book, must be known to the nurse, she can speak of loss of control. If this remark is challenged, a simple test is to investigate whether or not control is there. Any member of the family, and perhaps even the patient himself, could answer this question. Comparison with loss of control over an automobile is very often useful in illustrating to the layman the effect of alcohol; the removal of brakes, that is, controls, from an automobile increases the risk in driving the car.

The nurse should acquaint herself with the prevalence and epidemiology of alcoholism in such a way as to sound authoritative in her discussion and be able to convince the family that alcoholism is common enough to strike anyone.

The nurse must be particularly knowledgeable about the places offering help. Such recommendations as seeing the family physician, Alcoholics Anonymous, the clergy, or various social agencies must be part of the information the visiting nurse suggests when she detects alcoholism among her clients.

Above all, the nurse must have an optimistic attitude about the possibility of recovery. Her references to treatment must be positive, and she must be able to discuss the medical and psychiatric approaches to the disease adequately and objectively, much as she would discuss any disease, with no connotation of stigma in her remarks.

As a therapeutic agent the nurse can be of tremendous value. Her objective attitude and understanding must be accompanied by a constant awareness that the alcoholic is a sick person. She must appreciate the fact that he requires rest, assurance, and comfort. Very often these patients have a tremendous sense of remorse, guilt, and inadequacy, and it is up to the nurse whether on the hospital floor or in a home, to be patient and make him feel at ease. She should try to make him realize that he is not an evil person but a sick person, like any other patient under her care. Her attitude must not be one of fear or distrust. Frequently, bad behavior in an alcoholic patient in a hospital ward is more a manifestation of his resentment against the way he is being treated than it is a manifestation of the disease itself. All too often, nurses on hospital floors avoid the alcoholic, particularly in his acute stage, and this indicates rejection of such patients. Alcoholics have already been rejected by society, and they feel it more keenly when the same thing occurs with a professional person who, in their opinion, should know better.

The nurse must always be aware of the fact that withdrawing the patient from alcohol deprives him of his only means of getting comfort, the only medication he has found that gives him surcease from his suffering. This medication that is being withdrawn must then be replaced by kindness and interest on her part. The patient who suffers from alcoholism is frightened and unsure; she must give him assurance, confidence, and encouragement. There are times, of course, when the alcoholic patient is disagreeable, not because he is a mean person, but because he feels inferior and discriminated against. He wants to feel like anyone else, and he wants to assert himself, thinking that by such assertion he is convincing others. The nurse must understand this, and give him her sympathy and compassion.

In discussing the patient with the physician, the nurse must be able to describe his actions accurately and give the physician a complete report of his behavior and his attitudes. All this can be of great value to the physician for instituting and continuing treatment.

The nurse should never hesitate to engage the patient in conversation; she should encourage him to talk, for a good listener is a wonderful therapeutic agent. She must allow him to express himself freely and give vent to his resentments, his feelings, his inadequacies, his fears. In many instances the patient will confide things to a nurse that he will not or cannot tell his doctor. When the nurse relates these things to the doctor, he can often glean information that will be valuable in treating the patient.

The patient wants understanding and sympathy, not lectures, not harangues, and not preachments. He feels that people do not understand him or his suffering. Alcoholics, as a rule, are quite dependent people. They require someone upon whom they can lean, at least temporarily, until they can learn to stand on their own feet. The nurse represents such a rock to him, if her attitude is receptive.

Another function the nurse can serve is to help explain to the family the things she has learned about the alcoholic. What she herself has found will help the alcoholic, must be conveyed to the family so that they can carry on with her type of therapy after the patient leaves the hospital and comes home.

The nurse plays an extremely important role in the more serious cases during the hospitalization of the alcoholic patient. When delirium tremens or hallucinosis occur, her reassurance, her accepting attitude, and her motherliness can often help the patient to feel secure. While he is learning to get along without alcohol, she must make him stand on his own feet and get over his dependency on her. All this takes time and patience and learning, but these are the things that make the good nurse, whose allegiance to her profession is a source of pride, valuable in our society.

In addition, the nurse must never forget that she is also a citizen and a member of her community, and as such she must display the public spirit that helps the community to understand a disease like alcoholism. The nurse must take her place in community education on the subject. She must see that nurses' training schools and postgraduate courses include alcoholism in their curricula. She must acquaint herself with the various modalities of treatment and how they must be varied and tailored to the individual patient.

Intravenous treatment, with which she is familiar, will often be necessary for the alcoholic patient. Vitamins and minerals and various tranquilizing drugs must be administered. The nurse must also be aware of the danger of habit-forming drugs and of the danger of misleading advice, like tapering off, using barbiturates, and so on.

There is no need here to inform the nurse of the importance of the spiritual approach to this illness and how she can help to indoctrinate the patient with such values. The help of the nurse is also important to alleviate anxiety of the alcoholic patient about psychiatric treatment. She must be able to convince him of the importance and value of the psychiatric approach to his problem.

There are many organizations that disseminate information about alcoholism. The nurse should make it a point to become a member of these organizations so that she can carry on her work in the best possible way.

To most people a nurse is the personification of a ministering angel. She must practice her profession with this in mind. Her own life must be above reproach, and she herself must be careful about the use of alcohol. This does not mean that she must be a total abstainer, but she must be careful that she does not succumb to the illness.

The industrial nurse is in a position to be even more concerned about the problem of alcohol.[1] The alcoholic population in industry can have economic impact, and the industrial nurse has an additional responsibility in this area. The industrial nurse, personnel supervisors, management, union stewards, union officers, and in fact anyone engaged in industry must all cooperate in detecting alcoholism in a worker. Rumor, gossip, animosity, spite, misunderstanding, prejudice, and jealousy can all enter into comments about any individual in any organization; therefore, any information given about a fellow employee must be taken with extreme caution. Investigation of the employee must be done diplomatically and without embarrassment to either the employee or the employer. Here the union can be of great help, but understanding by all concerned is imperative before detection, proper evaluation, and proper disposition can be made of any particular case.

Industry employs about two million alcoholics. This repre-

---

[1] "Alcoholism in Industry"—M. A. Block. *American Association of Industrial Nurses' Journal*, April, 1959.

sents about 3 percent of all the job-holders in the country. The average working alcoholic usually loses two days per month more than an average nonalcoholic worker does. During a year the average alcoholic loses about twenty-two days from his work.

Absenteeism is one of the most common indications of alcoholism in an industrial worker. The industrial nurse is in a position to detect this, particularly when she examines her Monday morning absentee list. In following through and attempting to uncover these cases, she must be very diplomatic in ascertaining the reasons for absence. Among the signs she can look for are personality changes in the individual. Evidence of undue tensions or a change in working pace from the previous pattern may be indicative. Physical irregularities or temperamental outbursts where none appeared before may indicate trouble of this sort. Reports of unusual drinking behavior off the job should be investigated for accuracy. Growing domestic, financial, and community problems in an individual who previously did not have such problems may also indicate the beginning of alcoholism.

Certain physical manifestations of drinking, such as bloodshot eyes, flushed face, florid skin, carelessness in personal appearance, are not unusual, and the nurse must be aware of these in watching for the illness in employees.

Should she interview some of these patients, she must be sure that whatever information she gets is kept confidential. Her attitude toward the worker must be sympathetic. There must be apparent a desire to help the worker. Criticism, censure, scolding, and haranguing have never helped an alcoholic. Telling him to stop drinking is like telling an anxious person to stop worrying, and overlooks the fact that he does not drink because he likes it, but because he can't help it. Understanding the problem, the individual, and the illness is extremely necessary in handling these situations. Since it is a medical problem, it should be handled by medical personnel.

The nurse must be patient and give the worker an opportunity to tell her his troubles, and she must listen carefully and encourage him to seek help from the family physician, a clinic, or an individual the physician recommends. She may suggest Alcoholics Anonymous, or advise him to seek help from his clergyman. Above all, she must not sit in judgment or scold or threaten. This will not help. When there is any doubt, the patient should be referred to the medical department for further disposition of the case. But the nurse can do a tremendous job in helping alcoholics just by using the patience and understanding with which she was trained.

More about alcoholism in industry can be found in the chapter on Industry.

CHAPTER 21

The Clergy

PERHAPS no group can serve the alcoholic patient more effectively than the clergy. Respected from the day of his graduation from the divinity school, the clergyman, like the doctor and lawyer, enjoys the admiration and respect of his fellow men, whether he has earned them or not. Men in these professions carry a great responsibility. The clergyman, as a man of God, endowed with compassion, charity, mercy, and understanding of human beings and their frailties, is viewed with the greatest respect of all. It is to him that most people look for the love and understanding denied them by other people.

In the past, excessive drinking was considered a moral issue by many clergymen. They believed that alcoholism was a weakness of individual character, a sign of lack of moral fiber, and a failing of a human being to recognize right from wrong. Unfortunately, some clergymen still feel that way today. Most, however, have come to understand that alcoholism is an illness.

The clergyman, if he is to help the alcoholic must realize that he is not a pariah nor an immoral person, but simply one who has inadvertently become addicted to a drug that most people ingest without harm. The fact that he takes too much of it is not his choice. He is driven to it by his own discomfort. It is up to his clergyman to give him comfort and understanding, and to advise him. To sermonize and to criticize, to harangue and to lecture is of no avail, and will only drive the alcoholic patient away from his pastoral counselor. The clergyman must instead show faith in him as a human being and direct him to the right channels for help. If the clergyman has been trained for this work, he himself may act as counselor to the individual. If he is untrained, he must give the alcoholic the spiritual succor required and direct him to the proper sources for treatment.

Alcoholics Anonymous can be of great help to many alcoholic patients, but the clergyman must understand that the spiritual approach will not always work with all patients. First of all, an evaluation of the individual is necessary to determine whether there is an underlying condition that might account for this individual's alcoholism. Should there be something more complicated, helping him spiritually will be of little value if the other problems are ignored.

Many clergymen feel that kindness itself will help the alcoholic to stop drinking. Unfortunately, this is not true. There are some, of course, who will respond to this type of treatment, and because of kindness and acceptance from certain people, will cease drinking and try to assume the responsibilities of living. Many, however, are completely dependent people, and will accept the kindness and become even more dependent on the individual dispensing it. These patients must be encouraged to assume independence and responsibility. This cannot be achieved by giving them everything they would like to have.

Very often clergymen who are total abstainers and whose religious faith forbids them to drink have little patience with the alcoholic sufferer, especially if he is a parishioner who has violated the tenets of his church. This makes him a sinner and implies that further punishment is in order. To make the individual sinner feel more guilty does not help him to recover from his illness. It only drives him to further drinking, since this seems to be the only thing that will relieve his guilt. The clergyman's task is to make him see the error of meeting his problems in this way, not to add to his guilt by pointing out his sinfulness to him. Initially, his drinking may have been sinful in the eyes of his church; once he is addicted to the drug, however, drinking is no longer an act of sin but his only answer to the discomfort he feels—which in itself is punishment enough, compounded many times over.

Is it the duty of the clergyman to mete out punishment, or to condemn those who have sinned? Is it not his duty rather to help these individuals to health and stability through understanding and spiritual guidance, encouraging them to stop drinking not because it is a sin but because it is not the way to handle their feelings, since it represents only disaster and increased suffering.

To those clergymen who consider excessive drinking gluttony, it must be pointed out that once control has been lost, the individual is no longer a glutton but a slave to an addiction. At this stage he cannot be held morally responsible for continuing to drink. Compulsive drinking knows no denial. The suffering is too great.

The brochure of the Reverend John C. Ford [1] on the moral concept of alcoholism is very interesting. Other writings, such as those by Howard J. Clinebell, Jr., Ph.D., are exceptional in their approach to the treatment of alcoholism by the clergy.[2]

Religion plays an important part in the treatment of any disease. The faith of the patient is a factor that cannot be discounted in any illness. The patient's faith has a very definite effect on his physiology. The hope his faith gives him

[1] *Depth Psychology, Morality and Alcoholism,* John C. Ford, S.J., A.M., L.L.B., S.T.D. Weston College, Weston, Mass., 1951.
[2] *Understanding and Counseling the Alcoholic Through Religion and Psychology,* Howard J. Clinebell, Jr., Ph.D., Abingdon Press, New York and Nashville, 1956.

seems to help the physiological processes and builds greater resistance in his body. Often the patient who is sick and has no hope will succumb more rapidly than the one who has hope and a desire to live. It is no different for alcoholism. It is here that the clergyman can play his greatest role—to renew in the individual patient his faith and desire to live, to convince him that he is wanted and loved, and that there are people who care. After his lifetime of rejection, this is a difficult job. For many alcoholic patients the bottle has been the last refuge, the only comfort. It is with such patients that the clergyman can offer a ray of hope and be the agent to supply the incentive for the individual patient to go on to make the necessary battle for recovery.

The alcoholic patient has had lectures, scoldings, sermons, harangues, punishment, threats, and recriminations for years and years. When the clergyman approaches him, he expects more of the same. The understanding clergyman will not adopt this attitude but will assume instead an attitude of sympathy and understanding, and a desire to help. It appears obvious that this is the role of the clergyman. To be sure, there are many clergymen who do adopt the proper attitude and who have contributed enormously to the recovery of many alcoholics. But there are many clergymen who still feel that the alcoholic patient is a moral renegade, an irresponsible individual, a weakling who is unable to help himself and so has fallen by the wayside. Such advice as "Be a man," "Look what you are doing to your wife and children," and other guilt-producing suggestions have no place in the vocabulary of the clergyman who is to help the alcoholic. He must make the patient feel wanted and accepted. He must make him feel comfortable and convinced that the clergyman is there to help him. If the clergyman cannot provide this assurance, it would be better for him not to go near the alcoholic. Only if he can feel compassion and understanding and desire to help the alcoholic patient, can he help. He can in fact be of enormous aid in effecting a recovery.

CHAPTER 22

Young People and Drinking

NOT everyone who drinks becomes an alcoholic. There are those who would have us believe that a liking for alcoholic beverages assures eventual alcoholism. They insist that all drinking should be avoided. The consensus all over the world, however, is that drinking in moderation does no particular harm, and that people who drink excessively are ill. They are either suffering from a disease that renders them susceptible to the drug alcohol, or they rely on alcohol to help them meet the problems of living. In a further development alcohol is used as an escape from the realities of living. Since humans have always used alcohol, it is unlikely that the custom will be done away with, either by inspiring fear or by misrepresenting the facts. Prohibition does not seem to work. The greatest weapon against alcoholism is knowledge and recognition of the truth.

Sooner or later the question of whether or not to drink comes up in almost every home so every parent should know the basic facts about alcohol, where its dangers lie, who shouldn't drink at all, and how to recognize excessive drinking. It may be wise to discuss the problem in the home with young people.

The average young person in this country starts experimenting with drinking at about the age of fourteen. Recent studies in various parts of the United States indicated that it is at this age during the early high school years, that most people who eventually drink to any extent at all, started. There are exceptions: some people become accustomed to drinking at meal or during ceremonies at three or four; some do not drink any alcoholic beverages until they are eighteen or nineteen, or even later. The variation in drinking customs is tremendous.

Is the parent being old-fashioned if he feels that drinking is a problem? From the physician's viewpoint, not at all. Alcohol is a habit-forming drug, one that may lead to addiction. Unlike narcotics, however, alcohol in moderate amounts is socially acceptable in our culture, and herein lies some of its danger. Because it is so widely accepted and used, we tend to lose sight of the fact that for some people it is a dangerous drug.

The best way to teach our children about alcohol is by example. If the parents drink, their ability to use alcoholic beverages with discretion and control will go a long way toward determining the behavior of their children. If the parents do not drink, their reasons for refraining should be logical and reasonable, so that children will not become rebellious.

Knowledge about alcohol is the best safeguard against it. One of the first things both young people and parents should understand is just why people drink. An excellent book on this subject is *Young People and Drinking: The Use and Abuse of Beverage Alcohol,* by Dr. Arthur H. Cain, published by The John Day Company. Most often, in all probability, alcohol is used as a social lubricant, reducing shyness and inhibitions, making the world seem brighter, and relaxing nervous tension. Drinking for these purposes is generally considered respectable, although too often it results in the loss of the art of conversation and the capacity for quiet companionship.

The use of alcohol as a psychological crutch is a very different matter. The unhappy and insecure youth, often the product of bickering and conflict in the home, is unable to meet his problems with confidence. He seeks to escape from them, and finds that alcohol makes him more comfortable. Soon he begins to depend upon it as on a crutch, and here is a potential alcoholic. The over-indulged boy or girl who gets everything too easily, or the over-protected child, whose decisions are always made by dominating parents, who never gets a chance to make a mistake and so learn by experience, falls into the same pattern. When eventually he leaves such an over-protective environment he cannot cope with the problems of life, and in many instances seeks escape in alcohol.[1]

Another potential problem drinker is the child whose parents expect more of him than he can deliver. He is always frustrated, never feels any satisfaction, because what he does is never quite good enough. Drinking gives him, for the time being at least, the illusion of bigness and success.

If the present rate of alcoholism in our population continues, we can expect that about 6 per cent or one out of every fifteen of our young people, will become an alcoholic some time in the future unless something is done to prevent it. There are ways of preventing this illness, of helping the individual to grow up and meet his responsibilities without the escape into alcohol. Improvement of the home environment, understanding of the factors that contribute to alcoholism, suitable guidance and proper education can materially modify the estimate of a 6 per cent alcoholic population of the future. The young person's inherent characteristics may play a part in his susceptibility to alcoholism, but these can also be considerably modified. Personality characteristics are not as important as the total environment.

[1] "Could Your Child Become an Alcoholic?," M. A. Block. *This Week* Magazine, February 8, 1959.

Primary responsibility for education about alcohol rests in the home. Too many parents today expect the school to take over this responsibility. Parents should become acquainted with the early signs of alcoholism and the scientific facts about alcohol, and apply them not only to the education of their children but to themselves as well. If parents conduct themselves in an exemplary way and control their own emotional problems and behavior, the chances of their children having such problems are minimized.[2]

Children should be given a sense of confidence in the principles they are taught. They must be taught independence and the reasons for not conforming at all times. Withstanding conformity in some areas can give them stature, when such independence is accompanied by a feeling of confidence. Too often, children drink to conform to what other teen-agers are doing. Otherwise, they may feel self-conscious. They need to understand how independence and confidence about or nonconformity in drinking will give them stature in the eyes of their fellows.

There are times, of course, when children drink not as conformists but as nonconformists, because it makes them feel grown-up. They have a false idea of what constitutes being grown-up. If standards such as responsibility were associated with the term grown-up rather than superficial ones like drinking, this situation might be corrected. Insistence by parents on hurrying their children into adulthood, with formal parties for young teen-agers, cocktail parties before proms, kiddie cocktails, etc., encourage young people to imitate adults before they have gained the sense of responsibility that should accompany adulthood.

In the small percentage of young people who have trouble with their very first drink, there may be not only a psychological but a physiological basis for alcoholism. In fact, many physicians are of the opinion that there is something about a

[2] "How Teens Set The Stage for Alcoholism," M. A. Block and Fred V. Hein, *Today's Health,* June, 1962.

person's blood or glands or nervous structure that makes him become addicted to narcotics or alcohol. While most doctors think that addictions occur only after prolonged use, there are cases on record where a person shows signs of addiction with the very first drink. Such people must be extremely careful, because it is obviously unsafe for them to drink at all.

School teachers can be of tremendous help in confirming and reinforcing the principles taught at home. The teacher should help to develop a sense of responsibility in the children and teach them the value of self-discipline and respect for individual thinking, along with confidence in the reasons for such thinking. Independent thinking can be emphasized as a virtue. The history, traditions, and customs of drinking can make interesting teaching, but instructors must disclose the fallacies of many of these traditions. One of the common fallacies is that drinking is a manifestation of manliness.

As said before, surprisingly little is known about just how alcohol works in our bodies. As a drug, it can properly be placed among the anesthetics; for instance, ether. Contrary to the popular belief, its effect is that of a depressant. It gives the illusion of stimulation because it depresses the higher centers of thinking and judgment, and allows activity without control.

It is obvious that where judgment is poor and activity without a brake, harm can result. This is the condition that encourages fast driving, recklessness, the thoughtless deed that ruins too many young lives. Alcohol affects judgment whether the individual is an alcoholic or not; it therefore affects actions and even drinking itself. Parents may warn their children about such dangers, but unfortunately the individual doing the drinking cannot always ascertain when alcohol has affected his judgment and control.

The effects of alcohol on the body should be taught with as much scientific truth as we know; conflicting statements and half-truths should be avoided. Teachers should avoid frighten-

Young People and Drinking

ing students by talking about the lethal effects of alcohol, but they should explain in detail the early signs of trouble. Teachers should approach these subjects with objectivity; their own emotions must not be involved. Frequent meetings of teachers, parents, and youth leaders should be encouraged, and discussions on drinking should be part of their meetings, so that the principles of teaching and supervision coincide.

If a person never drinks alcohol, he can never become an alcoholic. The prohibition of alcohol, however, does not necessarily guarantee that it will not be used. Perhaps more of our young people learned to drink during Prohibition than at any other time. Rigid restraint can lead to earlier experimentation by youngsters; children are always attracted to the forbidden.

I think we all recognize that alcohol occupies far too important a place in our cultural background and in our society. Therefore the necessity for alcohol in our culture should be minimized. However, the changing patterns of drinking in our society should be realistically explained. Students must be taught to recognize the early signs of using alcohol as an escape mechanism in people who find the problem of living too difficult to face realistically. The reasons for avoiding such artificial escape must be carefully detailed. Half-truths or inaccuracies must be avoided, since this may lead to a loss of confidence when correct facts are later learned.

The use of alcohol in moderate amounts as an aperitif or as part of a meal has long been recognized as a social amenity, but when it us used to escape from reality or as a drug to relieve tension or anxiety, or in amounts sufficient to produce drunkenness or reduce or impair judgment, then its use has exceeded propriety and should not be tolerated socially.

Standards must be reliable for children. The ability to hold one's liquor is often the accomplishment of an individual who can do nothing else well; such excessive drinking, young people must learn, is the mark of inferiority feelings, and the more this fact is denied, the more accurate is the diagnosis. The knowledge that alcohol is potentially dangerous can keep children from falling prey to the excess that destroys so many lives today.

Respect for abstinence in others must be taught to all young people. Those who do not drink have a right to their abstinence without appearing inadequate. Refusal to drink is a matter of free choice and is to be respected.[3]

Alcoholism is a very insidious illness that is difficult to detect in its early stages. The line of demarcation between the early alcoholic and the heavy social drinker is not a sharp one; the victim slips from heavy social drinking into the early stage of alcoholism without noticing too much change. That is why it is so important that the early signs be recognized.

The beginning of every disease is usually mild and difficult to differentiate from health. The earlier we can detect it and institute treatment, the better is the chance of recovery. Young people assume that they are immune to diseases that usually occur among middle-aged and older people. It is therefore important that they learn enough about the agents with which they deal to know the risks involved, whether the agent be an automobile, where safety and judgment must be taught, or the use of alcohol, where the same safety and the same judgment must be exerted as much or even more.

Many feel that the disease concept of alcoholism offers the victim an alibi. This, I fear, is a misunderstanding of the severity of the disease itself. Social irresponsibility can hardly be considered a normal state of affairs. When a person uses a disease as an alibi to injure himself, it only demonstrates how much more ill he is than those with the same affliction who do not use the alibi. A small percentage of people are completely dependent and will require constant care. It is these who may use the disease concept as an alibi. To some extent, such inadequacy may be attributed to lack of proper education early in life, which could help reduce the number

[3] "Teen Age Drinking: Whose Responsibility?," M. A. Block, *Today's Health*, May, 1961.

of these inadequate individuals and help them to adjust to their limitations.

We cannot emphasize too strongly the need for a sound physical body, which helps maintain a healthy mind. However, a healthy body in itself will not prevent alcoholism. There are times when ideals of physical efficiency are carried too far; too much emphasis is placed on the muscles rather than the proper mental approach to living. Physical fitness is desirable, but mental fitness and emotional maturity are no less desirable.

If a young person finds himself in difficulty as the result of drinking, or begins to feel that alcohol is occupying too important a place in his life, or if his parents feel that this is the fact, there are many sources to which he may go for help. The medical profession, the church, the school, alcoholism information centers, and other social agencies are always willing to provide information and aid. Unfortunately, many individuals too often delay a request for such help, and too many parents hope that scolding and remonstrations will do the job.

Some of the early underlying symptoms of emotional problems in children that may eventually lead to alcohol as a method of escape should be watched for in any child. Such symptoms as daydreaming, withdrawal from activity with other children, inability to face the ordinary problems of life, guilts and anxieties and worries about school or friends or grades, bashfulness, self-consciousness, and other manifestations of inadequacy or inferiority should be noted.

These symptoms can be brought on by frustrations, inability to meet goals set by parents, rejection by parents or by parents who do not meet the emotional needs of the child, lack of love and understanding of the child, and quarreling between the parents themselves, any of which gives children a sense of insecurity or a feeling of not belonging. This may lead to drinking, especially when the young person finds that it obliterates these feelings. Drinking, the desire to drink more often when confronted with problems, or the necessity to drink before any problem arises can all be manifestations of alcoholism.

There are other signs that indicate insecurity, for instance, stuttering, stammering, and embarrassment. This does not mean that these symptoms in a child will inevitably lead to alcoholism, but, as a mental health prophylactic, all such manifestations should be observed early and subjected to treatment. They all indicate emotional instability that *could* lead to alcohol for relief, and eventually to dependence on it. After all, alcoholism is but one segment of a tremendous mental health problem, and we have no way yet of predicting who will or will not become alcoholic.

Parents and teachers must often walk a fine tightrope in discerning how far to go in considering these problems. Sometimes too much concern and worry on the part of parents can communicate itself to the child and give him a feeling of insecurity. Over-concern indicates an insecurity in the parent, a lack of confidence in himself to handle the problem.

It is impossible for a parent to prepare a child for all of life's contingencies. He can only lay down the principles and by example teach the child how to live a mature and well-adjusted life. If he can do this, the child will learn to use these principles when the need arises.

Children who do drink should learn to recognize early signs of trouble. Any feeling of dizziness, undue exhilaration or unusual activity, depression, silence, lethargy, sleepiness, violent swings of emotion, or carelessness may be an early sign of excessive drinking or dependence on alcohol. Ignoring the suggestion that there has been too much drinking or resenting criticism of drinking may also indicate that there is trouble ahead with alcohol.

Later on, some of the early signs can be frequent drinking bouts, drinking alone, early morning drinking, interference with work or loss of time from studies—these are the more serious signs of real alcoholism. Drinking too much or getting drunk when one did not intend to, which may occur early in the condition, is extremely important, as is sneaking drinks. All of these signs must be taught so that young people will recognize this problem in themselves and others.

I think it is generally recognized that drinking should be an exclusively adult activity. This does not mean that children who drink in their homes with their parents will necessarily become alcoholic. Sometimes this initiation into drinking customs, especially with parents who set a good example, will in no way harm these children. There are many intelligent and emotionally mature individuals who do share alcoholic drinks with their children, and no harm seems to come of it. It may be ceremonial drinking or drinking with meals, which is done customarily in many homes. As a matter of fact, in the homes where drinks are taken regularly with meals we see very little alcoholism, since children look upon such drinking as part of their home life; they rarely indulge in alcohol to excess later in life. This is true, also, of children who drink moderately with their parents, and where drunken behavior is never exhibited. It is of special importance, therefore, that parents never drink excessively.

There is no optimum age for children to drink if it is done at home. This is a matter of the atmosphere in the home and how drinking is regarded there. Only if it is done with the express purpose of achieving a state of exhilaration or reduced inhibition is there danger in this type of drinking. Whether the drinking is beer or wine or hard liquor seems to have no bearing on the possibility of the individual developing alcoholism. All beverages with alcohol represent the same risk to the kind of individual who may become an alcoholic.

The custom of feeding children "kiddy cocktails" is but one example of parents who are pushing their children into adult customs far before they are prepared to accept the responsibilities of adulthood. Children are not small adults, and it is a mistake, in my opinion, to encourage a child to imitate an adult in his actions. There are certain aspects of an adult's life to which a child is introduced only when he is ready for such activity, and only when he has learned the responsibilities that accompany these privileges is the child ready for them.

Exposure to movies and television greatly influence a child's attitude. Allusions to the need for a drink on television or in movies often give the impression that a drink answers a need in time of crisis. This is exactly the type of escape idea I feel it is important to avoid with children. If drinking is to be shown on the screen or on television, it should be done exactly as it is in the homes where it creates no problem. This would include having an aperitif or drinking as a part of a meal, but never as a necessity or as a separate social function dedicated only to drinking.

The general trend in our culture in the last several years is to overemphasize drinking. The tolerance in this country for drunken behavior and the social pressure for drinking are perhaps the two greatest factors that have led to this overemphasis on drinking. Much of our advertising suggests that drinking is glamorous, and gives the idea that alcohol is of greater importance in our lives than its qualities justify. I am sure the manufacturers of alcoholic beverages have no intention whatever of seeing an increase in alcoholism if they can help it. However, their advertising does generally give the idea that drinking enhances life and its pleasures, without indicating in that same advertising that there are a large number of people who should not drink.

The important fact for children to learn is that abstinence should not affect them socially, that alcohol is not a necessity of life, that some people may drink if they wish, but others would be harmed by it. If we could teach people that the real sophisticate never drinks excessively and that to do so means social ostracism, we would find less and less alcoholism. We must discourage tolerance of drunken behavior and regard abstinence more as a virtue than a peculiarity. For those whose drinking has an adverse effect on them, abstinence should be mandatory and respected.

Respect for law and order and for parental authority must be stressed, but the atmosphere of the home is extremely important. Family living should be more attractive. Although education alone will not prevent all alcoholism, it can help to do so if there is close cooperation between home and school. The formal elements of teaching can be handled in the schools, but behavior problems are best dealt with at home.

CHAPTER 23

The Spouse of the Alcoholic

ONE of the most important factors, if not the most important factor, in the life of the alcoholic patient is the spouse. This may be true not only in the etiology of alcoholism but in the recovery from it as well. Very few spouses of alcoholics have any appreciation of the importance of their role. Few indeed have any appreciation of the part they may play in bringing about the condition. Far too many fail to understand that the illness of their spouses is also an illness of the family, from which they cannot divorce themselves as participants. It has been said that to be the spouse of an alcoholic requires a certain type of personality. Certainly to remain the spouse of an alcoholic does require some unusual characteristics. Just as there are many kinds of alcoholics, so are there many kinds of spouses of alcoholics, but each in his own way is part of the illness.

There is very often a tremendous difference between the reasons for men marrying certain women and women marrying certain men. Among these differences is the attitude of each toward the prospective spouse. As a rule, the man marries the woman to whom he is attracted and with whom he has much in common, and he expects that the woman will remain the way she is at the time of marriage. Since it is the man who chooses the woman, he looks for the characteristics that to him seems desirable.

Women, on the other hand, do not always have such a choice, and unfortunately in many instances must wait for the man to ask them to marry. They depend to a large extent upon being sought. Their attitude toward marriage is that they do not expect or desire the characteristics of the man they marry to remain unchanged. They have usually married not the man they prefer over all the men they know, but the man they prefer to the other men who have proposed. They too often plan, after marriage, to mold their husbands according to the pattern and the characteristics they would like.

The objectives of the women who wish to change their husbands need not be carried out in a dominant or overbearing manner. Very often they are achieved only by long-term, kind, but steady suggestion. This can be done with love and as an act of dependence that actually masks a very aggressive personality. The very kindness, considerateness, and love that many of these women show are merely means of making the men depend on them enough to bring about the changes that were their original objectives. This molding of the individual by his spouse will in many cases make the male partner extremely dependent. This lack of independence and what might be called emasculation can even lead to excessive drinking, to avoid facing the realization that he has lost his male independence. Failure on the part of the woman to change the characteristics of her spouse, which means that the man insists on maintaining his independence, will often lead to a hostility sometimes so great, with the resultant frustration so devastating, that many times the woman herself may resort to alcohol. All these characteristics must be considered in dealing with the interpersonal relationship between spouses where a case of alcoholism is being considered.

The recognition of the spouse's role is so widespread now that Alcoholics Anonymous has formed a group made up of the spouses of alcoholics, known as Al-Anon (see Chapter 12). These people meet for the express purpose of understanding more clearly both the illness that afflicts their husbands and wives and for understanding themselves. It has proved very effective, for they learn that their spouses' drinking problems result from disease rather than from purposeful misbehavior. This understanding is often very helpful to the patient involved.

All too often the hostility that has been generated over the years has become so great that the so-called normal spouse resents any action at all on the part of the alcoholic, even beginning to think that the alcoholic is drinking purposely in order to annoy him or her, or to make his or her life miserable. It is not until they are properly indoctrinated that the spouses of alcoholics begin to see that they must help if there is to be any hope of rehabilitation for their sick mates. While Al-Anon is based upon the principles of Alcoholics Anonymous, and is a spiritual approach to helping the sick alcoholic in the family, it also teaches its members to live in this atmosphere and to understand that the sick mate is not deliberately annoying the rest of the family. It teaches that he is driven by a compulsion to drink, in most cases to relieve himself of feelings that make him miserably uncomfortable.

In treating alcoholics, medically or psychiatrically, it is extremely important that the spouse of the patient be interviewed, perhaps more than once, depending on the relationship between the two. It is surprising to find how much better a relationship can be established once the healthier member of the couple begins to understand the sickness that is affecting his or her spouse.

Perhaps the most common complaint that physicians hear from families of alcoholics is that the member is extremely ill, extremely difficult to deal with, and absolutely refuses to seek help for his illness from any source. In these cases the physician is often asked what can be done to put the individual under medical care, since he refuses to see a doctor or go into a hospital. My advice has been that the spouse of the alcoholic should always go to see the physician if the patient himself will not. It is surprising how many spouses, once they learn about the illness and do seek consultation with the family physician or with the specialist, succeed after several sessions of their own, in getting the patient himself to come for treatment. This is probably because the spouse who does seek such consultation begins to understand the disease and develop a new tolerance for the sick mate. As a result, the atmosphere in the home is so changed that the patient begins to feel less rejected and better understood, and after several weeks is much more susceptible to suggestion. Even though he or she may refuse to seek help for a long time, the very change in the spouse's attitude will often produce good results.

In two instances in the past five years I have been able to effect complete recoveries in an alcoholic without ever seeing the patient himself, by working completely through the spouse. In these two cases, the wives of the alcoholics were such intelligent people that it was possible to carry on a type of therapy that was conveyed to the patient through the wives' actions, attitudes, understanding, and care, without going into the psychiatric details of the patients' condition. Such wives have been able, in time, to induce their husbands to abstain from drinking alcohol at all.

In some cases, where the alcoholic patient is so severely ill that the entire family is disrupted, it is often necessary to treat the spouse simply to maintain an atmosphere in the home that will not affect the children too severely, even though the alcoholic patient does not have an immediate recovery.

In many instances we find that an overbearing or dominant wife may produce an alcoholic husband, who uses his drinking as an escape from such domination. In other cases, we may find that a wife cannot tolerate her husband's personality or actions, and she too uses alcohol as an escape from this unhappy environment. All too often, spouses of alcoholics are completely unaware of the effect they have upon their mates, and careful investigation and explanation will produce changes in those individuals who actually love their spouses and quite inadvertently have caused them to drink excessively. With proper indoctrination and understanding, many such spouses will change their ways, the relationship will improve, and excellent results can be achieved.

Too frequently, when suggestions are made that the spouse of the alcoholic come in for consultation, we get the response, "I am not the one who is sick—he is"; or "she is," as the case may be. A defense like this reveals a very immature attitude and a hostility between man and wife that may be at the bottom of the excessive drinking of the less stable personality.

Often, too, we find a wife whose husband has been alcoholic for a long time assuming a holier-than-thou attitude, and even though the husband eventually stops drinking and becomes exemplary in his behavior, she can find no forgiveness in her heart for him. This type of power wielded over a dependent individual by refusing forgiveness for past transgressions, as she looks upon them, does not improve the relationship and only maintains a kind of cowed behavior on the part of the remorseful husband, which eventually leads him to drink again.

Other factors enter into the relationship between the alcoholic husband and the wife. All too often the wife of an alcoholic has a martyr complex, and she enjoys the so-called nobility of her position. Her friends and acquaintances continually compliment her nobility and stoicism in maintaining a home with an alcoholic husband. She has the sympathy, understanding and compassion of all these friends, and she fancies herself one whe has devoted her life and sacrificed everything in order to live with the alcoholic husband. In many such instances, when a recovery is finally effected for the patient, the same friends and acquaintances, instead of looking upon the wife as a noble person, begin to comment on the husband's great improvement in character, in strength of will, and in his remarkable fortitude in bringing about his own recovery. The wife is forgotten, her recent nobility is no longer a source of comment, and her martyrdom is a thing of the past. I have heard such wives, after they have lost the attention they enjoyed previously, say that they wished their husbands would go back to drinking; they could again be martyrs. Characteristics like these in spouses of alcoholic husbands are not unusual. They are often present, too, in husbands of alcoholic wives, with the same result. Treatment of the spouses in these cases is of the utmost importance in bringing about a satisfactory relationship after recovery.

Another type of spouse is the one who refuses to stop drinking as a means of helping his or her alcoholic mate. "I am not the sick one. Why should I give it up?" is a rather common statement, particularly when there is hostility between the two, even though they are advised that such abstinence may be only temporary until the mate has become accustomed to going without drinking. Actually, of course, there is no real reason why the so-called healthy mate should abstain. The alcoholic must learn to abstain in a world where others drink, much as the diabetic must learn to live in a world where others eat everything that is denied to him. However, in the early stages of treatment, it is sometimes very helpful to the alcoholic patient not to have his spouse drink. When this request is refused, I often suspect that there may be a problem with the spouse as well as the alcoholic. A suggestion to this effect often elicits considerable indignation, but when it is pointed out that refusal to maintain abstinence at least for a while, is an indication of need for alcohol, it causes a somewhat rude awakening. The necessity of a drink is very often the precursor of problem drinking and alcoholism.

The spouse with an alcoholic mate has a responsibility to the rest of the family as well as to the patient himself. Children very often misunderstand the alcoholic parent, and the healthy parent must do everything in his power to explain to the children the condition that afflicts the sick parent. Children in their teens, particularly, are often ashamed of the alcoholic parent, and attribute his drinking to misbehavior rather than to illness. If properly educated about the results of excessive alcohol intake and the disease involved, children will often change their attitude toward the alcoholic parent. Their understanding and sympathy will often benefit the sick parent.

An organization known as Al-a-Teen is also affiliated with Alcoholics Anonymous. Unfortunately, however, too many of these Al-a-Teen youngsters develop a seriousness about their positions in the family that makes them old before their time. Many have taken the responsibility of caring for their parents long before they are prepared to do so, and it is unfair to saddle a youngster with such responsibilities so early in life. But understanding alcoholism is very helpful to these youngsters, and they feel less ashamed about the sick parent. In this sense the fellowship is of great value. Its basis in faith and a spiritual approach helps the young person to come through this trying period.

Any chronic, serious illness would be met with a tremendous amount of patience by spouses of the victims. But with alcoholism they soon lose patience. Furthermore, a surprising number of such spouses do not wish their sick wives or husbands to abstain completely. "I want him to drink the way I do. I don't want him to stop drinking altogether, but I see no reason why he should not drink and then stop whenever he should" is commonly heard. Since they themselves have no difficulty controlling their drinking, they cannot understand why their sick husbands or wives cannot do the same. They attribute the problem to weakness or purposeful misbehavior, and refuse to believe that their mates are sick. Convincing them is almost as difficult in many of these cases as convincing the alcoholic himself. As much patience must be taken with them as with the patient, and very often they may require as much consultation with the therapist as the patient himself.

The understanding of the spouse cannot be underestimated. It is perhaps the single greatest factor in helping the alcoholic to recover. There is no more difficult case to treat than the alcoholic who has no spouse or family to whom to appeal. The lone alcoholic is the most difficult case in the world to rehabilitate.

Another excellent function of the spouse is to administer a deterrent drug. Very often deterrent drugs are of extreme value, as explained in a previous chapter. The temptation to drink on certain occasions or under certain stressful situations is so great that very often the patient will subconsciously forget or completely neglect to take his drug. But with the spouse present to remind him and see that he does it, many a patient can be helped over this hump, and avoid a slip. To make sure that the patient takes these drugs as he should, it is of tremendous value to have the spouse administer such drugs.

The spouse can very often act as an intermediary between the therapist and the patient, who will often express things to his spouse that he will not tell his therapist, and the spouse can pass on the information to the therapist. On many occasions the patient may become discouraged, or may feel that therapy is no longer necessary, since he has stopped drinking, and here also the spouse can play a very important part.

Most patients who have remained abstinent for a reasonable length of time feel that treatment is no longer required, since they have the problem solved. This usually happens long before the therapist feels that such a stage has been reached, and the wife or husband, given adequate explanation can help convince the patient to continue. Abstinence alone is not enough. The individual must continue with treatment until he is happy in his abstinence, and until he has accepted the fact that alcohol is no longer for him. This type of acceptance is the only goal that will prove successful, for only then is drinking no longer a problem. The acceptance, however, must be on an emotional level, not an intellectual level, for much as most of us would like to believe that we are controlled by our intellects, in fact most of us are controlled by our emotions.

The spouse plays an extremely important part in encouraging the patient to remain abstinent. In many instances the alcoholic patient has a tremendous sense of inadequacy and dependence. By encouraging him or her, by inflating the ego when necessary, by giving approval to achievements, the spouse represents to the sick person a continuous source of reassurance, a pillar on which he can lean until he has learned to stand on his own feet. In many instances, the spouse can be the therapy itself.

CHAPTER 24

Mass Media and Communications

THERE used to be a character in practically every locality known as the village idiot. This person was imitated by comedians on the stage, laughed at by people his own age and by children, mocked in the streets, and generally held up to ridicule. The village idiot has practically disappeared from the American scene. The disappearance took place when it was recognized that this poor character—spastic, drooling, grimacing, and somewhat repulsive—was a very sick person suffering from what is now known as cerebral palsy.

A counterpart of the village idiot today is the drunk, or the alcoholic. He, too, is imitated by comedians on the stage, laughed at, ridiculed, and made much of as a subject of humorous discussion.

It is not unusual for those who do not understand to make fun of certain situations. Very often this is done as a defense against their own fears of the particular condition. It is strange how many people think that an intoxicated person, staggering from too much alcohol, is a comical sight. Little do they realize what a sad individual he is, how ill he is, and how impossible it is for him to handle himself in his circumstances. There is nothing funny about alcoholism. Ask any alcoholic or his family. Alcoholism is a tragic condition, which should excite the sympathy and understanding of the beholder rather than his scorn or ridicule.

To some extent responsibility for the persistence of this idea lies with newspaper reporters. When newspaper reporters are sent out to hear discussions on alcoholism or to interview those interested in the problem, we find that it is the young, inexperienced reporters who are usually assigned to the task. Apparently this is because the subject is not considered important enough for the more experienced and understanding newspapermen. Very often, the reports are given a humorous twist, usually because the young reporters do not understand the seriousness of the problem, and because so often they are defensive in their reaction toward the alcoholic. Fear of the condition in themselves, either at the time or for the future, prompts them to make light of the entire subject.

Of course, this is not true of all newspaper reporters. There are many who, having been educated sufficiently, understand the seriousness of the illness and the tragedy it manifests. All too many, however, are willing to consider the matter very lightly and to treat it humorously. Little thought is given to the effect of their attitudes on the public. Even less thought is given to the alcoholic himself and to his family, to whom the illness represents not only a problem, but a tragedy.

Radio and television announcers and interviewers very often have the same problem. If they are uninformed, they often make humorous allusions to the subject or to the individuals involved. There is no doubt that the reason is the same as that of the newspapermen who find an intoxicated alcoholic funny. It has been said often that there is some humor in all tragedy, and many jokes are told about alcoholics and drunks, particularly by comedians on the stage. This type of humor is declining with the growing understanding of alcoholism. Whereas in the early part of the century practically every comedian on the stage either imitated a drunk or alluded to him, today we see this only in rare instances. Even on television it has become less popular as a characterization because more writers and actors are coming to understand the seriousness of alcoholism as an illness and the tragedy it brings about.

Why do so many interviewers who discuss alcoholism on radio or television usually allude to their own patterns of drinking and attempt to have the speaker interpret the difference between their drinking patterns and alcoholism? There is tremendous consciousness now on the part of many of these people that their drinking patterns may be becoming pathological, and there is often justification for this fear. The difference between heavy social drinking and alcoholism is not a sharp line that can be easily determined. It is a hazy area, where one slips from social drinking into alcoholism without being aware of it. In some cases it is almost impossible to tell whether the individual is still a social drinker or has already become an alcoholic in the early stages. To try to pinpoint it at this stage is, therefore, somewhat risky. Nevertheless, many interviewers will try to elicit this specific information from the person whom they are interviewing. The discussion cannot be objective and this maneuver only points up the fears of the interviewer that his drinking may be getting out of hand.

As has already been stated, alcoholism is a very complicated problem from the viewpoint of both the individual and society. It represents not only an illness of the individual but a public health problem as well. Would it not be wiser, then, for mass media reporting on the subject to have those who do the interviewing or write the reports learn something about the illness beforehand? In those instances where a reporter or an interviewer has been interested enough to do so, we have found that the conversation is much more intelligent, there has been much more understanding between the individuals involved, and the resulting reports are much more clearly presented, much more educational, and much more understandable for the readers and listeners.

Just as the village idiot disappeared from the American scene when his pathological condition was better understood by everyone, so the drunk will also disappear from the American scene as an object of ridicule, and the seriousness of his condition will be understood by all who witness it. This does not mean that all the humor of any situation msut be removed. Humor is a necessary part of our existence, and even the most serious situations have their humorous points, but there is a difference between humor and ridicule. Intelligent people enjoy humor, and no matter what the subject or its seriousness are willing to appreciate its humorous aspects. To ridicule an individual who cannot be held responsible and who has no control over his situation is both unfair and a manifestation of ignorance. If all of the mass media used for communication were aware of this and the individuals involved were sufficiently informed, the stigma attached to the poor alcoholic would be more easily removed, and his chances of getting help would be much enhanced. He himself would be more likely to seek help were the condition not so stigmatized.

There is no doubt that those in charge of these mass media, when they understand and appreciate the seriousness of the situation, are willing to help. It is only a question of their being made aware of alcoholism as a disease and as a public health problem afflicting so many. It is necessary, however, to change the attitude of the younger and less informed individuals in their fields. A change in attitude would redound to the credit of the media and to the benefit of a tremendous number of ill people.

CHAPTER 25

Lawyers and Alcoholism

THE LEGAL profession has long been interested in public health problems. Alcoholism is one of the most important of such problems, one with which the law is necessarily involved. Not only is the behavior of the alcoholic very often antisocial and sometimes in violation of the law, but the differentiation between the sick alcoholic and the irresponsible social drinker is one with which the law is particlularly concerned.

The legal profession should interest itself in the education of its members about the various types of alcoholics and how they should be regarded from the legal viewpoint. Since alcoholism is but one of the addictive illnesses, it might be of benefit if each legal society were to have a committee on alcoholism and addictions. This committee could bring these matters to the attention of all members of the profession and thus they could have a working knowledge of these illnesses in relation to the law.

The Association of Municipal Judges, an organization that originated in the west, has been of inestimable value in bringing to the attention of the municipal courts the importance of regarding alcoholism as an illness rather than a violation of the law. It has been of tremendous help in seeing that people brought before the courts for drunken behavior, when they are alcoholic, are treated as sick people rather than punished because of their illness. Many municipal judges have become aware of the ill people standing before them, and have instituted treatment for them rather than punishing them.

Because the inebriate standing before the judge, having been arrested for public intoxication, so often has no resources, it is often up to the judge himself to ascertain whether or not the individual is ill or misbehaving. In those communities where facilities are available for differential diagnoses, treatment, and rehabilitation, they can be referred to these various facilities by the judge. All too often, however, it is up to the judge to make up his mind about the arrested individual right on the spot. Careful questioning can ascertain for him whether or not the person whom he is about to sentence should be punished or should be treated. Only a working knowledge of the illness will help him in making this decision. Properly, he should have the help of adequately trained professionals.

As is true in many cases when the individual has been before the court on many occasions, there is a tendency on the part of the judge to sentence him to incarceration as a means of calling his attention to the fact that he must respond in the way expected of him. Such incarceration, however, is of very litle value, since the individual, if he is an alcoholic, has not become intoxicated because he chose to do so. Very often he did so only because he started to drink and could not control his drinking after that. The judge's understanding of this will help him to decide what disposition to make of that particular case. If the individual is incarcerated, the least that can be done for him if alcoholism is suspected, is that he be put on some rehabilitative program while in jail. Not to do so is to waste the taxpayers' money and the time spent in incarceration.

Another interesting problem that often comes before the

court is that of the drunken driver. There is no doubt that the individual who can control his drinking and does not do so is irresponsible and should be punished. However, if the person is an alcoholic and unaware of the fact that he has lost control of his drinking, no amount of punishment will help him. There have been many accidents as a result of illnesses from which drivers suffer, but there is a reluctance, however, on the part of judges to punish people who have had strokes, heart attacks, diabetic incidents, or fainting spells, even when these illnesses were the cause of the accidents. There is, rather, a sympathetic attitude toward the victim of the illness, and he is admonished to take care of himself and his health so that risk of recurrence of the incident will be minimized. Why cannot this same attitude obtain with the sick alcoholic? It is because most people believe that he would only go out and repeat the drinking episode and again endanger the lives of others as well as his own life.

When a driver has been adjudged drunk and his license is revoked, he is considered to have been punished because the privilege of driving has been rescinded. However, many courts have held that the driver's license is no longer a privilege but a right, since the livelihood of so many drivers depends on their having automobile transportation. As a result of this new attitude, many judges hesitate to deprive a driver of his license for fear that he will be unable to work and support his family, and thereby become a public charge. As a matter of fact, many drivers, it appears, value their driver's license more than they do their lives. In some places where driver's licenses are revoked after three arrests for drunken driving it has been found that two arrests cause the individual to stop drinking rather than risk losing his license. A suggested procedure for handling the problem of the diagnosed alcoholic and his driving license is discussed in the chapter entitled "Alcoholism and the Law."

The laws of the various states regarding alcoholism are so diverse that it would be impossible to list them all. A law, which could become uniform for all states, is one that was drawn up by the Committee on Alcoholism and the Legal Department of the American Medical Association. It contains all the essentials that would allow for civil commitment of alcoholics so that treatment could be instituted. This is also described in the chapter on Alcoholism and the Law.

Many individual lawyers have recognized the importance of the relationship between alcoholism and the law.

The legal profession has a distinct responsibility to bend its best efforts toward producing a climate for sick alcoholics that will be conducive to their rehabilitation. To condone the present method of punishing such individuals rather than treating them is to waste not only human manpower, but also a great deal of the taxpayer's money in a revolving door recidivist type of punishment that consumes much of the court's time, and benefits no one. Were the legal profession to apply its knowledge and energies toward correcting this situation, a great service could be rendered not only to the individuals involved, but to the public at large.

CHAPTER 26

The Social Worker and Alcoholism

THE SOCIAL worker, professionally trained, has become one of the important members of the professional population of our civilization. It would be presumptuous to attempt to give in one short chapter the essential details of the training and function of the professional social worker. In the problem of alcoholism the social worker plays a tremendous role, not only as a case-finder, but also as a counselor.

Unfortunately, sufficient time is not given to the problem of alcoholism in the training of social workers. Even with training, which is excellent for the most part, social workers are usually so overworked that they are often unable to see details that would indicate the possibilities of alcoholism in a family. As most welfare departments are short-handed, it is almost impossible for the staffs to keep up with the case load imposed on them. They must of necessity therefore limit their work to the bare essentials of clothing, housing, and food that so many of their clients require. They have so many clients to interview and visit that it is almost impossible to get the detailed and accurate information necessary to uncover incipient cases of alcoholism in families under their care.

Because of the stigma attached to the illness, there is a tendency on the part of welfare clients, and even those who do not require welfare, to cover up the excessive drinking of members of their family who require the help of social workers. The worker must practically detect the individuals in the act of drinking excessively before they can be sure of it. Under these circumstances, the situation may be reported to superiors, and help can be offered the individual who is suspected of being sick. There is no way of forcing these people to accept help, and out of fairness to the rest of the family the social worker will often be forced to accept their explanation that the drinking is not excessive, or is at least only temporary.

Alcoholic welfare clients who go through the routine revolving-door procedures, in the hospital and out, drying out and again getting drunk, will often cause the welfare department to pay for numerous admissions to hospitals in the course of a year. The only recourse with these cases is to have them sentenced by law for public intoxication or chronic drunkenness. When such sentences are carried out, however, there is unfortunately no treatment rendered during the time of incarceration.

It would be of great value if all those who were arrested and convicted of drunkenness or public intoxication were screened sufficiently to ascertain whether or not they are suffering from alcoholism. If they are, they should receive sufficient treatment at least to give them a start toward rehabilitation. The social worker can play an important role in ascertaining the background of the individual and the chances of his being helped through proper treatment. Probation officers can also be of assistance.

In taking histories from clients, the social worker can get detailed drinking histories of the individual members of the family to uncover early cases of alcoholism. Not only must an accurate history be taken about the amount of drinking and the time of drinking, but also the reason for drinking. Since in most cases the clients before the social worker are not the ones who do the drinking, it is most important that the questions be asked in such an objective way that the informer will be truthful. This can only be done if the family member is put sufficiently at ease and assured that no judgment will be passed on the individual except in terms of health or illness. If the informing relative will not be held responsible, a great deal more information can be obtained. It is only when the relative feels that the afflicted individual will learn the source of the information that he or she will refrain from giving positive and truthful facts.

All schools of social work should have a course on alcoholism so that students can recognize early signs and symptoms. They should also be made aware of the facilities in the area where alcoholics can go for help. Visits to these various facilities by students and graduate social workers will help them to become acquainted with methods and places for rehabilitating sick people.

In many cases social workers become counselors in facilities for alcoholics, and they have done a remarkable job in aiding these patients. A thorough understanding of the illness and its complications, as well as a knowledge of the possible etiological factors in a background that might be conducive to the disease, is always helpful to the social worker in determining whether the given individual has already developed the illness or represents a potential alcoholic.

Close relationship between the medical and social work professions is always helpful, and can be encouraged by mutual understanding of the role each plays. Courses on counseling can be obtained from various clinics so that the social worker can become more adept at handling alcoholic cases. The important factor in this matter is the attitude of the social worker toward the alcoholic patient. A clearer understanding of the illness will result in a proper attitude.

CHAPTER 27

Alcoholism in Other Countries

THE EXISTENCE of alcoholism as a public health problem as well as a disease of individuals is universal. As has been stated previously, every country has its characteristic form of alcoholism, which depends upon the culture, historical background, geographical environment, and availability of raw product. Even in those countries where the prevalent religions forbid the ingestion of alcoholic beverages, a percentage of the population is still afflicted with this illness. Some countries have a greater percentage of alcoholics in their population than others. This, to a great extent, depends on the factors mentioned as well as social, economic, dietary, and psychological factors. Generally speaking, the severity of the alcoholic problem can be classified, according to the amount of alcoholism present in any given country, into the low range, the middle range, and the higher range groups.

Some years ago the International Institute for Research on Problems of Alcohol drew up a chart explaining the extent of true alcoholism in various parts of the world, and made the classification referred to above.[1] For each of the classifica-

[1] Personal correspondence with the late E. M. Jellinek, Secretary General, International Institute for Research on Problems of Alcohol, Geneva, Switzerland.

tions, the low, the middle, and the high ranges, there was a further subdivision into lower, middle, and upper ranges of each of the three. While this method of classifying did not pinpoint the exact percentages, it did to some extent give an idea of the severity of the problem in various countries of the world.

Some countries, of course, were not cooperative in providing information that would make the report of the International Institute complete. The Iron Curtain countries, particularly, were loath to admit that there was such a problem as alcoholism within their borders, and refrained from submitting sufficient statistics for an evaluation to be made. The report of the International Institute, therefore, did not include any of the larger of the Iron Curtain countries, although it is a well-known and recognized fact that the problem does exist in all of these countries.

Visitors returning from Russia and Poland have noted the amount of alcoholism in those countries, but cannot give any accurate measurement of the problem. Russia itself has admitted that the problem does exist by taking various measures to curb what has been considered an increase in the problem in that country. These, of course, are newspaper reports, whose accuracy may be doubtful, and certainly not statistically correct. What they are doing, and to what extent alcoholism exists, cannot be determined from these reports. That the condition is a fairly severe one in Poland is also reported by those who have visited that country, but again, no accurate statistics have been available in order to classify this country in any particular range.

The chart by the International Institute is produced here in order to give some indication of the relationship among the countries in the occurrence of alcoholism. The predominance of urban and/or rural populations where alcoholism is most prevalent is also noted, as is the predominant source of the alcohol—wine, beer, or distilled spirits.

INTERNATIONAL INSTITUTE FOR RESEARCH ON PROBLEMS OF ALCOHOL

	1	2	3	4	5	6	7	8
	Extent of True Alcoholism	Country	Predom. Type of Alcoholics	Predom. U or R	Predom. Occup. or Soc. Group	Mag. of "Other Alc. Problems"	Predom. Type of Damage through "Other Alc. Problems"	Predom. Source of Alc.
LOW RANGE	Lower Low Range	Argentina	Sy. & I.D.	R	Ag. & L	X	viol. ab.	W
		Spain	I.D.	U & R	Ag. & L	X	viol. acc.	W
	Upper Low Range	Brazil	Sy.	U (R)	L (O)	X	ab. f.b.	D
		Holland	Sy.	U (R)	All	—	ab. acc.	D
		Portugal	I.D.	R (U)	Ag. & L	XX	health	W
MIDDLE RANGE	Low	Belgium	Sy. (I.D.)	U	L (O)	X?	rowd. abs. acc.	B
		Czechoslo.	Sy.	U	All	?	?	BD
		Engl. & Wales	Sy.	U	L & Wh. C.		ab. acc.	B
		Finland	Sy.	U	All	XX	viol. acc. ab.	D
		Ireland (Rep.)	Sy.	U & R	All	OXO	ab. acc. ab.	B
	Middle Range	Italy	I.D. (Sy.)	U (R)	L & Ag.	OXO	?	W
		N. Zealand	Sy.		All	?	?	D
		No. Ireland	Sy.	?	?	?	?	B
	Upper Middle Range	Canada	Sy. (I.D.)	U (R)	All	?	?	BD
		Denmark	Sy.	U (R)	?	?	?	B
		Norway	Sy.	U (R)	All	X	ab. rowd.	D
		Peru	Sy. (I.D.)	U & R	L & Ag. (O)	X	?	BD
		Scotland	Sy.	U (R)	L (O)	?	?	DB
		Uruguay	I.D. (Sy.)	U	L & Ag.	OXO	ab. rowd.	WD
		Yugoslav.	I.D. (Sy.)	U & R		OXO	rowd.	WD
HIGH RANGE	Lower High Range	Australia	Sy.	U	All	OXO	ab. rowd.	B
		Sweden	Sy.	U (R)?	All	?	ab. acc. rowd.	D
		Switzerland	Sy. (I.D.)	U (R)	Ag. & L.	—	ab. acc. f.b.	WD
		U. of S. Afr.	Sy.	U	All	?	?	?
	Upper High Range	Chile	I.D. (Sy.)	U & R	L. & ag.	XX	ab. viol. f.b.	W
		U.S.A.	Sy.	U	All	?	?	B (D)
	Extreme	France	I.D. (Sy.)	U & R	L. & Ag. (O)	X	health ab. acc. rowd.	W (D)

Glossary of the Tabular Presentation of Some Aspects of the Problems of Alcohol in 27 Countries

The number of countries for which at least some aspects of the problems of alcohol can be described is at present limited to 27.

These aspects are shown in eight columns:

Column No. 1 divides the incidence of true alcoholism into Low Range, Middle Range, High Range, and Extreme. Each of the ranges is further divided into low and upper subranges. Thus, for the middle range there is a low middle range and an upper middle range, etc. The lower low range refers to an alcoholism rate of up to .4 of 1 percent of the adult population; the upper low range 0.5 to 0.9 percent; the low middle range from 1 to 1.4 percent; the upper middle range from 1.5 to 1.9 percent; the lower high range from 2 to 3 percent; the upper high range from 4 to 5 percent; and the extreme which contains France only, represents a rate of close to 10 percent of the adult population. "Incidence of true alcoholism" includes alcohol addicts as well as so-called problem drinkers.

Column No. 2 shows the countries according to the ranges to which they belong. However, within a given range no inference should be made as to the relative position of a given country. Thus, in the low middle range, eight countries are given, namely, Belgium, Czechoslovakia, England and Wales, Finland, Ireland, Italy, New Zealand, and Northern Ireland. It will be noted these countries are given within this range in alphabetical order and thus it should not be inferred that Belgium is the lowest in the low middle range and Northern Ireland the highest. We have refrained from determining the rank orders of countries within a given range.

Column No. 3 shows the predominant type of alcoholics in any given country. We have taken only two broad types of alcoholics, namely, symptomatic addicts or problem drinkers, that is, drinkers who start their drinking as a symptom of an underlying personality disorder. These are designated by the abbreviation Sy. and the second, "inveterate drinkers" abbreviated to I.D. By inveterate drinker we mean the alcoholic who because of the acceptance of very high alcohol intake in his social group develops tissue adaptation to alcohol in the course of many years of daily high alcohol intake in such a manner that although there may not be any apparent intoxication, alcohol is present in the bloodstream every hour of the day and night. The symbols Sy. and I.D. for a given country mean that symptomatic and "inveterate drinkers" are represented approximately equally. If, on the other hand, the symbols Sy. (I.D.) appear, it should be understood that while symptomatic addicts are predominating, the "inveterate drinkers" represent a large minority, that is 25 to 40%. If the symbol Sy. stands alone this indicates that the symptomatic is predominant in the given country, that the "inveterate drinkers" form a small minority if any.

Column No. 4, "Predom. U or R," indicates whether the predominant occurrence of alcoholism is in urban or rural areas. Of course, if only the symbol R is shown it should not be understood that the occurrence is entirely a rural phenomenon, but that the urban occurrence is less than 25% of the total. The symbols U & R denote approximately equal occurrence in urban and rural areas and the symbol U (R) means that while the urban occurrence embraces the majority, the rural occurrence represents anywhere from 25 to 40 percent of the total.

Column No. 5 indicates the predominance of certain occupational or social groups; Ag. denotes the agricultural workers, L denotes industrial labor, mining, construction work, etc.; All means all classes proportionately represented; Wh. C. means white collar class; and (O) designates that in addition to the predominant class denoted by L or Ag., etc., other classes contributed at least 25 percent of the total.

Alcoholism in Other Countries

In Column 6 it is attempted to show the magnitude of alcohol problems other than true alcoholism in comparison to the extent of the latter. These "Other alcohol problems" include the excessive consumption of alcoholic beverages by drinkers who drink on weekends only or drinkers who use alcohol as a form of rough recreation. In some countries, this might represent a greater problem than "true alcoholism" either numerically or through the extent of social damage occasioned. X means that the "other alcohol problems" are greater than true alcoholism; XX, much greater; OXO designates that other alcohol problems are about the same size as true alcoholism and a minus sign denotes that the other alcohol problems are smaller than true alcoholism. An X of course indicates that it was not feasible to determine the magnitude of "other alcohol problems" in that given country.

Column No. 7 indicates the predominant type of damage occasioned through "other alcohol problems." We distinguish between violence (viol.), and rowdyism (rowd.), absenteeism (ab.), accidents (acc.), interference with family budget, (f.b.), and health means undermining the health.

Column No. 8 shows the predominant source of alcohol. Beer, B; Distilled Spirits, D; and Wine, W. If any of these symbols stands alone, it indicates that the other two types of alcoholic beverages contribute less than 20% to the total pure alcohol. Two symbols standing together indicate an approximately equal share of the two types of beverages to the total alcohol consumption. If one of the symbols is in parentheses it designates that the indicated beverage contributes more than 20 percent to the total absolute alcohol consumption. Thus in the U.S.A. beer contributes slightly more than 50 percent of the total alcohol consumed and distilled spirits somewhat less than 40 percent. The symbols in Column 8 for the U.S.A. would read B (D). Wine, of course, does not contribute sufficient alcohol in the U.S.A. to be indicated by a symbol. It must be pointed out that in the instance of France the symbols read W (D) although distilled spirits contribute not more than 14 percent to the total alcohol consumption in that country. However, since the total consumption of pure alcohol is extremely high in France the 14 percent contribution represents one of the largest distilled spirits consumption in the world.

The chart gives a rough comparison of the problem in the various countries mentioned. So many factors enter into the production of alcoholics in these various countries that it is difficult, in many instances, to account for reasons why some countries should be more alcoholic than others. The absence of many countries in Asia and Africa from the list does not mean that alcoholism does not exist in these countries. Among the Indonesian and other Asiatic countries, where the religions forbid the drinking of any form of alcohol, there are, nevertheless, many alcoholics, but not enough to represent a problem to the country itself, nor can it be considered a public health problem, since the percentage is so low. Alcoholism, however, does exist in these countries, but in a much smaller proportion than in the countries named. In many of the African countries, none of which appear on the list except the Union of South Africa, there is, nevertheless, considerable alcoholism. Particularly in the Rhodesias and in Kenya, there are sufficient alcoholics to represent a problem. However, it is not a high enough percentage to represent the kind of problem that public health authorities would recognize as such. In addition, it must be borne in mind that alcoholics in the African countries who are counted are white only. The native blacks were not considered in any population determination numerically. That alcoholism exists in many of the native blacks, there is no doubt. On my visit to those countries, particularly the Rhodesias, and in Kenya, I learned that there are enough alcoholics to have caused people interested in the problem to create committees to alleviate the problem. Again, we are speaking of the white Rhodesians and the white Kenyans. Very little effort is made to control the problem among the native blacks. The only control used with them is forbidding of the sale of alcoholic beverages through usual channels. The illegal channels, however, are plentiful, and there is no lack of alcohol for the natives who wish it. Besides, no one seems to be very interested in doing anything about it among these people. There is a definite interest among the whites in doing something about the problem of alcoholism in their own population.

In the Union of South Africa there is about the same percentage of alcoholism among whites that we see in the United States, although the chart shows the range to be in the lower of the high range rather than of the upper as in the United States. However, here again we find that the interest in alcoholism is limited to the white population, and very little is being done about the black population. The blacks are allowed legally, or were allowed up to a few months ago, to buy a concoction known as "Kaffir beer," which is manufactured by the government and sold to the natives in "beer halls." They are only allowed to purchase it in beer halls, and must drink it right on the premises, where tables and chairs are provided for them. The Kaffir beer is a liquid of rather heavy consistency, reddish tan in color, and tastes somewhat like fermented buttermilk. It is thick with a heavy protein content, which is kept at a high level with the idea that this will prevent alcoholism or deterioration of the liver. It is served warm, and to the Westerner has a somewhat disagreeable taste. Apparently it must be palatable to those who drink it, since it is bought by them in containers varying from a quart to a gallon or more, and drunk right on the premises. There is a 3 percent alcoholic content in this beer, which supposedly will not allow the individual to get drunk. Recently, under pressure from the Liberals and the black natives themselves, the black natives in South Africa were allowed to buy distilled spirits. This does not mean distilled spirits were not available to them before. The so-called shebeens, or what we might call speakeasies, were very prevalent in South Africa, and any amount of distilled spirits was sold to the black natives illegally. Many of these shebeens were run by women, called shebeen queens, and were very popular with the blacks in South Africa. These also existed in the Rhodesias, where by now the blacks are also allowed to buy distilled spirits legally. What the result of this change in policy will be, only the future can tell. The distilled spirits, of course, are a great deal more expensive than Kaffir beer, but they also produce the kind of results that most people want much more quickly.

The South American countries, as a rule, do not have a great problem with alcoholism, although it does exist, particularly in those countries where wine is produced. However, in some of the smaller countries, and among some of the Indian tribes, alcoholism is rampant, but the numbers of alcoholics in these countries is so small that it can be hardly considered a public health problem. Among these tribes there is a status need for the ingestion of vast amounts of alcohol, particularly by the chiefs, in order to maintain their status as chiefs. Here is one of the places where alcoholism is hardly considered a disease, or even a social error, since the drunken state is an accepted matter in these tribes, and represents a certain amount of strength and prestige for those who achieve it. Numerically, however, the problem is not great in these countries.

While alcoholism is a problem in the British Isles, the attitude toward drunkenness there differs from the attitude in this hemisphere, particularly in North America. Most of the drinking in England is done in the so-called public houses, and beer is the favorite beverage. Just as the Germans drink beer, the English enjoy their pint, and become quite habituated to drinking.

A considerable number of alcoholics are to be found in the Scandinavian countries. Of these countries, Sweden is perhaps the most alcoholic, and distilled spirits is the popular drink. Excessive drinking in Sweden poses quite a problem for the law enforcement people, who are quite energetic in apprehending those individuals who drive while drinking. One is somewhat adversely impressed by the number of young people who are drunk on the streets of Stockholm, as compared with other capitals whose alcoholism problem may be as great or greater, but whose people do not drink in the same way that Swedish youth does. In this respect the Swedish type of alcoholism and excessive drinking resembles that of the United States. In Denmark, while there is considerable alcoholism, it is not of the same character as that of Sweden; this may be because beer is the preferred drink, not distilled spirits as in Sweden. Finland has even less of a problem, even though distilled spirits is the popular drink there. Norway is also classified in the middle middle range, and here distilled spirits is the preferred drink.

In all of the Scandinavian countries, the problem of alcoholism is vigorously combatted by the governments. In Sweden, the Government maintains alcoholic clinics, as does Alcoholics Anonymous. The hospitals admit alcoholics there, and they are treated in many instances through the use of legal pressure.

Norway has a very effective means of meeting this problem by community action. In many instances committees handle complaints of excessive drinking among individuals within their own city blocks. Any individual who is suspected of beng alcoholic can be reported to the committee. If the complaint is made and the family of the individual concurs that the individual is drinking excessively or is alcoholic, this person can be committed to a community hospital where he is treated for alcoholism on an inpatient basis, with all the facilities of psychiatry and medicine available to him. His follow-up treatment is also provided for the length of time necessary to rehabilitate him. There are several of these hospitals on the outskirts of the large cities, such as Oslo, and patients are followed up very energetically to determine how they behave after leaving the hospital. General hospitals in Oslo also accept alcoholic patients, both on their medical and psychiatric floors.

Denmark has a rather unique way of following up its treated alcoholic patients from the clinics provided for them. Many of these patients are treated with Antabuse, since this was the home of Antabuse—it was discovered by Erik Jacobsen, in Copenhagen—and the clinics in Copenhagen use it almost routinely. After hospitalization and successful treatment, the patient is put on Antabuse and referred to a clinic for follow-up treatment. He is then either sent to his own home or to some foster home, where he is allowed to remain while working, and must report regularly to the clinic. The clinic maintains an itinerant social worker. Whenever a patient slips, it is immediately reported to the clinic, and the social worker will go out looking for the patient. This occurs whether it is day or night, and eventually, knowing the haunts of the individual patients, the social worker will eventually find him and return him to the hospital. In this way, a record is kept of all patients for an indefinite time after they leave the clinic. Rehabilitation in many instances proved successful only through the efficient follow-up treatment.

Australia and New Zealand have a problem with alcoholism that is quite similar to that in the United States. Although New Zealand may be considered in the middle range, and it is no doubt true that the problem there is not as great as it is in Australia, the similarity of the two countries in their drinking habits is marked.

Australia prefers beer as its drink of choice, while New Zealand prefers the distilled spirits. In Australia, however, the beer-drinking is unusually extensive. The beer halls there are extremely popular, and a surprisingly large percentage of a man's income is spent on beer. The hours these beer halls are open vary with the various cities. In some cities they are required to close at six o'clock and in some cities they are allowed to remain open until ten or even later. I had occasion to investigate the drinking habits of the Australians in both Sydney and Melbourne, and was astounded at the amount of beer consumed by citizens of those cities. In both cities I did what is known as "pub crawls." This consisted of going from pub to pub, on one occasion with a fellow physician, and on another occasion with a newspaper reporter. The people of Australia are extremely friendly, very much like Americans, and great admirers of our country. It was not at all difficult to engage them in conversation, and they were quite candid about their drinking habits. I was surprised to learn that the boys come into the pubs right after work, and remain until closing time. At six o'clock, there is a half-hour period of closing time to enable the customers to go to their homes. In some cities the pubs simply closed at six o'clock for the evening, but the demand was so great that some were allowed to reopen at six-thirty, and though the wives of the customers complained that their husbands did not take them out, they were now allowed to accompany their husbands back to the beer halls and drink with them. Difficult though it may be to believe, I found, by inquiring from many of these young men, that they consume 25 percent of their incomes in beer-drinking. This was verified by asking several people what their earned income was and how much they spent on beer, both in different pubs and from different individuals in the same pub. I was so surprised by this experience that while riding in a taxicab I made the same inquiry of the taxi-driver, and received the same response.

In some of the higher-class pubs, and when I use the term higher-class I mean where the men of higher income gather, I found that they drank distilled spirits as well as beer. These men did not spend quite as much on their drinking as did the lower economic classes, but the habitual drinking was fully as great. Of course, this drinking did not necessarily mean alcoholism, but the drinking habits we see in Australia could account for the rather high range of alcoholism there.

As has been stated before, Chile and the United States are in about the same category, as far as percentage of alcoholics in the general population is concerned. Chile, of course, is a wine-drinking country, while the United States prefers both beer and distilled spirits.

According to the chart, and in all probability, France is the most alcoholic country in the world. For a long time it has been a recognized fact that France and its economy were geared to its vineyards, and the production of wine in France was one of its great industries. It not only consumed much of its own product, but also exported tremendous amounts. French wines are known throughout the world for their excellence and flavor. During the depression, however, there was very little money available for wine, and the wine industry of France suffered. In order to rescue the industry from the depth into which it had fallen, and with no outlook for an increase in the exportation of its wines, France called upon its own people to consume its product. As a matter of fact, it was announced that wine was the ideal food and contained all the necessary elements for health. This campaign, which continued for some time, had its effect, and Frenchmen began to drink more and more wine, consuming more of their country's product than any other country. France then became the most alcoholic country in the world.

A few years ago, a French psychiatrist reported the occurrence of delirium tremens in several children. She accounted for this by the fact that children were drinking wine instead of milk. Wine had become a staple of France, and was as much a part of its nutritional intake as any other food. The habit of drinking wine in France was so ingrained that many Frenchmen are addicted to wine but never know they are alcoholic because they have never been withdrawn from the beverage long enough to show any withdrawal signs. In France, apparently, alcoholism is simply absence of abstinence, and many Frenchmen are surprised to find that they are alcoholic when they are withdrawn from the drug and go into delirium tremens, never having known that they were addicted.

Alcoholism in Other Countries

In late years, however, France has attempted to correct this situation. There were more deaths from cirrhosis of the liver per thousand in France than anywhere else in the world. There was sufficient cause, then, for alarm, and the health authorities began seeking some method of correcting this situation. After generations of being indoctrinated with the health-giving qualities of wine, it was difficult, indeed to un-sell the public from this rather popular notion. It had been said that the average Frenchman several years ago was drinking two liters of wine a day. The health authorities felt that if this were continued, the population would become more and more alcoholic. A drive was therefore launched to convince Frenchmen that no one should drink more than one liter of wine a day. Some years previously, one of the famous premiers of France became quite unpopular because he insisted that the French drink milk instead of wine. He did not stay in office long enough to carry out his threat of substituting milk for wine.

A few years later, however, the severity of the problem and the seriousness of the illness impressed the health authorities of France sufficiently for them to try to discourage the amount of wine-making. Since the economy of the country was geared to its vineyards, and so many people were engaged in this industry, it was no small problem to reduce the production of wine. A few years ago one of the health ministers tried to convince the vintners, by subsidizing them, to raise products other than grapes. Suger beets was the one product they felt could be a substitute for grapes. The health minister who inaugurated this program, which was going along very well, was not in office long enough to achieve real success, since at that time the premiers of France were changing unusually rapidly.

Several years ago, however, the drive to cut down on the wine-drinking in France was inaugurated. Posters, placards, radio announcements, television programs, and educational forums of all kinds were held throughout the country urging people to drink no more than one liter of wine a day. All the subway stations and subway cars had pictures and placards depicting the value of cutting down on wine consumption, always proclaiming that one liter of wine was sufficient for any adult. This campaign has begun paying off, and if this continues, the wine-drinking of France may decrease. In discussing this matter with the health minister of France some years ago, we agreed that this was a matter of generations rather than years. Such educational campaigns take a long time before they have an effect, and it is only the children of the children of the period when the campaign is started that will benefit from such educational measures.

This same theory could be applied to our attitude toward excessive drinking and alcoholism in our own country. All too often, we expect too much too soon from our educational programs. As has been said many times before, alcoholism represents but one aspect of a tremendous mental health problem. We can improve one aspect of the problem only by improving all aspects of the problem. This, of course, applies not only to alcoholism but to other addictions as well—narcotics addiction, gambling, barbiturates, and even work addiction, which can also be a mental health problem.

It is interesting to note that in Europe two adjacent grape-bearing countries, which produce a great amount of wine, have such divergent ratios of alcoholism in their population. France, which is considered to be the most alcoholic country in the world, is next door to Spain, which has one of the lowest alcoholism problems in the world. Italy, also a wine-drinking country, and culturally conditioned to drinking daily with meals, also has a comparatively low range compared with neighbor France. The same divergence can be noted in South America, where Argentina, Brazil, Peru, and Uruguay can be considered low-alcoholism countries. The not too distant Chile is one of the highest-ranking countries. The lowland countries of Belgium and Holland have their problems with alcoholism, but we see them ranked among the lower percentages compared with Switzerland and France, their not too distant neighbors.

We have no definite knowledge of the rate of alcoholism in the Far East. For a long time, alcoholism was practically unknown among Chinese people, but their predilection for opium has been a long-recognized fact. Until comparatively recently, Japan had very little alcoholism, which, up to the time of the American occupation, presented no public health problem whatever. However, since occupation by American troops and the introduction of a great deal more drinking, the problem of alcoholism has become apparent in Japan, particularly in the northern section of the islands. In the last several years, there has grown up in Japan, particularly in the large cities, the so-called dance palaces and entertainment centers, which cater to those who can afford it. Here drinking is a very common occurrence. The drinking of hard beverages, as well as beer, is extremely popular. Although Japan has always had its alcoholic beverages made from rice, it was not until comparatively recent years that the problem of alcoholism became apparent. If the trend continues, it will represent one of the health problems that Japan must face before long.

All countries of the world have not been described here in terms of their problems of alcoholism, but it is generally conceded that any country has some alcoholics. Those not mentioned, however, do not show the presence of alcoholism to an extent great enough to be noted as a public health problem. It can be expected, however, that with the new freedom attained by many of the countries, particularly in Africa and Asia, and with the increase in the economic advantages many of these countries will experience, there will be an imitation of the Western world in both its industrialization and its leisure-time activities. It seems characteristic of the economies of countries that as incomes rise and the trials of living diminish, drinking increases. In reviewing the histories of many countries and civilizations, it also seems apparent that the complexity of growing civilization increases the strain on individuals in that society, and as the generations pass, the ability to contend with these stresses is often diminished. In such cases, it appears historically evident that escape into unreality is characterized in many instances by the use of alcohol. It is very possible, therefore, that for coming generations increased economy and more leisure time, and the resultant complications of competitive living in a modern world, may result in alcoholism in those countries that hitherto showed little incidence of this illness. If alcoholism is to be prevented in these countries, it is advisable that their education on the problem be started very soon, concurrent with their indoctrination into modern Western world industrialization. Perhaps if proper education were carried out now, the problem of alcoholism, which has affected so many countries can be avoided in the newer ones.

Glossary

A

ABSTINENCE—forbearance from the use of alcoholic beverages.
ADDICTION—enslavement to a habit, especially drugs, where cessation of drug produces "withdrawal" signs.
ADEQUATE—equal to the requirement or occasion.
ADVERSE—antagonistic in purpose or effect; unfavorable.
ALLERGY—a state of hypersensitiveness to certain things as pollens, food, fruits, etc., to which an individual is abnormally sensitive in comparison with the majority of people who remain unaffected.
AMBIVALENT—having equal power or value in both directions.
ANALEPTIC—restorative; invigorating.
ANCILLARY—serving as an aid, adjunct or auxiliary.
ANESTHETIC—an agent that produces insensibility to pain or touch. Partial or complete loss of sensation with or without loss of consciousness.
APHRODISIAC—an agent which stimulates sexual desire.
AQUEOUS—like or containing water; watery.
ATHEROSCLEROSIS—senile type of fatty desquamation of walls of arteries.
AUDITORY—pertaining to sense of hearing.

B

BEHAVIORAL SCIENCES—psychology, sociology and anthropology. Also often included, political science and economics.

C

CEREBELLUM—lower or back brain.
CEREBRAL CORTEX—the forebrain, the outer layers of the larger part of the brain (Gray matter).
CEREBRUM—the forebrain—the larger part of the brain where sensory stimuli are received and motor impulses originate.
CHOLESTEREMIA—a fatlike substance (a monatomic alcohol) in the blood.
CHRONIC—long-drawn-out; a prolonged disease.
COMATOSE—an abnormally deep stupor; patient cannot be aroused.
COMMUNICABILITY—characteristic of being transmitted directly or indirectly.
COMPULSIVE—a strong irrational impulse to carry out a given act—particularly against one's wishes and/or better judgment.
CONCOMITANT—taking place at the same time.
CONCUSSION—a common result of a blow on the head, usually causing unconsciousness, either temporary or prolonged.
CORTICAL—pertaining to the cortex or outer layers (particularly the brain).
CUSTODIAL—guardianship keeping in charge or in care of.

D

DEBILITATION—weakness of tonicity in functions or organs of the body; functions of body are feebly discharged.
DEHYDRATION—withdrawal of water from the tissues, naturally or artificially.
DELIRIUM—disorientation of time and place, usually with illusions and hallucinations; a state of mental confusion and excitement.
DELIRIUM TREMENS—a psychic disorder involving hallucinations, both visual and auditory, found in habitual users of alcohol.
DEPRESSANT—an agent that will depress a body function or nerve or brain activity.
DETERIORATION—retrogression; said of impairment of mental or physical functions.
DEVIATION—departure from normal.
DEXTROSE—chemical name for sugar.
DIDACTIC—intended for instruction.
DIETARY—a regulated selection of food materials.
DISEASE—a pathological condition of the body or mind. Literally, lack of ease. A group of signs, and symptoms which sets the condition apart from other normal or pathological body states.
DISORIENTATION—inability to estimate direction or location or to be cognizant of time, place or persons.
DYSFUNCTION—absence of complete normal function.

GLOSSARY

E

EGO—that part of the unconscious that has been influenced by the senses and which has taken on consciousness in its contacts with reality.
ENDOCRINE—internally secreting glands.
ENTERITIS—inflammation of the intestines.
EPIDEMIOLOGY—the study of diseases not of local origin which attack many people at the same time and spread from person to person.
EPITOME—a summary or condensed amount.
ETIOLOGY—the study of the causes of disease which result from an abnormal state producing pathological conditions.

F

FALLACY—a deceptive, misleading or false notion.
FRUCTOSE—fruit sugar.
FRUSTRATION—nullification; planning to no avail; defeat; bafflement.

G

GASTRITIS—inflammation of the stomach.
GLYCOSURIA—the presence of sugar in the urine.

H

HABIT—a motor pattern executed with facility because of constant repetition; habituation—act of becoming accustomed to anything from frequent use.
HALLUCINATION—false perception bearing no relation to reality and not accounted for by any external stimuli.
HARANGUE—passionate, vehement speech; noisy and intemperate address.
HEMIPLEGIA—paralysis of only one half of the body.
HEMOPTYSIS—expectoration of blood; hemorrhage from the lungs.
HORMONE—a chemical substance originating in an organ, gland or part which is conveyed through the blood to another part of the body, stimulating it to increase functional activity and increase secretions.
HOSTILITY—unfriendly, antagonistic, animosity.
HYPERACIDITY—an excess of acid.
HYPERACTIVE—excessive action.
HYPERTENSION—high blood pressure.
HYPOGLYCEMIA—deficiency of sugar in blood.
HYPOTENSIVE—low blood pressure.

I

INCIPIENT—beginning.
IMMATURE—not fully developed or ripened.
INADEQUACY—insufficiency; incompetence.
INANE—empty; void.
INARTICULATE—not uttered or emitted with expressive or intelligible modulations; not able to express properly.
INCARCERATION—imprisonment; confinement.
INCENTIVE—that which incites to action; stimulus; motivation.
INFLATE—to distend, puff or swell; dilate.
INGESTION—the process of taking material (food) into the gastrointestinal tract.
INTRAVENOUS—within or into a vein.

L

LAVAGE—washing out of a cavity.

M

MENOPAUSAL—climacteric; that time which marks the cessation of a woman's reproductive period.
METABOLIC—the successive transformation to which a substance is subjected from the time it enters the body to the time it or its decomposition products are excreted and by which function of nutrition is accomplished and energy provided.
METHODOLOGY—the science of the conduct of scientific inquiry.
MORES—folkways of control; importance accepted without question and embodying the fundamental moral views of a group.
MOTIVATION—something that prompts a person to act in a certain way; incentive.
MUCOUS MEMBRANE—the lining passages and cavities communicating with the air and which secrete mucous.

N

NARCOLEPSY—overwhelming attacks of sleep which patient cannot control.
NARCOTIC—drug producing stupor, complete unconsciousness, and allaying pain.
NEURAL—pertaining to nerves.
NEUROSES—psychoneuroses; emotional disorders in which feelings of anxiety, obsessional thoughts, compulsive acts, and physical complaints without objective evidence of disease, in various patterns, dominate the personality.
NYSTAGMUS—constant involuntary movements of the eyeball.

GLOSSARY

O

OBSESSION—an uncontrollable deisre to dwell on an idea or an emotion or to perform a specific act.
OPPROBRIUM—disgrace or reproach incurred by conduct considered disgraceful.

P

POLYNEUROPATHY—diseases of many nerves.
PARTURITION—childbirth.
PATHOLOGICAL—diseased.
PERSONALITY CHANGES—changes in totality of an individual's characteristics and emotional trends, interests and behavior tendencies.
PETECHIAE—minute hemorrhagic spots.
PHYSIOLOGICAL—concerning body function; function of cells, tissues, and organs.
PLETHORA—overfullness; excessive amount of blood or other fluid in the body.
POTENCY—strength of a medicine; sexual strength; power.
POTENTIATING—increasing the power of.
PRECURSOR—one or that which precedes.
PREREQUISITE—required beforehand.
PROLIFERATION—reproduction rapidly or repeatedly; as by cell division. Rapid reproduction.
PROJECT (projection)—distortion of a perspective as a result of its repression, resulting in such a phenomenon as hating without cause, one who has been loved.
PROPHYLACTICALLY—warding off disease.
PSYCHIATRIC—the science of dealing with mental ailments.
PSYCHOPATH—one with a constitutional lack of moral sensibility although possessing normal intelligence.
PSYCHOSIS—any mental derangement; insanity.
PSYCHOTHERAPY—any mental method of treating disease.
PUNITIVE—concerned with or inflicting punishment.

R

RAPPORT—a relationship of sympathy and confidence.
RATIONALIZE—plausible explanation of behavior or belief activated by unknown motives.
RECIDIVISM—repeated or habitual relapses.
REFRACTORY—not responsive to ordinary treatment.
REHABILITATION—process of restoring or of undergoing restoration to health or efficiency.

REMORSE—deep and painful regret for wrongdoing, compunction.
RESENTMENT—the feeling of displeasure or indignation at something regarded as an injury or insult.
RETROGRESS—to go backward into an earlier or worse condition.

S

SEDATIVE—an agent allaying irritability or nerve action.
SEQUELAE—condition following or the result of a disease.
SKID ROW—the area in a community usually inhabited by homeless men and chronic alcoholics, drunkards, derelicts and vagrants.
SOMNOLENT—sleepy, drowsy; tendency to sleep.
STIMULANT—any agent temporarily increasing functional activity.
STOICISM—repression of emotion; indifference to pleasure or pain; philosophy of the Stoics.
SYMPTOMATOLOGY—the study of the changes in the body or its functions which indicates disease or the kind or phases of disease.

T

TOLERANCE—capacity for enduring a drug, food or poison which may be harmful if taken in excess; power of resistance to such, or point at which resistance ends.
TENSIONS—states of stretching or being strained.
TERMINOLOGY—the study of terms used in any special field.
TOXIC—cumulative effect of an agent resulting in poisoning which in small amounts would be innocuous.

U

UNINHIBITED—without restraint; without control.
UNTOWARD—unfavorable or unfortunate; perverse.

V

VISUAL—pertaining to vision or sight.
VENTILATION—to submit to free examination and discussion; to give free utterance and expression.

Index

Absenteeism in industry, 197, 252
Abstaining alcoholic, the, treating, 121-32
Abstinence, total, 35, 67, 85, 86, 107, 108, 131, 143, 227, 264, 268-69, 277-78
Abstract Archives of the Alcohol Literature, 186, 187
Acetaldehyde, 107
Acetic acid, 107
Addiction, 39, 41, 43, 54, 55-56, 65, 75, 131, 159, 222
Adelstein, Joseph, 173
Adrenal cortex extract, 93, 96-97
Adrenal glands, 120
Adrenocorticotropic hormone, 99
Advertising, alcoholism and, 268
Africa, alcoholism in, 296
Age bracket for alcoholics, 63
Agranulocytosis, 96
Alabama, alcoholism program in, 171
Al-Anon, 155-56, 272
Al-a-teen, 156, 276
Alberta, alcoholism program in, 171, 174
Alcohol, absorption of, 215-16; affect on humans, 50-59; anesthetic drug, 34, 42, 50-51; dependence on, 54; effect on the body, 116-20; food value of, 218; habit-forming tendency of, 222; heredity and, 47, 222; manufacture of, 32; medicinal value of, 220; sexual behavior and, 165-66, 219-20
Alcoholics, age bracket for, 63; behavior of, characteristics of, 55-57; conformed, 84, 85; court case, the, 142-44; evaluation of condition of, 91-92; homeless, 133-44; hospitalization of, 85-86, 89-91, 182; labeling of, 74-75; personal history of, need for obtaining, 123; punishment of, 70-71; questions posed to, 57-58; rehabilitation of, see Rehabilitation of alcoholics; rejection, sense of, 76-77, 83; self-consciousness of, 124, 166-67; spouse of, 270-78; treatment of, see Treatment of alcoholics; types of, 23, 25-29, 122; understanding, 74-81; women, 157-67
Alcoholics Anonymous, 69, 85, 86, 114, 124, 129, 141, 143, 145-56, 159, 175, 183, 200, 202, 223, 241, 248, 253, 255, 271, 272, 276, 299; advantages in, 155; affiliated organizations, 155-56; appeal of, 153-54; history of, 150-53; responsibility of, 154; twelve steps, the, 146-47; twelve traditions, the, 147-48
Alcoholism, allergy, 21; causes of, 34-42; chronic, 61; clergy and, 254-57; communicability of, 47-48; communications and, 279-82; complications of chronic, 110-14; compulsive character of, 61; cure for, 222-23; definitions of, 19-25, 62; diagnosis of, 44, 45, 48-49, 57-58, 61, 73; disease concept of, 15, 22, 29-30, 54, 57, 61-62, 70, 75, 76, 264; education on, see Education on alcoholism; government and, 168-81; hospital and, 229-37; industry and, 190, 196-210; inheritance of, 47, 222; law and, 60-73, 285-86; lawyers and, 283-86; lethal, acute, 114; mass media and, 279-82; medical profession and, 182-95; medical treatment of, see Medical treatment of alcoholics; mental health aspect of, 46; New York State program on, 70; nurse and, 194-95, 246-53; in other countries, 290-306; prevention of, 44, 46-49; programs on, 70, 72; progression of, 55-57; public health matter, 43-49; recognition of, 29-30; signs of, early, 49; social worker and, 143-44, 287-89; stigma attached to, 75, 232-33; teacher and, 211-28, 262-63, 266; treatment for, see Treatment of alcholics; young people and, 258-69

313

INDEX

Allis-Chalmers Corporation, 200
Alpha type of alcoholic, 26
American Association of Medical Colleges, 188
American Bar Association, 73
American Hospital Association, 187, 233, 237
American Medical Association, 73, 80, 183-86, 187, 188, 190, 192, 193, 200, 208, 233, 237, 240, 286
American Psychiatric Association, 80
American Telephone Company, 200
Amnesia, 113
Amobarbital (Amytal), 98
Amphetamine (Benzedrine), 92
Anderson, Carl L., 174
Andrews, Elmer V., 172
Anesthesia, 50-51, 89
Antabuse, *see* Disulfiram
Antihistaminics, 96, 105
Anti-Saloon League, 214
Archibald, H. David, 72, 174
Argentina, alcoholism in, 292, 304
Arkansas, alcoholism program in, 171
Armstrong, John D., 174
Ascorbic acid, 105
Asia, alcoholism in, 296
Association of American Medical Colleges, 188
Association of Municipal Judges, 283-84
Atherosclerosis, 45
Atlanta (Ga.) Rehabilitation Program, 80
Australia, alcoholism in, 292, 300-01
Azacyclonol (Frenquel) hydrochloride, 110

Bacon, Selden, 186 n.
Bailey, Margaret, 79
Baker, Art S., 172
Bar associations, 70
Barbiturates, 96, 98, 131
Beaton, Lindsay E., 193 n.
Beer, 33
Behavior, alcoholics, characteristics of, 55-57; antisocial, 14, 60; sexual, alcohol and, 165-66, 219-20
Belgium, alcoholism in, 292, 293, 304
Bell, Gordon, 72, 174
Benactyzine hydrochloride (Deprol), 93
Beta type of alcoholic, 26
Beverages, alcoholic, 31-33
Blacker, Edward, 172
Block, Marvin A., 22 n., 42 n., 49 n., 121 n., 186 n., 193 n., 229 n., 251 n., 261 n., 264 n.

Blood concentration tests, 91
Bloomquist, Edward R., 193 n.
Blue Cross corporations, 188-89
Body, the, effect of alcoholism on, 116-20
Bourbon, 32, 33
Boyle, Terrence J., 173
Brain, the, deterioration of, chronic, 61; effect of alcohol on, 117
Brandy, 32
Brazil, alcoholism in, 292, 304
Breen, Ruth, 172
Brill, Henry, 193 n.
British Columbia, alcoholism program in, 171, 174
Brody, Nathan, 172
Buffalo University, 184
Buffalo University Medical School, 184
Bureau of Family Services, 180
Burnett, William H., 68
Business administration, schools of, education on alcoholism in, 241-42
Butler, John, 172

Caffeine sodium benzoate, 92, 101, 105
Cain, Arthur H., 33 n., 259
Cain, Vashti, 172
California, alcoholism program in, 171-72; rehabilitation program in, 72
California State Medical Society, 191
Cameron, Dale C., 193 n.
Canada, alcoholism in, 292; alcoholism programs in, 171, 174
Cancer, stigma attached to, 75
Capone, Antonio, 173
Carbon dioxide, 107
Cardiovascular system, effect of alcoholism on, 118
Central nervous system, drugs that depress, 93-98; drugs that stimulate, 92-93
Cerebral palsy, 279
Ceremonial drinking, 33
Children, alcoholic parents and, 275-76; drinking and, 258-69
Chile, alcoholism in, 292, 301-02, 304
Chloral hydrate, 97
Chlordiazepoxide (Librium), 93, 95-96, 103, 111
Chlorpromazine, 93, 94, 95-96, 102, 103, 105, 111
Cholesteremia, 45
Christie, Keith M., 174
Chronic Disease Institute, 184
Cirrhosis of the liver, 61, 86, 220-21; treatment, 112-13

INDEX

Citrated calcium carbimide (Temposil), 106-07, 114
Civilizations, decline of, 52-53
Clergy, the, alcoholism and, 254-57; education on alcoholism for, 242-43
Cleveland Rehabilitation Program, 80
Clinebell, Howard J. Jr., 20, 256
Cohen, Wilbur E., 181
Colleges, education on alcoholism in, 240-42
Colorado, alcoholism program in, 171, 172; rehabilitation program in, 72; school of alcoholic studies, 79
Comatose state, treatment, 101
Committee on Alcoholism, A.M.A., 185, 186, 187-89, 190-91, 192, 193, 286
Committee on Alcoholism and Addictions, A.M.A., 193
Committee on Aviation Medicine, A.M.A., 208
Committee on Mental Health, A.M.A., 184, 185
Committee on the Problems of Alcoholism, A.M.A., 183-84
Commonwealth Edison (Chicago), 200
Communicability of alcoholism, 47-48
Communications, alcoholism and, 279-82
Communications personnel, education on alcoholism for, 244
Community Health Services, 177
Compulsory treatment of alcoholics, 66, 71-72
Compulsive drinking, 40, 55
Concussion, 91
Conditioned response therapy, 108-09
Confabulation, 113
Congress, U. S., appropriation for mental health, 174; legislation for relief of alcoholics, 61
Connecticut, alcoholism program in, 171, 172; rehabilitation program in, 72
Consolidated Edison (New York City), 200
Convulsions, 57, 110; treatment, 101-02
Cooperative Commission on the Study of Alcoholism, 175-77
Cordials, 32
Cortical control centers, depression of, 50-51
Corticotropin (ACTH), 99, 110, 111
Council on Education and Hospitals, A.M.A., 188
Council on Mental Health, A.M.A., 185, 186, 187, 189, 190, 197
Council on Scientific Exhibits, 185
Court case, homeless alcoholic, 142-44

Curare, 99
Custer, Walter, 172
Custodial institutions, 86, 169
Czechoslovakia, alcoholism in, 292, 293

Daniel, Ralph W., 172
Dehydration, 91
Delahanty, Edward and Mary, 172
Delirium tremens, 27, 57, 99, 233, 302; treatment, 110-11
Delta type of alcoholic, 27
Demone, Harold W., Jr., 72
Denmark, alcoholism in, 292, 299, 300
Dental schools, education on alcoholism in, 240
Depression, drugs that counteract, 92-93
Dermatitis, 96
Deterioration, *see* Brain, the; Mental deterioration; Physical deterioration
Deterrent drugs, 114, 123, 124, 277
Deterrent therapy, 104-08
Detoxification, 66
Detroit Rehabilitation Program, 80
Dextroamphetamine (Dexedrine), 92
Dextrose, 91, 101, 105
Diabetes, 91
Diagnosis of alcoholism, 44, 45, 48-49, 57-58, 61, 73
Dietary cause of alcoholism, 41
Dietary regimen, 100-01, 102-03, 112, 113, 231
Dimas, George C., 173
Diphenhydramine hydrochloride (Benadryl), 96, 105
Diphenylhydantoin (Dilantin) sodium, 102
Disability, permanent, payment for, 61-65
Distillation of alcohol, process of, 31-32
District of Columbia, alcoholism program in, 171
Disulfiram (TETD or Antabuse), 104-06, 114, 130, 143, 144, 300
Disulfiram-alcohol reaction, 105
Disulfiram therapy, 104-06
Dorsch, Graydon, 172
Drinking, ceremonial, 33; compulsive, 40, 55; control of, 20; criticism of, reaction to, 58; customs, 23; escape from problems, 38-39, 54-55; excessive, 20, 23, 36, 39-40, 43, 52-53, 56, 61, 85, 120, 125, 159, 215, 258; patterns of, 23; problem, 24-25, 32, 45, 48, 49, 54-55, 84-85, 158, 234, 260; psychological phenomenon, 216-17; reasons for, 33-42; for relaxation, 34-35, 38,

51; social, 33-34, 35, 51, 54; young people and, 258-69
Driving under influence of alcohol, 55, 65-67, 209, 285
Drugs, abstaining alcoholic and use of, 131-32; adrenal cortex extract, 93, 96-97; azacyclonol (Frenquel) hydrochloride, 110; barbiturates, 96, 98, 131; central nervous system depressing, 93-98; central nervous system stimulating, 92-93; chloral hydrate, 97; chlordiazepoxide (Librium), 93, 95-96, 103, 111; chlorpromazine, 93, 94, 95-96, 102, 103, 105, 111; citrated calcium carbimide (Temposil), 106-07, 114; depression counteracting, 92-93; deterrent, 114, 123, 124, 277; diphenhydramine hydrochloride (Benadryl), 96, 105; disulfiram (TETD or Antabuse), 104-06, 114, 130, 143, 144, 300; hydroxyzine (Atarax), 99; mephenesin (Tolserol), 94, 99-100; mephobarbital (Mebaral), 96; meprobamate (Miltown or Equanil), 93, 94-95, 96, 99, 103; muscle system relaxing, 98-99; paraldehyde, 97; promazine hydrochloride (Sparine), 93, 94-95, 96, 102, 103, 105, 111; Rauwolfia serpentina, 94, 96, 103; reserpine, 93-94, 96, 103; tranquilizing, 93-98, 110, 111, 114, 131
Du Pont de Nemours, E. I., 200

Edema, 101
Education on alcoholism, components for effective programs on, 238-45; need for, 46-48, 49, 75, 78-81, 170, 171, 224
Electroencephalograms, 102
Encyclopedia of Problems of Alcohol, 176
Endocrine glands, 103, 120
Endocrine system, effect of alcohol on, 120
England, alcoholism in, 292, 293, 298
Enteritis, 111
Ephedrine, 92
Epsilon type of alcoholic, 27-28
Esophagus, hemorrhage of, 86, 111-12
Ethchlorvynol (Placidyl), 98
Ether, 89
Etiology of alcoholism, 48
Excessive drinking, 20, 23, 36, 39-40, 43, 52-53, 56, 61, 85, 120, 125, 159, 215, 258
Excessive ingestion, definition of, 20
Excretory system, effect of alcohol on, 118-19

Family service agencies, 170
Far East, alcoholism in, 305
Federal government alcoholism programs, 174-77
Feldman, Hyman, 68
Felix, Robert H., 174
Ferguson, William, 79
Finland, alcoholism in, 292, 293, 299
Fleming, Robert, 186 n.
Florida, alcoholism program in, 171, 172; rehabilitation program in, 72, 80
Florida State Rehabilitation Program, 80
Food value of alcohol, 218
Ford, John C., 56 n., 256
Foster homes, 137-38
Fox, Vernelle, 72, 172
France, alcoholism in, 292, 302-04, 305
Fronczak, Francis, 182
Freeman, Macon W., 173
Fructose, 91
Frustrations, ability to overcome, 46, 161

Gamma type of alcoholic, 26-27
Gardiner, Yvelin, 79
Garrard, Mrs. Robert, 173
Gastritis, acute, 111
General Motors Corporation, 200
Georgia, alcoholism program in, 171, 172; rehabilitation program in, 72
Gibbs, W. T. Dixon, 172
Glandular products, 99-100
Glutethimide (Doriden), 98
Gooderham, Clyde W. and Marie, 173
Gorman, James, 173
Government, alcoholism and, 168-81; programs on alcoholism, 72, 174-77; responsibility of, 49, 72, 81
Government departments, education on alcoholism in, 243-44
Grennell, R. G., 50 n.

H.R. 7225, statement concerning, 61-65
Habit-forming tendency of alcohol, 222
Halfway house, 138-39, 169
Hallucinations, 57
Hallucinosis, 110
Hangover, 57
Harris, Grant B., 172
Harrison, Ray, 68, 69
Health, Education, and Welfare Department, U. S., 177, 178-81, 192
Heart disease, alcohol as medication in, 118
Hein, Fred V., 261 n.
Hemiplegia, 91
Hemorrhage of the esophagus, 86, 111-12

INDEX

Hemorrhagic poliocephalitis, superior, *see* Wernicke's disease
Heredity, alcohol and, 47, 222
Himwich, Harold, 186 n.
Hinchliffe, Leonard, 173
Hofstra College, 225 n.
Holland, alcoholism in, 292, 304
Hormonal products, 99-100
Hormone glands, 41
Hospital administrators, education on alcoholism for, 243
Hospitalization of alcoholics, 85-86, 89-91, 182
Hospitals, alcoholism and, 229-37; board members of, education on alcoholism for, 243; government, 66; mental, 168-69; state, 141; for treatment of alcoholics, 67-68
Hydroxyzine (Atarax), 99
Hypnosis, 109
Hypothyroidism, 100

Illinois, alcoholism program in, 171; rehabilitation program in, 72
Illinois State Medical Society, 191
Indiana, alcoholism program in, 171; rehabilitation program in, 72; school of alcoholic studies, 79
Indonesia, alcoholism in, 296
Industry, alcoholism and, 190, 196-210; nurse in, 251-52; rehabilitation program for employees, 71
In-hospital service, 136-37, 169, 170
Institute for the Study of Human Problems, 175
Insulin, 92, 101
Insulin shock, 91
International Institute for Research on Problems of Alcohol, chart of, 290-96
Intoxication, acute alcoholic, 88-89, 230-31; arrest for public, 67, 169, 284; pathological, 113; treatment of, 82-102
Intravenous therapy, 91
Ireland, alcoholism in, 292, 293
Irish, attitude toward drinking, 37-38
Iron Curtain countries, alcoholism in, 291
Irresponsibility, drinking a matter of, 40
Italy, alcoholism in, 292, 293, 304

Jacobsen, Erik, 300
Japan, alcoholism in, 305
Jaundice, 96
Jellinek, E. M., 20, 23 n., 25, 26, 43 n., 122, 186 n., 290 n.
Jews, attitude toward drinking, 36-37

Joint Commission on Accreditation of Hospitals, 187, 189
Jones, Thomas, 172
Journal of the American Medical Association, 186, 187

Kaffir beer, 297, 298
Kansas University, 226 n.
Kelly, Norbert L., 172
Kentucky, alcoholism program in, 171
Kenya, alcoholism in, 296-97
Korsakoff's syndrome, 61, 86; treatment, 113
Kruse, H. D., 22 n.

Lampert, Kenneth, 172
Law, the, alcoholism and, 60-73, 285-86
Law enforcement agencies, education on alcoholism for, 242
Law schools, education on alcoholism in, 241
Lawyers, alcoholism and, 283-86
Legislators, education on alcoholism for, 242
Lethal alcoholism, acute, 114
Lieberman, Ben, 173
Lipscomb, Wardell R., 23 n.
Liver extract, 112
Logan, Albert B., 68
Louisiana, alcoholism program in, 171
Lovell, Harold W., 21
Lungs, infection of, 101
Lysergic acid (LSD 25), 109
Lysergic acid therapy, 109-10

Maine, alcoholism program in, 171
Manitoba, alcoholism program in, 174
Manitoba Rehabilitation Program, 80
Manliness, drinking to prove, 35-36
Mann, Marty, 21, 79
Manual on Alcoholism, 187-88
Marchiafava's disease, 113-14
Margulis, Elizabeth, 190
Maryland, alcoholism program in, 171, 172
Maryland Department of Health, 80
Massachusetts, alcoholism program in, 171, 172
Mass media, alcoholism and, 279-82
McCambridge, Clyde, 72
McCambridge, Frona, 172
McGuire, H. Thomas, 186 n.
McKay, James R., 172
McRae, E. D., 174
Medical profession, alcoholism and, 182-95

Medical School of the State University of New York (Buffalo), 184
Medical schools, education on alcoholism in, 240
Medical treatment of alcoholism, 87-115; acute lethal alcoholism, 114; chronic alcoholism, complications of, 110-14; cirrhosis of the liver, 112-13; conditioned response therapy, 108-09; delirium tremens, 110-11; deterrent therapy, 104-08; disulfiram therapy, 104-06; drugs that depress the central nervous system, 93-98; drugs that stimulate the central nervous system and counteract depression, 92-93; enteritis, 111; gastritis, acute, 111; glandular products, 99-100; hallucinosis, 110; hormonal products, 99-100; hospitalization, 89-91; hypnosis, 109; intoxication, acute alcoholic, 88-89, 100-02, 230-31; Korsakoff's syndrome, 113; lysergic acid therapy, 109-10; Marchiafava's disease, 113-14; not in acute stage, 102-04; pathological intoxication, 113; patient's condition, evaluation of, 91-92; varices of esophagus and cardiac end of stomach, 111-12; Wernicke's disease, 113
Medicinal value of alcohol, 220
Mental deterioration, 86
Mental health, alcoholism and, 46, 168-69
Mental Hygiene Department, New York State, 70
Mephenesin (Tolserol), 94, 99-100
Mephobarbital (Mebaral), 96
Meprobamate (Miltown or Equanil), 93, 94-95, 96, 99, 103
Metheson, J. P., 174
Methvin, Charles B., 72, 172
Methylphenidate hydrochloride (Ritalin), 92
Methyprylon (Noludar), 98
Michigan, alcoholism program in, 171, 172; rehabilitation program in, 72
Michigan Rehabilitation Program, 80
Miller, Dudley Porter, 171-72
Miller, Welles, 172
Minerals, 112, 113, 231
Minnesota, alcoholism program in, 171
Mississippi, alcoholism program in, 172; rehabilitation program in, 72
Mississippi School of Alcoholic Studies, 79
Montana, alcoholism program in, 171, 172

Municipal courts, 67, 68-70, 284-85
Murtagh, John, 69-70
Muscular system, effect of alcohol on, 119

Narcosis, 50-51
Nassau County, New York, 225
National Association of Municipal Judges, 68-70
National Committee on Alcoholism, 184
National Council on Alcoholism, 21, 70, 79, 171, 181, 184, 202
National Institute of Health, 173
National Institute of Mental Health, 173, 175, 177, 184
Nervous system, effect of alcohol on, 116-17
Neuroses, 64
Nevada, alcoholism program in, 171, 172; rehabilitation program in, 72
New Hampshire, alcoholism program in, 171, 172; rehabilitation program in, 72
New Jersey, alcoholism program in, 171; rehabilitation program in, 72
New Mexico, alcoholism program in, 171
New York State, alcoholism program in, 171, 172; rehabilitation program in, 72
New York State Bar Association, 70
New York State Health Department, 184
New Zealand, alcoholism in, 292, 293, 300
Nilsson, Gertrude, 172
Nitrous oxide, 89
Nonconformists, society's attitude toward, 77-78
Nondrinkers, fear of conspicuousness, 77
Norris, John, 72, 172
North American Association of Alcoholism Programs, 171, 175, 177-78
North Carolina, alcoholism program in, 171, 172-73; rehabilitation program in, 72; school of alcoholic studies, 79
North Dakota, alcoholism program in, 171; rehabilitation program in, 72; school of alcoholic studies, 79
Norway, alcoholism in, 292, 299
Nova Scotia, alcoholism program in, 171 174
Nurse, the, alcoholism and, 194-95, 246-53
Nursing schools, education on alcoholism in, 243

Oblivion, desire for, 39, 46-47, 134
Observer, 80

Ohio, alcoholism program in, 171, 173
Ontario, alcoholism program in, 72, 171, 174
Ontario Commission on Alcoholism, 80
Oregon, alcoholism program in, 171, 173
Ostracism, social, 48
Outpatient facilities, 137, 169, 170, 232
Oxford Movement, 150
Oxygen, 105

Paraldehyde, 97
Parents, responsibility of, 36, 47-48, 259, 261, 266, 267-68
Pathological intoxication, 113
Patton tube, use of, 112
Pennsylvania, alcoholism program in, 171, 173; rehabilitation program in, 72
Pentobarbital (Nembutal), 98
Pentylenetetrazol (Metrazol), 92
Personnel for rehabilitation of homeless alcoholics, 141-42
Peru, alcoholism in, 292, 304
Phenobarbital, 98
Physical deterioration, 85, 86
Pipradrol hydrochloride—alpha-(2-piperidyl) benzhydrol hydrochloride—(Meratran), 92
Plasma, 105
Pneumonia, 222
Poland, alcoholism in, 291
Portugal, alcoholism in, 292
Potter, Milton G., 183
Pregnancy, effect of alcohol during, 119-20
Presnall, Lewis F., 79
Prevention of alcoholism, 44, 46-49
Problem drinking, 24-25, 32, 45, 48, 49, 54-55, 84-85, 158, 234, 260
Prohibitionist Party, 214
Prohibition of drinking, 47-48, 78, 258, 263
Promazine hydrochloride (Sparine), 93, 94-95, 96, 102, 103, 105, 111
Psychoses, 57, 73, 85, 107, 130-31, 164, 233
Psychotherapy, 102, 103, 107, 111, 114, 128-29, 154
Publications on alcoholism, 79-80
Public health problem, alcoholism as, 43-49, 168; Skid Row as, 133-44
Public Health Service, U. S., 177
Public Welfare Amendments (1962), 178-81
Purdue Opinion Poll, 214
Purdue University, 214

Quarterly Journal of Studies on Alcohol, 79

Racine County, Wisconsin, 225-26
Radioactive uptake test, 100
Raskin, Herbert A., 193 n.
Rauwolfia serpentina, 94, 96, 103
Rehabilitation of alcoholics, 62, 63, 66, 67-68, 71, 72; government responsibility in, 169-70; homeless alcoholics, 133-44
Rehabilitation center, 139-40
Relatives, responsibility of, 83-84
Relaxation, drinking for, 34-35, 38, 51
Reproductive system, effect of alcohol on, 119-20
Reserpine, 93-94, 96, 103
Respiratory system, effect of alcohol on, 117-18
Responsibility, escape from, 62; sense of, decline of, 52
Rhode Island, alcoholism program in, 171, 173
Rhodesias, alcoholism in, 296-97
Riegelman, Harold, 70
Rogers, Stanley S., 172
Rum, 32
"Rum fits," 57
Russia, alcoholism in, 291
Rutgers School of Alcoholic Studies, 79
Rye, 33

Safety Council, 192
Saline solution, 91, 101, 105, 112
Salvation Army, 141
Sands, Edward S., 177
Saskatchewan, alcoholism program in, 171, 174
Scandinavian countries, alcoholism in, 298-300
Schizophrenia, 130, 164
Scotch, 33
Scotland, alcoholism in, 292
Secobarbital (Seconal), 98
Sedita, Frank, 70
Seevers, Maurice H., 193 n.
Self-destructive tendencies, 39
Senate Committee, statement before, concerning H.R. 7225, 61-65
Sengstaken, use of, 112
Sexual behavior, alcohol and, 165-66, 219-20
Shepard, Ernest A., 172
Shere, Norbert, 172
Skeletal system, effect of alcohol on, 119
Skid Row, 44, 57, 133-44

INDEX

Sleep, continual, desire for, 39
"Slip, the," treatment of, 127-29
Smith, Jackson A., 186 n.
Smithers, Brinkley, 79
Snow, J. M., 174
Social drinking, 33-34, 35, 51, 54
Social work, schools of, education on alcoholism in, 241, 289
Social worker, the, alcoholism and, 143-44, 287-89; lack of understanding among, 15; rehabilitation program and, 64-65
Society, responsibilities of, 124-27
Sociologists, lack of understanding among, 15
Sociology, schools of, education on alcoholism in, 241
Sodium benzoate, 92
South Africa, alcoholism in, 297-98, 304
South America, alcoholism in, 298
South Carolina, alcoholism program in, 171
Spain, alcoholism in, 292, 304
Spouse of the alcoholic, 270-78
Standard Oil of New Jersey, 200
State hospitals, 141
State programs on alcoholism, 171-74
Stewart, William, 177
Stimulant, alcohol as, 50
Stomach lavage, 101
Stomach ulcers, 221-22
Strachan, J. George, 174
Stress, ability to cope with, 46
Subcommittee on the Problems of Alcoholism, A.M.A., 184-86
Suicide, 57
Supervision, permanent, 140-41
Supportive therapy, 131
Sweden, alcoholism in, 292, 298-99
Swinyard, Chester A., 116 n.
Swinyard, Ewart, 173
Switzerland, alcoholism in, 292, 305

Teacher, the, alcoholism and, 211-28, 262-63, 266; lack of understanding, 15
Tennessee, alcoholism program in, 171, 173
Tensions, acceptance of, 46, 75
Tequila, 32
Terminal cases, 86
Texas, alcoholism program in, 171, 173
Thiopental (Pentothal), 98
Thyroid dysfunction, 100
Tranquilizing drugs, 93-98, 110, 111, 114, 131
Treatment of alcoholics, 48, 49, 64, 82-86, 114-15, 223-24; abstaining, 121-32; compulsory, 66, 71-72; medical, see Medical treatment of alcoholics; "slip," the, 127-29; women, 165-66
Tuberculosis, stigma attached to, 75

Union of South Africa, alcoholism in, 292, 296, 297-98
Unions, labor, alcoholism and, 200-01
United States of America, alcoholism in (chart), 292
Universities, education on alcoholism in, 240-42
Uruguay, alcoholism in, 292, 304
Utah, alcoholism program in, 171, 173
Utah University School of Alcoholic Studies, 79

Vermont, alcoholism program in, 171; rehabilitation program in, 72
Virginia, alcoholism program in, 171
Vitamin B Complex, 91
Vitamins, 112, 113, 231
Vodka, 32
Volunteers of America, 141

Wales, alcoholism in, 292, 293
"War on Poverty" program, 181
Washington, alcoholism program in, 171; rehabilitation program in, 72
Welfare agencies, 170
Welfare rolls, alcoholism and, 66
Wells, John P., 173
Wernicke's disease, 61, 86; treatment, 113
Western Electric Company, 200
Wettrick, Marian, 72, 173
Whiskey, 32, 33
Whitney, Elizabeth, 172
Wines, 32, 33
Wisconsin, school of alcoholic studies, 79
Wisconsin University, 226 n.
Withdrawal signs, 222
Women alcoholics, 157-67
Women's Christian Temperance Union, 214
World Health Organization, 20, 21
Wyoming, alcoholism program in, 171

Yale School of Alcoholic Studies, 79
Yale University, 186
Young people, drinking and, 258-69
Young People and Drinking (Cain), 259
Yugoslavia, alcoholism in, 292

Zwerling, I., 28